THE

99%

AlterNet Books

101 Spear Street, Suite 203, San Francisco, CA 94105

AlterNet.org

Cover photograph by Nina Berman/NOOR

Design by designSimple | First printing, 2011

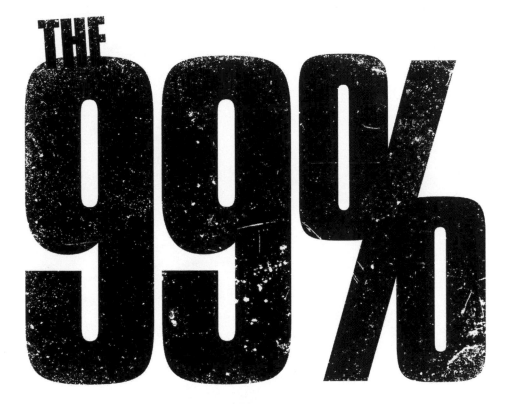

THE 99%

HOW THE
OCCUPY WALL STREET MOVEMENT
IS CHANGING AMERICA

EDITED BY

Don Hazen, Tara Lohan and Lynn Parramore

CONTENTS

ACKNOWLEDGEMENTS

As the Occupy Wall Street Movement was heating up and gathering momentum, AlterNet writers and editors were working feverishly to cover the rapidly breaking and developing story (even as one of our editorial team members, Kristen Gwynne, was arrested on the Brooklyn Bridge).

Strong voices were emerging, excellent writing was being produced and the OWS movement was dominating the national discourse. It dawned on us that we were in the midst of an historic moment.

So we decided to document what happened in the first two months of OWS for both inspiration and historical record. We wanted to provide a detailed documentation for why OWS was happening now, and offer some analysis of how OWS can tackle the corporate dominance of America and the globe.

We produced this book in about three break-neck weeks – with the cooperation and support of many.

This book was made by three staff-superstars, along with great support from other editors, writers and activists who aided our effort.

• Tara Lohan, who served as managing editor (she has had experience producing two fantastic books on water, including *Water Matters*), was a terrific juggler, overseer, photo editor, and she brought all around calmness to the hectic process;

• Roxanne Cooper, savvy publisher that she is, handled all the keys to making a book—printing, design, coordination—all with remarkable skill and steadiness;

• Lynn Parramore brought her fine creative sense, and keen editing scalpel to many of the pieces, making sure everything fit;

• Key members of the AlterNet editing team were consistently terrific: each was responsible for sections of the book – both for their own writing, and finding the best material to include: Joshua Holland, Tana Ganeva, Sarah Jaffe, Sarah Seltzer, Julianne Escobedo Shepherd, Lauren Kelley, Kristen Gwynne and Rania Khalek;

• Kristen Lee for great attention to detail, proofing the book at the last second;

• Bill Smith for his excellent design, ability to work long and hard in a very tight time frame;

• Photographers Nina Berman and Michael Gould-Wartofsky, and graphic artist Cristian Fleming for donating their fantastic work to the cause;

• And to all the writers, photographers and activists whose passionate speaking and writing brought diversity, depth and creativity to our project.

—Don Hazen, Executive Editor

The 99%

INTRODUCTION

We have picked a fight with the most powerful economic and political forces on the planet.

—Naomi Klein

Summer, 2011. Nearly four years after Wall Street blew up the economy, the country was stuck in a quagmire. Americans were gripped by bleak realities:

- Wealth inequality was near an all-time high
- 50 million people lacked health insurance
- 16 percent of Americans lived in poverty
- Nearly one out of five homeowners was "underwater" and likely to default
- Outstanding student loans hit a record high of over $1 trillion
- 14 million people were unemployed
- The biggest banks were even bigger than before the financial crisis
- One third of U.S. deaths could be linked to economic inequality

As the long summer of heated partisan gridlock (captured in these pages by economist James K. Galbraith) staggered to its end, Americans grew exhausted. We had watched with disgust the machinations of a deficit commission bent on squeezing ordinary people to pay for an economic disaster driven by Wall Street greed. Disillusioned and drowning in debt, we could see plainly that a growing concentration of wealth was making a mockery of our democracy. We were perfectly aware that innocent people were losing their homes in a mortgage crisis created by the fraudulent activity of big banks. We felt intuitively that coddled elites were throwing us overboard as they sailed away in their yachts—the ones we paid for. And we knew damn well that the foundation of our society was crumbling.

We were hungry for change. But what could we do? Popular uprisings abroad had inspired us in the spring, but oppressors at home trampled us with abandon. Purchased politicians lectured on how we must "sacrifice" to feed the ravenous maw of unchecked capitalism. Mainstream media pundits complied with their corporate masters to spin economic fairy tales that distorted the causes of unemployment and deficits. Caught in a cycle of doom, we waited for the next round of job cuts. The next assault on working people. The next banking crisis.

Then something happened. Only a few sensed it at first—a whiff of electricity in the air. An obscure magazine called *Adbusters* published a whimsical picture of a dancer poised on the back of the iconic Merrill Lynch bull, calling for the occupation of Wall Street. A few weeks later, a small group of activists and anarchists converged on Manhattan, one of them anthropologist David Graeber, who reveals here how a haphazard gathering transformed into a leaderless coalition determined to challenge the powerful few. On September 17, surrounded by the glinting towers of finance, these activists set up camp at Zuccotti Park under the banner of a simple, arresting slogan: "We are the 99 percent."

At first, the Lords of Wall Street merely peered down from their towers with amusement. Mayor Bloomberg scoffed. Passersby puzzled over the scruffy young people who pitched tents and restored their new home to its original name, Liberty Plaza. The media snarked, baffled by this alternative community where protesters relayed messages through echoing calls and wiggling fingers because amplifiers had been banned.

The cops had intended to keep them quiet with that ban.

They would not be quiet.

This book records the voices of those who shared the anxiety and excitement of those early days—the sights, the sounds and the solidarity. Participants take you on a drama-charged journey; from the first spark struck on the concrete of lower Manhattan to the mass marches that ignited the entire nation.

When did the spark catch fire? For some, it was October 1, when police arrested hundreds of protesters on the Brooklyn Bridge, among them Kristen Gwynne, who tweeted and phoned in reports of frightened people huddled under umbrellas singing "This Little Light of Mine." One by one, the peaceful protesters were hauled away in cuffs, the wild spark passing from one to another; soon to thousands, then to millions glued to social media and cable news.

Well-known progressives soon heeded what the *Indypendent*'s Arun Gupta describes as a "clarion call" for "all-out commitment." Nobel-laureate Joseph Stiglitz, journalist Naomi Klein, philosopher Cornell West and actress Roseanne Barr were among those who embraced the protesters and caught the exhilaration of hearing their words transmitted by the people's mic in Liberty Plaza. Their stirring addresses are included here, along with the observations of the many curious and courageous citizens—from Iraq War veteran Shamar Thomas to rapper Immortal Technique—who joined an open-source movement in which all voices would be heard and all races, ages, creeds and genders would be welcome.

The flame burned still brighter on October 5, when a triumphant gathering of community groups, students and brothers and sisters from organized labor joined protesters—20,000 in all—to march from Foley Square to Liberty Plaza hoisting colorful signs highlighting student debt, attacks on workers' rights and the plight of unemployed millions.

If there was any hope on the part of the 1 percent that the flame would be doused, it died in the gray dawn of October 15 when occupiers stared down the NYPD to hold Liberty Plaza against the threat of eviction. All who linked arms in the park, including several AlterNet staffers, risked arrest to protect what was now a sacred temple of possibility. In a wondrous piece of urban theater, choreographed through social media, protesters pushed the boundaries of what is permissible and forced the billionaire mayor to back down. The next day, a massive rally at Times Square reported by Sarah Seltzer confirmed that possibility was passing into inevitability. Barricades wouldn't stop this. Cops in riot gear wouldn't stop this.

In just a few spectacular weeks, the movement had altered the conversation across the country. A bold idea had sprung from a tiny park: that ordinary people can mount a challenge to the entire economic and political system. AlterNet writers and other journalists and participants take you through the myriad creative actions that have occurred in New York since the movement's inception, from a "Millionaire's March" on the Upper East Side to a Harlem rally against police racial profiling.

In a section called "The Model Society," playwright Eve Ensler, Working Families Party organizer Nelini Stamp, AlterNet reporter Sarah Jaffe and others bring to life the movement's experimental nature and its emphasis on nonviolence, inclusiveness, open processes and unconventional approaches. They escort you inside the general assemblies, the reclaimed spaces and the working groups in which new ideas and bonds have flourished.

This book follows the spark of hope as it has leapt from city to city, state to state, across the ocean and around the world, along with the challenges and crackdowns that have pursued it. Rania Khalek reports on Occupy uprisings across the U.S., while Nick Turse examines international synergies. Adele Stan reports on flareups between protesters and those who would silence them at Occupy DC, while at Occupy Oakland, Joshua Holland records a violent confrontation with police as it unfolds before his eyes. At Occupy Boston, icon Noam Chomsky explains why he views the movement as "unprecedented."

The interaction of police with the movement forms its own section of this book in firsthand reports of protesters like teacher and playwright Barbara Schneider Reilly, who found herself locked behind bars for daring to speak her mind. Journalists like Tom Engelhardt, Pam Martens, Tana Ganeva, and others pose tough questions about our relationship to authority and responsibility toward each other. They provide analyses of disturbing trends of aggression, coordinated suppression and high-tech surveillance that have marked this new era of protest.

Why did all this happen now? To help answer this question, we delve into the root causes and long-term trends that have driven the movement, from the corrupt influence of money in politics (exposed by political economist Thomas Ferguson) to the foreclosure crisis (explained by financial writer Yves Smith and economist Nomi Prins). Experts in law, history, environmental issues, unemployment and war examine the ills that drove the 99 percent to finally take matters into their own hands. We also share accounts of the cultural reactions to OWS, from the drumbeat of media propaganda to the responses of corporate players like MTV. Julianne Escobedo Shepherd reveals how contemporary songwriters have taken the baton from the music giants of yesterday to produce a vibrant soundtrack for a revolutionary movement.

Finally, we bring you the insights of visionaries who explore the deeper meaning of the protests, like economist Robert Johnson, who sees the spirit of Gandhi soaring among the peaceful activists. We share the perspectives of those who urge us to find new ways to work together as we confront the outer forces of oppression, like AlterNet executive editor Don Hazen. And we look ahead with people like journalist Charles Eisenstein, who sums up why the movement must seek more than mere tweaks to the system. "Practical is not an option," he writes. "We must seek the extraordinary."

The 99% tells the gripping story of the emergence, expansion and influence of a phenomenon that is poised to transform our ideological landscape and unleash our potential to reinvent our society. Like all sea-changing movements in our history—the abolition of slavery, women's suffrage, the civil rights movement—this quest for economic equality and the dignity of ordinary people seems to reach for the impossible. The task, as early OWS organizer Yotam Marom warns us, will not be easy. It will require patience, long-term commitment and fortitude in the face of setbacks, like the November 15 crackdown that swept through encampments across the country and the globe.

But there's no turning back now. Occupy Wall Street has already helped us to see a new world: a world where students are not crushed by debt, where the elderly do not choose between food and medicine, where wars are not waged for profit, where we care together for the Earth and for principles like acceptance and nonviolence, where the people control the political system and where human values drive our society instead of corporate greed.

As you travel along with the remarkable citizens, journalists, artists, teachers, students, parents, thinkers and activists whose reports fill these pages, you'll discover what most of the pundits have yet to grasp. The movement is the message. Pluralistic, organic and punctuated by passionate actions, it has already done something wildly exciting.

It has occupied our imagination.

—Lynn Parramore
Contributing editor, AlterNet
New York, NY
November 16, 2011

I.

THE

BEGINNING

INTRODUCTION

IN THE FIRST few weeks of the Occupy Wall Street movement, people were drawn to Liberty Plaza out of curiosity, frustration and solidarity with their fellow global citizens, out of their concern about the future and the grave injustices that threaten the 99 percent. They are young and old, professional and student, thriving and struggling. They are celebrities and everyday people (whose voices were captured in on-the-spot interviews with Kristen Gwynne).

All of them have the common experience of finally standing up to a system that too often serves the powerful and the wealthy. These individuals, and the thousands who stand with them, are participants in a growing grassroots, international dialogue on economic and cultural equality.

THE REVOLUTION BEGINS AT HOME: A CLARION CALL TO JOIN THE WALL STREET PROTESTS

BY ARUN GUPTA

WHAT IS OCCURRING on Wall Street right now is truly remarkable. For over 10 days, in the sanctum of the great cathedral of global capitalism, the dispossessed have liberated territory from the financial overlords and their police army. They have created a unique opportunity to shift the tides of history in the tradition of other great peaceful occupations, from the sit-down strikes of the 1930s to the lunch-counter sit-ins of the 1960s to the democratic uprisings across the Arab world and Europe today.

While the Wall Street occupation is growing, it needs an all-out commitment from everyone who cheered the Egyptians in Tahrir Square; from everyone who said "We are all Wisconsin," and stood in solidarity with the Greeks and the Spaniards. This is a movement for anyone who lacks a job, housing or healthcare, or thinks they have no future.

Our system is broken at every level. More than 25 million Americans are unemployed. More than 50 million live without health insurance. Perhaps 100 million Americans are mired in poverty, using realistic measures. Yet the fat cats continue to get tax breaks and reap billions while politicians compete to turn the austerity screws on all of us.

At some point the number of people occupying Wall Street—whether that's 5,000, 10,000 or 50,000—will force the powers-that-be to offer concessions. No one can say how many people it will take or even how things will change exactly, but there is a real potential for bypassing a corrupt political process and for realizing a society based on human needs, not hedge fund profits. After all, who would have imagined a year ago that Tunisians and Egyptians would oust their dictators?

At Liberty Plaza, the nerve center of the occupation, more than 500 people gather every day to debate, discuss and organize what to do about our failed system that has allowed the 400 richest Americans at the top to amass more wealth than the 180 million Americans at the bottom.

It's astonishing that this self-organized festival of democracy has sprouted on the turf of the masters of the universe, the people who play the tune that both political parties and the media dance to. The New York Police Department, which has deployed hundreds of officers at a time to surround and intimidate protestors, is capable of arresting everyone and clearing Liberty Plaza in minutes. But assaulting peaceful crowds in a public square demanding real democracy—economic and not just political—would remind the world of the brittle autocrats who brutalized their people demanding justice before they were swept away by the Arab Spring. And the state violence has already backfired. After police attacked a Saturday afternoon march that started from Liberty Plaza, the crowds only got bigger and media interest grew.

The Wall Street occupation has already succeeded in revealing the bankruptcy of the dominant powers—the economic, the political, media and security forces. They have nothing positive to offer humanity, not that they ever did for the Global South, but now their quest for endless profits means deepening the misery with a thousand austerity cuts.

Even their solutions are cruel jokes. They tell us the "Buffett Rule" would spread the pain by asking the penthouse set to sacrifice a tin of caviar, which is what the proposed tax increase would amount to. Meanwhile, the rest of us will have to sacrifice healthcare, food, education, housing, jobs and perhaps our lives to sate the ferocious appetite of capital.

That's why more and more people are joining the Wall Street occupation. They can tell you about their homes being foreclosed upon, months of grinding unemployment or minimum-wage dead-end jobs, staggering student debt loads, or trying to live without decent healthcare. It's a whole generation of Americans with no prospects, who are told to believe in a system that can only offer them "Dancing With the Stars" and pepper spray in the face. Yet against every description of a generation derided as narcissistic, apathetic and hopeless they are staking a claim to a better future for all of us. That's why we all need to join in. Not just by "liking" it on Facebook, signing a petition online or retweeting protest photos, but by going down to the occupation itself.

There is great potential here. Sure, it's a far cry from Tahrir Square or even Wisconsin. But there is the nucleus of a revolt that could shake America's power structure as much as the Arab world has been upended. Instead of one to two thousand people a day joining in the occupation there needs to be tens of thousands of people protesting the fat cats driving Bentleys and drinking $1,000 bottles of champagne with money they looted from the financial crisis and then from the bailouts while Americans literally die on the streets.

To be fair, the scene at Liberty Plaza seems messy and chaotic. But it's also a laboratory of possibility, and that's the beauty of democracy. As opposed to our monoculture world, where political life means flipping a lever every four years, social life means being a consumer, and economic life means being a timid cog, the Wall Street occupation is creating a polyculture of ideas, expression and art.

Yet while many people support the occupation, they hesitate to fully join in and are quick to offer criticism. It's clear that the biggest obstacles to building a powerful movement are not the police or capital—it's our own cynicism and despair.

Perhaps their views were colored by the *New York Times* article deriding protesters for wishing to "pantomime progressivism" and "Gunning for Wall Street with faulty aim." Many of the criticisms boil down to "a lack of clear messaging."

But what's wrong with that? A fully formed movement is not going to spring from the ground. It has to be created. And who can say what exactly needs to be done? We are not talking about ousting a dictator; though some say we want to oust the dictatorship of capital.

There are plenty of sophisticated ideas out there: end corporate person-hood; institute a "Tobin Tax" on stock purchases and currency trading; nationalize banks; socialize medicine; fully fund government jobs and genuine Keynesian stimulus; lift restrictions on labor organizing; allow cities to turn foreclosed homes into public housing; build a green energy infrastructure.

But how can we get broad agreement on any of these? If the protesters came into the square with a predetermined set of demands it would have only limited their potential. They would have either been dismissed as pie in the sky—such as socialized medicine or nationalize banks—or if they went for weak demands such as the Buffett Rule their efforts would immediately be absorbed by a failed political system, thus undermining the movement. That's why the building of the movement has to go hand in hand with common struggle, debate and radical democracy. It's how we will create genuine solutions that have legitimacy. And that is what is occurring down at Wall Street.

Now, there are endless objections one can make. But if we focus on the possibilities, and shed our despair, our hesitancy and our cynicism, and collectively come to Wall Street with critical thinking, ideas and solidarity, we can change the world.

How many times in your life do you get a chance to watch history unfold, to actively participate in building a better society, to come together with thousands of people where genuine democracy is the reality and not a fantasy? For too long, our minds have been chained by fear, division and impotence. The one thing the elite fear most is a great awakening. That day is here. Together we can seize it.

'SOON THE WHOLE WORLD WILL HEAR US:' ROSEANNE BARR ADDRESSES OCCUPY WALL STREET

Barr, award-winning actress and comedian, spoke to Liberty Plaza on September 19.

I WANT A NEW capitalism. Not fueled by wars. One that doesn't pass on its wealth to a handful of white guys and call that free trade. One wherein the elderly actually get paid their retirement monies. We'll have capitalism, but we'll also have socialism. And education and basic compassion and healthcare. I'm talking about a system that rewards hard work and ambition, but cares for its weakest child—and being called a feminazi for saying these things will be considered treasonous.

We will simply combine capitalism and socialism and create people-ism, where ideas work together for a functional system. No one will cling blindly to single, unyielding ideology just because of a bloated, obese talk radio host who tells the starving to tighten their belts or because of that goddamn Ayn Rand book. We will actually compromise, adjust and make reasonable choices. We will have common-sense solutions.

I'm so glad to see you guys here. I'm just so thrilled that so many of us have been actually able to crack our program—our mind control program that we've been living under for all of these years—and I salute you. I salute you for thinking freely. [*reading protestor's sign*] "The corrupt fear us, the honest support us, the heroes join us." I love your masks. I love you guys. We all love freedom. I'm going to quote from a wonderful writer, a wonderful woman, her name is Mary Daly. She's my idol: "There is no liberty without truth."

How do we get more people here? I'll tell you what we have to do—we have to merge small ego into large ego. That's what fractured the left the first time around in the '60s when I was there and saw everyone's supposed small ego keep them from coalescing and uniting. That's what we have to do—put it aside. Don't say, I'm starting my own Web site. Get with people who already have a Web site and have already done the work and just walk in and volunteer. That's what we do. We unite. We get the Teamsters on our side. And after we have that, we close down every branch and every road. It's hard. How do you do it? You just walk over there and do it. We get the police on our side against those people who are taking their retirement funds. We will ask for unity from the police and also the military.

I mean, we're all royally screwed. Anyone who makes less than $250,000 a year is royally screwed in this country and it's only going to get worse until they have labor camps and they get your free labor. And that is where it's headed. It's not going to stop. Just want you to know that I hear you and I know you hear me and pretty soon the whole world will hear us. Pretty soon it won't be 500 people. There won't be a choice. We've already won by sheer numbers alone. We're asking the police and the people in the military to join us, because we're on the same side against the same people. Same hands, same people. Just let it sink in.

INTERVIEW WITH SANDRA NURSE

Nurse, 27, is a graduate student at the New School, where she is finishing her thesis on post-disaster elections in Haiti. She is a conflict and development consultant at the Center on Global Counterterrorism.

I'M FROM EVERYWHERE. My parents were in the U.S. military so I traveled a lot outside the country. I've lived in Cuba, South Korea, Australia, Japan, Kenya ... I spent my high school in South Korea and Japan and I did my middle school in Maine and a couple years of elementary in Vermont and Cuba. The exposure to the variety of standards of living around the world, and seeing very extreme ends of that—seeing people who have everything at their disposal and people who have nothing—made me very interested in the projection of power.

The draw of what's happening here, at Occupy Wall Street, for me, would be that people are finally making that connection in a very loud and angry way—the connection between corporations, politicians, and the effects it has on not only us but people around the world. That's what makes me happy to be here—that people are really trying to raise awareness about this and take action to expose it and expose everyone's anger over it.

I think OWS has the foundation, the wide-reaching message of a movement to really address power structures in the United States and how those power structures are projected onto the world. I would really like to see a very active, very engaged citizenry. I would really like to see people reflect on the current political culture and recognize that just because we have a tradition doesn't mean it's right, doesn't mean it reflects the current needs.

I would really like to see local politics amplified and people coming together and not depending on electoral politics to help solve their problems. I would like to see a real change in the ways we relate to each other. At OWS, I think a lot of people have been attracted to the idea of being inclusive and everyone having a voice, in some shape or form, in decision-making. And I think that that kind of spirit, that nature of interaction, can be replicated or adopted in communities.

The 99%

THE STRANGE SUCCESS OF OCCUPY WALL STREET

BY DAVID GRAEBER

JUST A FEW MONTHS ago, I wrote a piece for *Adbusters* that started with a conversation I'd had with an Egyptian activist friend named Dina. "All these years," she said, "we've been organizing marches, rallies. And if only 45 people show up, you're depressed, if you get 300, you're happy. Then one day, 200,000 people show up. And you're incredulous. On some level, even though you didn't realize it, you'd given up thinking that you could actually win."

I am suddenly beginning to understand a little of how she felt.

On August 2, I showed up at a 7 p.m. meeting at Bowling Green. A Greek anarchist friend had told me it was meant to plan some kind of action on Wall Street in mid-September. I was only vaguely aware that a month before, the Canadian magazine *Adbusters* had put out the call to "Occupy Wall Street," but had really just floated the idea on the Internet to see if it would take hold. A local anti-budget cut coalition top-heavy with NGOs, unions and socialist groups had tried to take possession of the process and called for a general assembly at Bowling Green.

The term "general assembly" proved extremely misleading. When I arrived, I found the event had been effectively taken over by a veteran protest group called the Worker's World Party. They had already set up their banners and megaphones, and were making speeches—after which, someone explained, they were planning on leading the 80-odd assembled people in a march past the Stock Exchange itself.

The usual reaction to this sort of thing is a kind of cynical, bitter resignation. Why advertise a general assembly if they're not actually going to hold one? But as I paced about the Green, I noticed something. To adopt activist parlance: this wasn't really a crowd of "verticals"—that is, the sort of people whose idea of political action is to march around with signs under the control of one or another top-down protest movement. They were mostly "horizontals"—people more sympathetic with anarchist principles of organization, non-hierarchical forms of direct democracy and direct action.

I quickly spotted at least one Wobbly, a young Korean activist I remembered from some Food Not Bombs event, some college students wearing Zapatista paraphernalia, and a Spanish couple who'd been involved with the *indignados* in Madrid. I found my Greek friends, an American I knew from street battles in Quebec during the Summit of the Americas in 2001 (now turned labor organizer in Manhattan), and a Japanese activist intellectual I'd known for years. My Greek friend looked at me and I looked at her and we both instantly realized the other was thinking the same thing: "Why are we so complacent? Why is it that every time we see something like this happening, we just mutter things and go home?" Although, I think the way we put it was more like, "You know something? Fuck this shit. They advertised a general assembly. Let's hold one."

So we gathered up a few obvious horizontals and formed a circle. After about an hour of drama, almost everyone abandoned the rally and came over to our side. We created a decision-making process (we would operate by modi-fied consensus), broke out into working groups (outreach, action, facilitation) and then reassembled to allow each group to report its collective decisions and set up times for new meetings. It was difficult to figure out what to do. We only had six weeks, not nearly enough time to plan a major action, let alone bus in the thousands of people that would be required to actually shut down Wall Street—and anyway the advertised day, September 17, was a Saturday. We also had no money.

Two days later, we were brainstorming what to put on our first flyer. Who were we? Who did want to appeal to? Who did we represent? Someone—this time I remember quite clearly it was me, but I wouldn't be surprised if a half-dozen others had equally strong memories of being the first to come up with it—suggested, "Well, why not call ourselves the 99 percent? If 1 percent of the population have ended up with all the benefits of the last 10 years of eco-nomic growth, control the wealth, own the politicians, why not just say we're everybody else?"

The Spanish couple quickly began to lay out a "We Are the 99 Percent" pamphlet, and we started brainstorming ways to print and distribute it for free.

Over the next few weeks a plan began to take shape. The core of the emerging group, which began to meet regularly in Tompkins Square Park, were very young people who had cut their activist teeth on the Bloombergville encampment outside City Hall earlier in the summer. There was also a smat-tering of activists who had been connected to the global justice movement with skills to share (one or two of whom I had to drag out of effective retire-ment), and a number of New Yorkers originally from Greece, Spain and even Tunisia, with connections to those who had been involved in occupations there. We wanted to do something like what had already been accomplished in Athens, Barcelona or Madrid; occupy a public space to create a New York general assembly, a body that could act as a model of genuine, direct democracy contraposed to the corrupt charade presented to us as "democracy" by the U.S. government. The Wall Street action would be a stepping-stone.

It was almost impossible to predict what would really happen on the 17th. There were supposed to be 90,000 people following us on the Internet. *Adbusters* had called for 20,000 to fill the streets. That obviously wasn't going to happen. But how many would really show up? We were keenly aware that the NYPD numbered close to 40,000; Wall Street was, in fact, probably the single most heavily policed public space on the face of Planet Earth. The greatest concern during those hectic weeks was how to ensure the initial event wouldn't turn out a total fiasco, with all the enthusiastic young people immediately beaten, arrested and psychologically traumatized as the media, as usual, simply looked the other way.

We'd certainly seen it happen before.

This time it didn't. True, there were all the predictable conflicts. Most of New York's grumpier hardcore anarchists refused to join in. The more open, "small-a" anarchists, who were largely responsible for organizing the facilitation and trainings, battled the verticals in the group to prevent a formal leadership structure from forming. There were also bitter battles over the Web page, as well as minor crises over the participation of various fringe groups. On September 17 itself, I was troubled at first by the fact that only a few hundred people seemed to have shown up. The spot we'd chosen for our general assembly, a plaza outside Citibank, had been shut down by the city and surrounded by high fences. Around 3 p.m., word went around we were moving to location #5—Zuccotti Park. By the time we got there, we were surrounded by at least 2,000 people.

The real credit for what happened after that—within a matter of weeks—belongs mainly to the students and other young people who simply dug themselves in and refused to leave, despite the endless (and in many cases, obviously illegal) acts of police repression designed to intimidate and make life so miserable in the park (refusing to allow activists to cover their computers with tarps during rainstorms, that sort of thing) that its inhabitants would simply become demoralized and abandon the project. And, as the weeks went on, there were calculated acts of terrorism involving batons and pepper-spray. Still, dogged activists have held out heroically under such conditions before, and the world simply ignored them. Why didn't it happen this time?

My first take on the question came when the *Guardian* asked me to write an op-ed on Occupy Wall Street a few days later. At the time I was inspired mainly by what Marisa Holmes, another brilliant organizer of the original occupation, had discovered in her work as a video documentarian, doing one-on-one interviews of fellow campers during the first two nights at Zuccotti Park. Over and over she heard the same story:

"I did everything I was supposed to—I worked hard, studied hard, got into college. Now I'm unemployed, with no prospects, and fifty- to eighty-thousand dollars in debt."

These were kids who played by the rules. They were rewarded with a future of constant harassment, of being told they were worthless deadbeats by agents of those very financial institutions that—after having spectacularly failed to play by the rules, and crashing the world economy as a result, were saved and coddled by the government in all the ways that ordinary Americans such as themselves were not. I wrote: "We are watching the beginnings of the defiant self-assertion of a new generation of Americans, a generation that is looking forward to finishing their education with no jobs, no future, but still saddled with enormous and unforgivable debt."

Three weeks later, after watching more and more elements of main-stream America clamber on board, I think this is still true. In a way, the demographic base of OWS is about as far as one can get from the Tea Party, with which it is so often, and so confusingly, compared. The popular base of the Tea Party was always middle-aged, suburban, white Republicans, most of middling economic means, anti-intellectual, and above all terrified of social change, for fear that what they saw as their one remaining buffer of privilege (basically, their whiteness) might finally be stripped away. OWS, by contrast, is at core a forward-looking youth movement. Just a group of people who have been stopped dead in their tracks; of mixed class back-grounds but with a significant element of working-class origins; their one strongest common feature being a high level of education. It's no coincidence that the epicenter of the Wall Street occupation, and so many others, is an impromptu library; a model of an alternative economy, where lending is from a communal pool, at zero percent interest, and the currency being loaned is knowledge, but also the means to understanding.

Obviously, what happened is exactly what we hoped would happen. The politics of direct action is based, to a certain degree, on a faith that freedom is contagious. It is almost impossible to convince the average American that a truly democratic society is possible. One can only show them. But the experience of watching a group of a thousand people making collective decisions without a leadership structure, or of watching thousands of people, motivated only by principle and solidarity, linking arms to hold their ground against a phalanx of armored riot cops, can change one's most fundamental assumptions about what politics—or for that matter, human life—could actually be like.

The 99%

Say what you will about Americans, this is a country of deeply democratic sensibilities. The idea that we are, or are supposed to be, a democratic society is at the very core of what makes us proud to be Americans. If Occupy Wall Street has spread to every city in America, it's because our financial overlords have brought us to such a pass that anarchists, pagan priestesses and tree-sitters are about the only Americans left still holding out for the idea that a genuinely democratic society might be possible.

A longer version of this essay appeared on NakedCapitalism.com.

'YOU GOT ME SPIRITUALLY BREAKDANCING:' CORNEL WEST ADDRESSES OCCUPY WALL STREET

West, professor at Princeton University, activist and author, spoke to Liberty Plaza on September 27.

THERE IS A SWEET spirit in this place. I hope you can feel the love and inspiration of those Sly Stone called the "everyday people" who take a stand with great courage and compassion, because we oppose the greed of Wall Street oligarchs and corporate plutocrats who squeeze the democratic juices out of this country and other places around the world.

I am so blessed to be here. You got me spiritually breakdancing on the way here, because when you bring folk together of all colors and all cultures and all genders and all sexual orientations, the elites will tremble in their boots. Yeah! And we will send a message that this is the U.S. Fall responding to the Arab Spring. It is going to hit Chicago and Los Angeles and Phoenix, Arizona, and A-Town itself, moving on to Detroit.

We gonna hit Appalachia. We gonna hit the reservations with our red brothers and sisters. And Martin Luther King, Jr., will smile from the grave and say we moving step by step for what he called a revolution. And don't be afraid to say "revolution," because we want a transfer of power from the oligarchs to ordinary citizens, beginning with the poor children of all colors and the orphans and the widows and the elderly and the working folk, that we connect the prison-industrial complex with the military-industrial complex, with the Wall Street-oligarchy complex and the corporate media multiplex.

So I want to thank you, and it's a blessing to be a small part of this magnificent gathering. This is the general assembly consecrated by your witness and your body and your mind. Yeah! God bless you!

INTERVIEW WITH THOMAS McALLISTER

McAllister, 40, is a Teamster from Long Island, New York.
A former Sotheby's employee, he was locked out over a labor dispute.

THE FIRST TIME I was here, I brought my kids because I'm worried about their future.

Right now we're losing our jobs, we're losing our houses, we're losing ourselves. This is about regaining the American dream. My expectation is change. We change the way we think, we change the way we live.

At Sotheby's, we've been locked out for three months, going into the fourth month. We didn't strike. We wanted to work. We wanted continued employment and to bargain a good contract while we were working and they just said no. They locked us out and said, "accept these concessions, all 70 of them, or go out on the street." We drew a line and said we can't accept this because you're breaking our unions. You're breaking the backs of America. It's just another example of big corporations demonizing the workers.

Sotheby's made $680 million in profit last year. They had their best year in history. The CEO gave himself a 125-percent raise, so he's making $6 million, plus he's making stock options. And how do they repay their workers? They throw us on the street with no pay, no benefits. They want to take away our pension, reduce our salary by 15 percent, and they want to abolish collective bargaining rights. It already happened in Wisconsin. We can't allow that to happen here.

OCCUPY WALL STREET: THE MOST IMPORTANT THING IN THE WORLD NOW

BY NAOMI KLEIN

I was honored to be invited to speak at Occupy Wall Street on October 6. Since amplification is (disgracefully) banned, and everything I said had to be repeated by hundreds of people so others could hear (aka the human microphone), what I actually said at Liberty Plaza had to be very short. With that in mind, here is the longer, uncut version of the speech.

I LOVE YOU.

And I didn't just say that so hundreds of you would shout "I love you" back, though that is obviously a bonus feature of the human microphone. Say unto others what you would have them say unto you, only way louder. Yesterday, one of the speakers at the labor rally said: "We found each other." That sentiment captures the beauty of what is being created here. A wide-open space—as well as an idea so big it can't be contained by any space—for all the people who want a better world to find each other. We are so grateful.

If there is one thing I know, it is that the 1 percent loves a crisis. When people are panicked and desperate and no one seems to know what to do, that is the ideal time to push through their wish list of pro-corporate policies: privatizing education and Social Security, slashing public services, getting rid of the last constraints on corporate power. Amidst the economic crisis, this is happening the world over. And there is only one thing that can block this tactic, and fortunately, it's a very big thing: the 99 percent. And that 99 percent is taking to the streets from Madison to Madrid to say, "No—we will not pay for your crisis."

That slogan began in Italy in 2008. It ricocheted to Greece and France and Ireland and finally it has made its way to the square mile where the crisis began.

"Why are they protesting?" ask the baffled pundits on TV. Meanwhile, the rest of the world asks: "What took you so long? We've been wondering when you were going to show up." And most of all: "Welcome." Many people have drawn parallels between Occupy Wall Street and the so-called anti-globalization protests that came to world attention in Seattle in 1999. That was the last time a global, youth-led, decentralized movement took direct aim at corporate power. And I am proud to have been part of what we called the movement of movements.

But there are important differences too. For instance, we chose summits as our targets: the World Trade Organization, the International Monetary Fund, the G8. Summits are transient by their nature, they only last a week. That made us transient, too. We'd appear, grab world headlines, then disappear. And in the frenzy of hyper-patriotism and militarism that followed the 9/11 attacks, it was easy to sweep us away completely, at least in North America. Occupy Wall Street, on the other hand, has chosen a fixed target. And you have put no end date on your presence here. This is wise. Only when you stay put can you grow roots. This is crucial. It is a fact of the information age that too many movements spring up like beautiful flowers but quickly die off. It's because they don't have roots. And they don't have long-term plans for how they are going to sustain themselves. So when storms come, they get washed away.

Being horizontal and deeply democratic is wonderful. But these principles are compatible with the hard work of building structures and institutions that are sturdy enough to weather the storms ahead. I have great faith that this will happen.

Something else this movement is doing right: You have committed yourselves to nonviolence. You have refused to give the media the images of broken windows and street fights it craves so desperately. And that tremendous discipline has meant that, again and again, the story has been the disgraceful and unprovoked police brutality. Which we saw more of just last night. Meanwhile, support for this movement grows and grows. More wisdom. But the biggest difference a decade makes is that in 1999, we were taking on capitalism at the peak of a frenzied economic boom. Unemployment was low, stock portfolios were bulging. The media was drunk on easy money. Back then it was all about startups, not shutdowns.

We pointed out that the deregulation behind the frenzy came at a price. It was damaging to labor standards. It was damaging to environmental standards. Corporations were becoming more powerful than governments and that was damaging to our democracies. But to be honest with you, while the good times rolled, taking on an economic system based on greed was a tough sell, at least in rich countries. Ten years later, it seems as if there aren't any more rich countries; just a whole lot of rich people. People who got rich looting the public wealth and exhausting natural resources around the world.

The point is, today everyone can see that the system is deeply unjust and careening out of control. Unfettered greed has trashed the global economy. And it is trashing the natural world as well. We are overfishing our oceans, polluting our water with fracking and deepwater drilling, turning to the dirtiest forms of energy on the planet, like the Alberta tar sands. And the atmosphere cannot absorb the amount of carbon we are putting into it, creating dangerous warming. The new normal is serial disasters: economic and ecological.

These are the facts on the ground. They are so blatant, so obvious, that it is a lot easier to connect with the public than it was in 1999, and to build the movement quickly.

We all know, or at least sense, that the world is upside-down; we act as if there is no end to what is actually finite—fossil fuels and the atmospheric space to absorb their emissions. And we act as if there are strict and immovable limits to what is actually bountiful—the financial resources to build the kind of society we need.

The task of our time is to turn this around, to challenge this false scarcity. To insist that we can afford to build a decent, inclusive society, while at the same time, respect the real limits to what the earth can take. What climate change means is that we have to do this on a deadline. This time our movement cannot get distracted, divided, burned out or swept away by events. This time we have to succeed. And I'm not talking about regulating the banks and increasing taxes on the rich, though that's important.

I am talking about changing the underlying values that govern our society. That is hard to fit into a single media-friendly demand, and it's also hard to figure out how to do it. But it is no less urgent for being difficult. That is what I see happening in this square. In the way you are feeding each other, keeping each other warm, sharing information freely and providing health-care, meditation classes and empowerment training. My favorite sign here says "I care about you." In a culture that trains people to avoid each other's gaze, to say, "Let them die," that is a deeply radical statement.

A few final thoughts. In this great struggle, here are some things that *don't* matter.

- what we wear
- whether we shake our fists or make peace signs
- whether we can fit our dreams for a better world into a media soundbite

And here are a few things that *do* matter.

- our courage
- our moral compass
- how we treat each other

We have picked a fight with the most powerful economic and political forces on the planet. That's frightening. And as this movement grows from strength to strength, it will get more frightening. Always be aware that there will be a temptation to shift to smaller targets—like, say, the person sitting next to you at this meeting. After all, that is a battle that's easier to win. Don't give in to the temptation. I'm not saying don't call each other on shit. But this time, let's treat each other as if we plan to work side by side in struggle for many, many years to come. Because the task before us will demand nothing less.

Let's treat this beautiful movement as if it is the most important thing in the world. Because it is. It really is.

This story originally appeared in The Nation.

'THE SYSTEM IS NOT WORKING:' JOSEPH STIGLITZ ADDRESSES OCCUPY WALL STREET

Stiglitz, the winner of the 2001 Nobel Prize in economics, spoke to Liberty Plaza on October 2.

BEFORE TALKING ABOUT economics, I want to say something about democracy. In July, I was in Spain talking to the *indignados*, the protesters. There, I could use a bullhorn. I didn't have to go through this echo chamber. I realize the pedagogy of having you repeat what I say is very valuable, but it makes the whole process much longer. The fact that you are not allowed to use a megaphone on a Sunday is outrageous! We have too many regulations stopping democracy and not enough regulations stopping Wall Street from misbehaving. You should have the right to peacefully demonstrate your views and not be arrested and not be sprayed with pepper spray.

So now I want to talk a little bit about what I said in Spain, and then about the banks. The protesters there are called the *indignado*s, and I said, "You are right to be indignant." The fact is, the system is not working right. It is not right that we have so many people without jobs when we have so many needs that we have to fulfill. It's not right that we are throwing people out of their houses when we have so many homeless people.

Our financial markets have an important role to play. They're supposed to allocate capital and manage risk, but they've misallocated capital and created risk. We are bearing the cost of their misdeeds. There's a system where we've socialized losses and privatized gains. That's not capitalism! That's not a market economy. That's a distorted economy, and if we continue with that, we won't succeed in growing, and we won't succeed in creating a just society.

One of the things the banks did was to prey on the poorest Americans through predatory lending. We knew about it. There were some people who tried to stop it, but Wall Street used its political power to stop those who would stop them.

After the bubble broke, they continued in their way of disobeying the law, in a sense—throwing people out of their houses, even in some cases when they didn't owe money. The balance of rights has been distorted. We bailed out the banks with an understanding that there would be a restoration of lending. All there was was a restoration of bonuses! Unless we deal with the anti-competitive practices, with the reckless lending and speculative behavior, unless we restore finance to the function it should serve, we won't have a robust recovery.

INTERVIEW WITH NAN TERRIE

Terrie, 27, is from East Oakland Park, Florida and a law student at the New School. Her father is from Germany and her mother is from Ethiopia. She was an early organizer of OWS.

MY FATHER ACTUALLY watched his great-grandfather die—executed at a Nazi camp. He always reminds me that he made a promise when he was nine years old and arrived here that he would not, and I repeat would not, watch his children suffer.

I'm here to make a difference. I'm here to be a voice for those that wish to be here but they cannot. This economy, this society, separates us by race, color, gender. We are sick and tired of being manipulated by the media. We are sick and tired of being manipulated by society, the press, the movie stars. You have to look a certain way, walk a certain way, have money to be valuable. *Everybody* is valuable.

I'm a college student and I'm going to graduate with a lot of student loans and I do not want anybody to have to go through what I'm going to go through after I graduate. They're going to be inside the grave paying student loans with a high interest rate while the big schools—the big corporations—get that money, and the interest rate is ridiculous. There is no more freedom. It's like you become 21st-century slaves, and I'm very concerned.

As a law student, I'm going to graduate with over $120,000 in student loan debt. Society says you have to have a good education in order to have a good job so you can make it in life. Right, I'm getting that good education. But when I graduate, then what?

The American dream—they told you growing up—you go to school, get good grades, get an education, work 50, 60 percent of your life, and then you retire. Now you have to make choices when you retire that make you wonder if you made the right decision all your life. I'm also here because of kids who haven't been born yet or are already here and can't make a decision for themselves. We're going to pass all that debt to them? That's really not fair.

I would like to see the government make companies that went overseas to save their money pay higher taxes, and take that money and put it toward the debt. I would like to see jobs—real jobs, serious jobs with real pay—the way America used to be, where you actually work and you make money, you make a living, and you get to live the American Dream. But I know that I might still be daydreaming.

OCCUPY WALL STREET'S EARLIEST VICTORIES AND HOW WE CAN KEEP WINNING

BY YOTAM MAROM

THE OCCUPATION OF Wall Street is now in its third week. Thousands of people have worked and fought for it, used their bodies as shields, sent letters of solidarity, marched, slept out, donated, tweeted, and more. There are still thousands more who have not been with us, whether because of geographical reasons or because they are busy struggling elsewhere.

I have been involved, in some way, with the occupation on Wall Street since the first planning meeting a number of months ago, and I have been out there almost every day since the occupation began, though mostly keeping quiet and working on the sidelines. I have participated in assemblies and working groups, done outreach to community organizations, pushed demands, been to dozens of meetings, gone hoarse from chanting about the banks, been bruised by metal police batons while marching for Troy Davis, and had about a million incredible conversations, at the occupation at Liberty Plaza itself, in other political contexts around New York, and even in jail with the 87 friends I made during the mass arrests of September 24. I am not an authority, and others have struggled and sacrificed much more than I have, but I have learned a lot.

The struggle is still very much underway. Those of us who can, who have that privilege, should be out in the streets, so now might not be the time for the most thorough analysis. It is, however, important for occupiers to be writing in our own words; to reach out to the many around the world who want to be a part of this in some way, to offer our own analyses and to counter the media blackout we are experiencing.

Though the press is now somewhat intrigued by us, and alarmed by police brutality, it still has very little to say about the actual content and processes of this occupation. Maybe it's because they don't care, or maybe it's because we are a threat to their sponsors (and we are). But, honestly, maybe it is because we speak a new language, one we have to translate for them.

The 99%

WHAT WE HAVE ALREADY WON

I have to admit, I was skeptical. I saw too many young white college kids and not enough of those communities hardest hit by neoliberalism and austerity. Having helped organize Bloombergville (a two-week occupation against the budget cuts in NYC) only a few months earlier, I didn't see how this would aid in the overarching aim of building a movement, beyond a single uprising. But I was wrong about some of those assumptions, and—though we are still far from being a huge, unified movement with clear goals—things have steadily improved.

First of all, the occupation has lasted more than two weeks and it's growing every day. Tens of thousands of people have participated in this occupation in some way or another, from the thousands who have slept out or marched or stopped by, to the thousands of pizzas ordered for us, the thousands of dollars sent our way, and the thousands watching the livestream and emailing and calling and tweeting. Add this to occupations being planned in more than 100 cities in the U.S. alone, not to mention in other countries (both those in solidarity with us, and those that were our inspiration). Labor, student and community groups from around the city are joining, and they bring with them serious organizers and community members from the most oppressed and marginalized communities in New York. They also bring their own concrete demands, which are easy to support because they are obvious, as they have always been.

Next, we have taken steps to define ourselves and to write documents to that affect. I have always been a strong proponent of clear demands. I do want to point out that we have been able to continue to grow despite a lack of demands. I also think our demands really aren't as mysterious as some people are letting on; I think our critics are playing dumb.

We wouldn't be on Wall Street if we didn't already have an implicitly unifying message: We hold the banks, the millionaires and the political elite they control responsible for the exploitation and oppression we face, from capitalism, racism and authoritarianism to imperialism, patriarchy and environmental degradation. We have planted ourselves in the financial capital of the world because we see it as one of the most deeply entrenched roots of the various systems of oppression we face every day. The clue is in the title: Occupy *Wall Street*.

Every day, the occupiers see themselves more and more connected to a movement—a movement around the country and the world. Every day more people from different communities join, and they bring their people, their demands, their languages, their struggles. Every day more grassroots organizations—struggling around housing or healthcare, for adjunct professors or postal workers—join the fight, bringing with them the clear message that this movement must be grounded in the hard organizing work that took place before this occupation and will continue after it. This realization of the connection between the different struggles we wage will be among the most important things to come out of this.

We have already taken back some space—space for new forms of democratic participation, for a type of rebellion that rejects permits, pens and sidewalks, one that demands streets and bridges instead, and someday also buildings and governments.

These are enormous victories in the creation of a new narrative, one that refuses to accept the myth that Americans don't struggle, that things really aren't so bad and that we're willing to let injustice happen because we get a bigger piece of the bounty our military and capitalists extract from others.

We are rewriting the story, telling it ourselves. And the story will be an important force not only in this struggle, but in the many to come. We will tell the story while we are at work and at school, on the picket lines, in marches, at our next occupations and sit-ins, in jail when the bosses get frightened enough to tell their henchmen to arrest us in the hundreds as they did on October 1, and the story will help us remember and imagine our boundless potential while we fight on.

BATTLES TO COME

Occupations are an incredibly important mode of resistance, an expression of a dual power strategy. On one hand, they give us the space and time with which to create an alternative, to practice, to learn, to create new relations, to become better revolutionaries, and to experience community. At the same time, they serve as a base camp from which to wage a struggle against the institutions that oppress us. Both are important. And yes, we face challenges in each realm.

Internally, we have to find and create new and diverse ways for people to participate, especially those too busy or too threatened by the daily brutalities they already face to be able to join us in occupations or marches. We have to continue to work to formulate a message together, not only because it will clarify our multitude of voices for the outside world, but also because the process will be educational for us and it will ground us in the real struggles we have inherited from being part of a movement together.

Externally, it is simple. We have to draw clear lines from the oppression heaped on this society to the agents responsible for it. If Chase Bank is foreclosing on homes, we need to foreclose on Chase Bank. If the city government is cutting schools and homeless shelters, we need to shut it down. They want business as usual, and that's what we have to take from them.

Liberty Plaza is not the struggle; it is the home for the creation of the alternative, and the staging ground for the fight that takes us out into the streets, to make business as usual truly untenable.

We win when we build diverse movements led by the most oppressed people in society, capable of proposing an alternative, laying the seeds for it, and taking the power necessary to transform it from the alternative to the norm. We win when we raise social costs to the point that those hopeless few elites find themselves left with no carrots to wave before us and no sticks big enough to do us any harm. We win when we show no signs of weakening, when we refuse to go home. We win when the movement grows and grows and grows with no sign of letting up. We win when losing is not an option, when winning is the only way to really be human.

'THEY ARE KLEPTOMANIACS:' MICHAEL MOORE ADDRESSES OCCUPY WALL STREET

Academy-Award winning filmmaker and best-selling author Moore spoke to Liberty Plaza on September 26.

THEY ARE THIEVES. They are gangsters. They are kleptomaniacs. They are trying to take our democracy and turn it into a kleptocracy: their kleptocracy. The 400 richest Americans own more wealth than 150 million combined. They think they're going to get away with it, because they have so much more than everyone else.

But they're afraid of one basic thing—there's only 400 of them! And there are 150 million, 200 million, 250 million of us! Now what happens when 250 million are pitted against 400 people. You don't have to be into sports to understand the outcome of that game. All we have to do—not just us here—but all Americans, is to realize how much more power we have than they have. They think their power is derived from their bank accounts, but our power is derived from the people—all the people! Not the 400. All the people!

Do not despair because there's only a few hundred here right now. All great movements start with just a few people … Whatever you do, don't despair, because this is the hard part. Everyone will remember, three months from now, six months from now, a hundred years from now … we started this movement. Thank you, all of you for everything you've done.

INTERVIEW WITH NICOLE CASTY

*Casty, 23, is from Atlanta, Georgia. She first visited Occupy
Wall Street on October 1, the day of the Brooklyn Bridge march.
She kept coming back.*

THE ECONOMY AND politics affect everyone, every second of every day.
We all live with the effects of politics and society. Of debt and the economy.
My parents, we used to be solidly middle-class and we lost a lot of money in
the failing of the tech bubble and later we lost a lot of investment with the
housing collapse. My mom's in real estate. We have a lot of debt now; we used
to have this kind of surplus. That's from an upper-middle-class perspective.
These are not new issues. This has been life for decades for a lot of communities. We can't forget that lower-income neighborhoods have been in a depression, not just a recession, for decades.

It's important to visibly connect our interests. All the people—anti-war,
feminist, against stop-and-frisk, against the prison industrial complex—we
are all interconnected. The problems are all related to corruption, putting
profit before people. Why do we criminalize and lock away black and Latino
men? Because there's money in it. What kind of dystopian future are we setting ourselves up for? The human factor becomes null when you profit from
selling weapons for war and also profit from refugee camps. There's no way
to go forward without dismantling structures because they are all so interconnected.

YEARS OF DISCONTENT TRIGGER AMERICAN AUTUMN

BY LEO GERARD

TO CONVEY THE significance of the Occupy Wall Street movement, NBC News anchor Brian Williams this week quoted the 1960s Buffalo Springfield song, "For What It's Worth."

There's something happening here
What it is ain't exactly clear.

Maybe it's unclear what the Occupy Wall Street movement will ultimately accomplish. But what's happening—for the past three weeks in New York and now in hundreds of towns across North America—is a roiling, inspirational, grassroots expression of anger, disgust and revolution.

And, frankly, given what's been going on in the United States since the bank bailout, it's amazing this uprising didn't precede the Arab Spring. The powers-that-be, from the rich and influential to their coin-operated politicians and corporate-owned media, have mocked and belittled and ignored the protesters, the 99 percenters as they call themselves—everyone but the richest 1 percent. No matter what the critics say, these people, with righteous outrage and new-age communication, have launched the American Autumn.

This revolt could have started in the spring of 2009, immediately after the Bush administration pushed through Congress the Troubled Asset Relief Program (TARP), the $700 billion in taxpayer money spent to prop up banks that had gambled and lost untold trillions. A Bloomberg News investigation would later show that the United States lent, spent or guaranteed as much as $12.8 trillion to save the banks. Despite that help, the Wall Street recklessness ruined the American economy, throwing tens of millions out of jobs and homes.

Poverty and hunger skyrocketed in the richest country in the world. As tax revenue fell, states, towns and school districts slashed essential public services and laid off teachers, librarians, firefighters and police officers. Maybe it just took this long for the middle-class to grasp all the horrible effects of the Wall Street gambling and to realize that a government held hostage by country club conservatives bent on cutting public services just made matters worse. Maybe young people looked at unrestrained war spending, Pell Grant slashing and voter disenfranchising and decided they were fed up and were not going to take foreclosure of their futures anymore.

Whatever the spark, the American Autumn began three weeks ago in New York City's Zuccotti Park. Late in September, some of the 1 percenters sipped champagne on an upscale restaurant balcony as they looked down on the protesters in the streets below. This week, as protests spread, wealthy risk-takers at the Chicago Board of Trade put signs in the windows of their ritzy offices bragging, "We are the 1 percent." They don't get it.

Nor does Bank of America. Here's a bank bailed out by taxpayers that announced it would begin imposing a new fee—$5 a month, $60 a year—on debit card users (since rescinded). This bank also just announced it would worsen the recession caused by bankster recklessness by laying off 30,000 workers.

This is a bank that engaged in the habitual, anti-capitalistic Wall Street practice of rewarding poor executive performance by giving its CEO Brian T. Moynihan a $9 million bonus immediately after the institution he runs lost $2.2 billion in 2010. Moynihan responded to criticism of the $5 fee by saying customers—and ultimately taxpayers—must line his pockets and that of shareholders, regardless of how badly he runs the bank or how stupidly he gambles with its money. That's because, he asserted, the bank has a "right to make a profit." No matter what.

The media and country club conservatives belittled the protesters. Here's what Herman Cain, a Tea Partier seeking the GOP nomination for president, said: "Don't blame Wall Street, don't blame the big banks if you don't have a job or you're not rich. Blame yourself!"

He continued, "It's not a person's fault because they succeeded. It's a person's fault if they failed. And so this is why I don't understand these demonstrations and what it is that they're looking for."

He called the protesters "anti-capitalist," although it was the banks that sought a socialist bailout from the government when they got themselves in trouble.

Cain didn't blame banksters for unemployment, even though it was Wall Street gambling that took down the economy. He blames the teachers and police officers thrown out of work by local governments that are cash-strapped as a result of the recession caused by Wall Street recklessness. Cain and the media keep saying they don't understand what the protesters want. They just don't get it.

A specific list of demands is unnecessary. What the 99 percenters want is obvious. They want the American Dream restored. Good public education for everyone. Equity in opportunity. Shared sacrifice so the rich pay a tax rate at least equal to that charged the middle-class. An end to poverty and unemployment in the richest country in the world. In the Buffalo Springfield song, "For What It's Worth," lyrics talk of 1960s youths criticized for their protests:

Young people speaking their minds
Getting so much resistance from behind.

This time protesters will get backing. The members of my union, the United Steelworkers, get it. Members of the unions of the AFL-CIO and Change to Win federations get it. We're here to support the people of the American Autumn.

The 99%

INTERVIEW WITH IMMORTAL TECHNIQUE

Born in Peru and raised in Harlem, Immortal Technique is a rapper and activist who has been one of Occupy Wall Street's strongest supporters in the hip-hop community.

KRISTEN GWYNNE: *Why are you here?*

IMMORTAL TECHNIQUE: I'm here because this is one of the most powerful expressions of democracy that I've seen in America in decades. And I'm here because in other countries in the world this is illegal, and it's sad that they're trying to make this illegal here. They're trying to discourage people from expressing their democratic right. There is no more love for a nation than you can have than to refuse to see it fall into the hands of people who do not have the people's interest at heart. That's the problem of so many nations that have collapsed before.

To think that America is unique in a way that it will exist forever you have to understand that Muslims held Spain for three times as long as America has existed as a nation. If we're going to last and we're going to create a better future and a better semblance of democracy then we cannot proliferate anti-democratic movements, we cannot proliferate dictatorships the way that we have in Africa, the Middle East, and all over Latin America for the past couple centuries.

We have to be the shining example of what democracy is. Does that mean that some of these businesses will fail? Absolutely, but isn't that the same Darwinism they want to impose on the rest of the world? Yes, some of you billionaires are going to have to go bankrupt. Oh, you're breaking my fucking heart. That's capitalism, right?

KG: *What do you think about Occupy the Hood?*

IT: I think that there's many movements that are going to branch off of this. I think the most important thing that we should realize is it doesn't matter where it is. Realistically speaking, Wall Street has detached itself from the democratic process here. It's detached itself from the hood everywhere. As a matter of fact Wall Street sees everywhere as the hood because it's not insulated in the small tiny island nation of corporations that it only represents. There is no democracy on Wall Street. There's no election to see what kind of brutal regime they're going to install so they can rape the natural resources of some place. I think the only democracy Wall Street knows is when we vote them out by not buying their products, when you vote them out by divesting in their companies.

KG: What do you think about people saying this is an all-white movement?
[*pointing*] 1, 2, 3, 4, 5, 6, 7, 8, 9, 10. I'm surrounded by people of color. I mean, there's so much diversity here it's crazy. There's more diversity here than a Tea Party rally! And this isn't corporate-funded. This isn't funded by the Koch brothers. It's an organic movement. They should learn the difference in that.

KG: Growing up in Harlem, how did you see the effects of corporations?
IT: One word, gentrification. You come to make the neighborhood nicer, but you didn't make it nicer for me, you made it nicer because you wanted to replace me. Because when you see a black or a brown face, automatically the property value goes down. Because they wanted to replace individuals. That's not just corporate America's fault, that's black and brown people's fault. When those brownstones were on sale for $1,000 all these niggas that was talking about hustling and getting money back in the '80s, why didn't you buy 12 brownstones, you idiot? What did you waste it all on—a fucking chain, a Mercedes Benz, jewelry? You're responsible for your own colonization, too. The best way to get somebody off your back is to stand up straight.

INTERVIEW WITH SGT. SHAMAR THOMAS

Sgt. Thomas is a U.S. Marine who confronted the NYPD at the global solidarity march on Times Square. The video went viral. Now a regular at the marches, he encourages fellow Marines and military servicepersons to join the movement. Here is what he said to the cops in Times Square.

THIS IS NOT a war zone. It doesn't make you tough to hurt these people. There's nothing tough about it. You are hurting U.S. citizens. Where's that in the contract? Leave these people alone. They don't have guns! Why are you hurting these people? It doesn't make any sense. How do you sleep at night? Do you get honor out of hitting people with batons? Nobody is trying to hurt you guys. There are no bullets flying out here. How tough are you?

Question posed by cameraman: What did you see tonight that bothered you?

I was here October 5. I saw them beating people, people who had nothing to do with anything, just grabbing people out of the crowd. There is no honor in that. I did 14 months in Iraq. My father was in Afghanistan. My mother did a year in Iraq. We fought for this country. I'm in New York City, I am from New York City—and these cops are hurting people that I fought to protect. There is no reason for this. There is no honor in hurting unarmed civilians and I won't let that happen.

As a part of the 99 percent, I think it's my duty as a leader, as somebody who chose to protect and serve this country, to continue my job. It's not an oath that I take lightly and that stopped once I left the Marine Corps.

WE CAME, WE STAYED

BY ANNA LEKAS MILLER

I WAS AT OCCUPY Wall Street the first day. I didn't believe it was going to actually happen. I knew that organizers from the organizing meetings were expecting "anywhere between 1,000 and 50,000" and I knew that as activist estimates tend to be, this was overly optimistic.

Still, it was all I could think about. I plagued friends with hushed conversations about the revolution that entire week—on campus, in cafes and bars, and over g-chat. I thought that if enough people were talking about it, it might actually happen. I thought the radical notion that my country—somewhere that I had been ashamed to say I was from while I was living abroad—might actually wake up and at least show that they are alive by being pissed off.

I wanted my anger towards the corporate regime to go from being seen as radical to being seen as mainstream.

I checked Twitter when I woke up the morning of September 17. Someone had tweeted, "With love to New York, from #SidiBouzid to #OccupyWallStreet" and I knew it was actually happening.

I didn't know the time it was going to happen—and I was anxious that if something did happen I would miss it. It was all I could think about—so I packed a notepad, a camera, and scrawled the Legal Aid number on my arm, another move that seemed premature and slightly idiotic at the time. I got to Wall Street, and it was completely blocked off—at 11 in the morning. The only other people there besides the slough of police officers were a Vietnam veteran wearing a tie-dyed shirt and a group of confused European tourists who were disappointed the police wouldn't let them in to see Wall Street.

I almost told a police officer I was there for the protest, to politely ask if he would please let me in to peacefully demonstrate.

Gradually, a few journalists and bloggers arrived—many of them left when it seemed like the police had shut down the protest before it began. Protesters followed, some carrying signs, a few in costume, but mostly plain-clothed people simply wondering what was going to happen. Organizers decided to re-assemble at Bowling Green Park—some decided to march around the bull, which had also been barricaded by the police.

Still, something felt significant. I didn't want it to die. I wanted to stay—being another body, keeping this precious moment of dissent and patriotism alive for as long as possible. Protesters seemed discontented—the police were threatening to arrest and kettle the protesters, Wall Street had already been shut down, and places like Egypt and Spain set a high global standard for what revolutionary uprisings should look like.

We finally marched—there didn't seem like there was anything else to do. We found Zuccotti Park.

The rest is history.

INTERVIEW WITH FRANK WHITE

White, 54, is a farmer living in Lebanon, New York. He spent seven years in Vermont as a licensed clinical mental health counselor specializing in severe mental illness. He works out of the medical tent.

I FIRST CAME DOWN as a tourist. I was drawn by curiosity to the electricity of the movement. And I saw mental health issues. I wasn't looking to stretch those brain cells and deal in that field but I found the best way to plug in was to use those skills. The balance has shifted where homeless people have plugged in more and more, and with that comes issues of not only homelessness, but drug abuse, alcohol abuse—quite a lot of mental illness.

I'm encouraging media and people to reform their thinking: that homelessness is here, it showed up, and it's a very essential element of the the 99 percent. The homeless are the bottom 2 percent or 5 percent, and that could not be more poignant. To grab the moment and talk about the reality happening on the ground is better than denial. We're talking about the movement having two themes, greed and poverty. And so it's germane to what we're talking about. This is the bottom of the 99 percent on the streets of New York. People should step up and embrace that.

Occupy Wall Street started with the Arab Spring. Is homelessness going to end it? What's real on the ground are all the issues we're talking about, under the same banner. It's a turning point in how history books will see it—it's how the media reports it, how you report it, it's holding it in a different light.

INTERVIEW WITH VLAD TEICHBERG

Teichberg, 39, holds a math degree from Princeton University. He is a former derivatives trader and a founder of Occupy's Livestream, Global Revolution TV. He works on the media team at Occupy Wall Street.

AFTER I GRADUATED, me and a bunch of my comrades who were actually activists, we all went to Wall Street. We decided that it was pretty impossible to reform the system, and the best way to reform it was to do it from the inside. Two of us actually had pretty long careers in it. One person is still inside. None of us had any success changing it. I was seeing how the system was basically corrupt.

I first quit in 2001. I quit credit derivatives and switched into computer-based arbitrage which at that time was not malignant. But it became cancerous as well. All these great mathematical ideas in finance start out as really beautiful concepts supposed to make the world a better place. Derivatives, for example, are supposed to spread the risk around the world and create this super insurance company where all the risk is naturally distributed in an organic way which would create a system that is much more robust against earthquakes or collapses or whatever. But combined with greed and unethical behavior it became a huge problem. It became the bomb.

The first week of Occupy Wall Street was a total media blockade. Then the police screwed up and brutalized some protesters on the march to Washington Square Park, and that went viral. Then the blockade was lifted. And because we had this 24-hour news stream coming out, we became the reference point for what this protest was about. So mainstream news was not able to shape or define us. We were able to define us and put our humanity, our people first, in front of the whole world. And we think that's why the process went viral—people saw the same kind of humans that they are. The mainstream media was not able to demonize the protesters as the Other because it was so obvious we are the same as everybody else.

INTERVIEW WITH KELLEY BRANNON

Brannon, 27, is an artist living in Queens, New York.

MY MOM HAS a master's degree and she makes $10 an hour as a special education teacher for students with mental and physical disabilities. And she literally goes year to year, contract to contract. She has no safety net. And that's been the case my whole life. They just keep bouncing her around. She's also at retirement age right now—she's 65. She can't afford to retire. So it's also a matter of how long the system will let her work.

She couldn't help me pay for school. Nobody could. I didn't have a cosigner for my loans, so my first two years of college I worked 30-40 hours a week. I was working so much it was very hard to concentrate on school and actually do art work, which takes a crazy amount of time. So my last year I got $10,000 and I took that. My debt is up to $23,000 dollars. It's not completely astronomical, but I think I probably have another $2,000 to $3,000 just in interest that's accumulated because I put them in forbearance because I really don't have any way to pay.

I started paying $50 per month in the beginning, but when you pay $50 per month and then only see your balance go down by $10 it's a little disenfranchising. I was literally just paying off the interest. I decided I would wait until I could make bigger payments. And honestly there's a part of me that just thinks I'm going to live with that forever—or until the revolution happens.

II.

THE

MODEL

SOCIETY

INTRODUCTION

THE FACT THAT Occupy Wall Street took off when so many attempts to jumpstart progressive protests targeting the big banks have failed may be due in part to the occupations themselves. More than just a tactic, they are tiny nerve centers for a new society, reclamations of public space by the people.

Inside those public spaces, protesters do more than camp out. They provide food and medical care, free of charge, and create their own media, with livestreams and Twitter feeds and in more than one space, a print newspaper. (In New York, the *Occupied Wall Street Journal* is a full-size broadsheet that nicked its style from the real *Wall Street Journal* and runs full-color photographs along with its articles.)

Beyond that, though, the occupations have become what writer Matthew Stoller called "a church of dissent," where a broad spectrum of activists, organizers, writers, thinkers and teachers come together to discuss, plan, debate, read and create. The center of the Liberty Plaza occupation in New York is a lending library, which sprawls across the northeast corner of the park.

The space is, as reporter Laurie Penny put it, its own demand: a demand for a place where people can gather and learn, create, help one another, and simply be in contact with their fellow humans for a while. Whether you sleep there or pass through on lunch break, you can stop, pick up a book, chat with a stranger, grab a bite to eat or get a free flu shot, donate an old coat, or hear a lecture on global capitalism.

Occupation is more than just a symbolic move, it's an act of creation. Here we've gathered some of the best writing about the alternative society the protesters are creating for themselves, day by day, night by night.

The 99%

Susie Cagle writes and draws true stories. She is usually for hire. Susie is also the founder of the Graphic Journos collective.

UPSPARKLES FROM THE HEART OF THE PARK

BY EVE ENSLER

I HAVE BEEN WATCHING and listening to all kinds of views and takes on Occupy Wall Street.

Some say it's backed by the Democratic Party. Some say it's the emergence of a third party. Some say the protesters have no goals, no demands, no stated call. Some say it's too broad, taking on too much. Some say it is the left's version of the Tea Party. Some say it's communist, some say it's class warfare. Some say it will burn out and add up to nothing. Some say it's just a bunch of crazy hippies who may get violent.

I have been spending time down at Zuccotti Park and I am here to offer a much more terrifying view. What is happening cannot be defined. It is happening. It is a happening. It is a response to injustice and inequity and poverty and Wall Street corruption and soaring college debt and unemployment and homelessness, institutionalized racism and violence against women, the murdering of the earth, fracking and the Keystone pipeline and the wars the U.S. has waged on other countries that have destroyed them and bankrupted us here.

It is a cry against what appears to be scarcity and what Naomi Klein calls a distribution problem, and I would add, a priority problem. It is a spontaneous uprising that has been building for years in our collective unconscious. It is a gorgeous, mischievous moment that has arrived and is spreading. It is a speaking out, coming out, dancing out. It is an experiment and a disruption.

We all know things are terribly wrong in this country. From the death of our rivers to the bankruptcy of our schools to our failed healthcare system, something at the center does not hold.

A diverse group of teachers, thinkers, students, techies, workers, nurses, have stopped their daily lives. They have come to gather and reflect and march and lay their bodies down. They have come from all over the country and the world. Some have flown in just to be here. I met students last night from a college in Kentucky who had just arrived and were committed to sleeping out for two nights in solidarity.

Occupy Wall Street is a work of art, exploding onto a canvas in search of form, in search of an image, a vision.

In a culture obsessed with product, the process of creation is almost unbearable. Nothing is more threatening than the moment, the living, breathing ambiguity of now. We have been trained to name things, own things, brand things, and in doing so control and consume them.

Well, the genius of Occupy Wall Street is that so far it is not brandable and that's what makes its potential so daunting, so far-reaching, so inclusive and so dangerous. It cannot be defined and so it cannot be sold, as a sound-bite or a political party or even a thing. It can't be summed up and dismissed.

What is also most unusual about Occupy Wall Street is that the evolving self-governing practices at the twice-daily general assembly and the organic way the park is being organized, are literally modeling a vision of the desired new world. A rotating group of facilitators, a constant check to make sure all voices are heard, timekeepers, free medicine and medical help, composting, learning groups, a free library, learning circles, workshops on human rights, arts and culture, history, extraordinary speakers at open forums.

I had the fortune to spend the night with a group of about 30 occupiers—the talk could have gone on through the early morning. The depth of the conversation, the intensity of the seeking, the complexity of ideas were startling. But, what moved me even more was the respect, the way people listened to each other and honored and appreciated each other.

I would like to encourage another take on Occupy Wall Street. I would like to ask that perhaps we stop trying to define it or own it or discount it or belittle it, but instead to celebrate it. It should make New York proud. It should make this country proud.

We say all the time how we believe in democracy, that we want the people to speak and be heard. Well, the people are speaking. The people are experimenting. The people are crying out with the deepest hunger to build a better world. Maybe instead of labeling it, we could join it. There is so much to be done.

Copyright Eve Ensler

THE HUMAN MICROPHONE
BY RICHARD KIM

ANYONE WHO'S BEEN down to Occupy Wall Street and stayed for a general assembly will instantly recognize the call and response that begins, and frequently interrupts, each meeting.

"Mic check?" someone implores.

"MIC CHECK!" the crowd shouts back, more or less in unison.

The thing is—there's no microphone. New York City requires a permit for amplified sound in public, something that the pointedly unpermitted Occupy Wall Street lacks. This means that microphones and speakers are banned from Liberty Plaza, and the NYPD has also been interpreting the law to include battery-powered bullhorns. Violators can be sentenced up to 30 days in jail. Further complicating the matter is the fact that Liberty Plaza is not actually a public park. It's privately owned by Brookfield Office Properties, landlords to Bank of America and JPMorgan Chase, and in addition to amplified sound, they've also sought to ban sleeping bags, tents and other equipment from the property they call Zuccotti Park.

So despite all the attention given to how Twitter, Facebook and livestream video have helped spread the word, the heart of the occupation is most definitely unplugged. But the protesters aren't deterred one bit; they've adopted an ingeniously simple, people-powered method of sound amplification. After the mic check, the meeting proceeds:

with every few words / WITH EVERY FEW WORDS!

repeated and amplified out loud / REPEATED AND AMPLIFIED OUT LOUD!

by what has been dubbed / BY WHAT HAS BEEN DUBBED!

the human microphone / THE HUMAN MICROPHONE!!! (jazz hands here).

The overall effect can be hypnotic, comic or exhilarating—often all at once. As with every media technology, to some degree the medium is the message. It's hard to be a downer over the human mic when your words are enthusiastically shouted back at you by hundreds of fellow occupiers, so speakers are usually pretty upbeat (or at least sound that way). Likewise, the human mic is not so good for getting across complex points about, say, how the Federal Reserve's practice of quantitative easing is inadequate to address the current shortage of global aggregate demand (although Joe Stiglitz tried valiantly), so speakers tend to express their ideas in straightforward narrative or moral language.

There's something inherently pluralistic about the human mic, too; it's almost impossible to demagogue, to interrupt and shout someone down or to hijack the general assembly for your own sectarian purposes. That's clearly been a saving grace of this occupation, as the internecine fights over identity and ideology that usually characterize Left formations haven't corrosively bubbled over into blood feuds—yet. The human mic is also, of course, an egalitarian instrument, and it exudes solidarity over ego. No doubt, a great frenzy erupts when Left gods like Michael Moore or Cornel West descend to speak, but many people only hear their words through the human mic, in the horizontal acoustics of the crowd instead of the electrified intimacy of "amplified sound." Celebrity, charisma, status, even public-speaking ability—they all just matter less over the human microphone.

But the greatest hidden virtue of the human mic has been the quality that almost every observer has reflexively lamented: it is slow. I mean incredibly, agonizingly, astonishingly slow; it can take over an hour for the general assembly just to get through a nightly refresher course on group protocols before starting in on announcements, which precede debate about anything new, like whether or not the occupation should make a list of demands and if so, what those demands should be. Imagine collectively debating and writing the Port Huron Statement by consensus, three to five words at a time.

But really, what is the goddamn rush? As my colleague Betsy Reed points out, it's Occupy Wall Street's raw anger and simple resistance to being beat down (sentiments well-suited for the human mic) that have captured the public's imagination, not the elaborate policy proposals of other efforts. As days go by and as the press attention heats up, the occupiers will be under increasing pressure to speed things up: to issue a list of demands, appoint spokespeople, nominate leaders, enumerate an agenda. I'm not sure they should go there—they did manage, over two weeks, to arrive at a consensus for a first statement, which if you think about it is a mind-boggling achievement—but if they do decide on demands, it will be at a plodding pace over the human mic. That's a good thing. The longer Occupy Wall Street can stay relatively indeterminate, the longer it has to capture the symbolic power of resistance itself.

The rest we can figure out; the protesters plan to be there through the winter, so we have plenty of time. Think of it as slow growth activism, one that poses a provocative counter-model to Wall Street's regime of instant profits. After all, it was in the offices and exchanges surrounding Occupy Wall Street that the financiers sliced and diced assets with mind-numbing speed. Enabled by vast and unregulated databases of information, the genius of quants and fancy algorithms and the whirl of flash trades, they ruled the economy on the principles of simultaneity and speed.

That did not work out so well.

It is, of course, ironic that New York City's attempt to crackdown on political protest by restricting "amplified sound" unwittingly ended up contributing to the structural strength of its rowdiest protest in decades. But like in Egypt or Argentina or Belarus or other places where the authorities sought to silence speech, the people found a way to be heard.

So how about it, can I get a mic check for this one: The people have the power.

Reprinted with permission from the October 3, 2011 issue of The Nation.

THE RADICAL INFRASTRUCTURE OF OCCUPY WALL STREET

BY SARAH JAFFE

"WE ARE NOW creating a society that we envision for the world. Being responsible for ourselves is at the heart of that," the woman facilitating the general assembly calls through the people's microphone. That responsibility took center stage at this emergency general assembly (GA), where the occupiers committed to an intense cleaning of Zuccotti Park to stave off an incursion by the police and cleaners purportedly hired by the park's ownership.

Occupy Wall Street, as many have noted, isn't just a protest; it's a reclamation of public space, a new commons for people who feel left out and left behind by the current system. Arun Gupta, editor of the *Indypendent* and one of those who helped create the *Occupied Wall Street Journal*, says, "You have this uncommodified radical public space right in the heart of global capital. There is no money being exchanged, and that's remarkable in a city that is kind of the height of the idea that we exist to consume."

He points out that the people claimed the space, and from there came up with the idea of the "We are the 99 percent" slogan that has taken hold across the country. "The mere presence itself," in the park, he notes, "became almost the politics of it. It's through the space that we can bring real democracy into being."

Symbolically snatching that space back just shouting distance from the New York Stock Exchange and holding onto it would be protest enough, but inside that space the protesters built a model for the communities they'd like to see. They created infrastructure, and the infrastructure they chose to build stands in stark contrast to the hacking and slashing at public infrastructure spending done over the last 30 or so years and rapidly accelerated in the age of austerity.

"People who couldn't afford food or healthcare, that's no longer the case. They can come here and get what they need," says Red, a street medic at the medical station. "It's probably my favorite part of this movement."

Red explains that the medical station is staffed by anywhere from five to 12 people at a time, some of whom are EMTs or trained medics, others are nurses or doctors. "We have five or six doctors who rotate in and out," he says, "They work for free, sometimes they stay up all night."

The medical station can't provide every bit of healthcare that people might need, of course—it's hardly set up for surgery or treatment of serious illnesses. But it's surprisingly well stocked, with donations from 1199 SEIU and the National Nurses United as well as supplies bought with cash donations. In a country that still balks at the idea of "socialized medicine," having a place where one can get a free doctor visit is all too rare.

It's not just healthcare and free food that the occupiers are modeling in the park, it's everything from greener lifestyle techniques to support for arts and books.

The People's Library might be the most impressive structure in the park. It's now extended from the concrete benches along one wall onto tables, and the books have been stickered, labeled and had their barcodes scanned and catalogued onto the web. This, as libraries across the U.S. face budget cuts and closure.

"Our working group has 15 or 20 people," Betsy Fagin, a Brooklyn librarian who is currently not working, tells me. Instead, she spends her days at Liberty Plaza, labeling and cataloging books, and her nights working on the online catalog. "We have a librarian in Indiana who is cataloging online for us," she notes. As of Tuesday, October 11, the library had around 400 records, and more donations are coming in all the time.(That's Day 25 of the occupation, according to a board that also provides a weather report, a donations count of more than $40,000 and an arrest count of 834-plus.)

As I make my way through the park, I see a sign declaring the arts and culture space, and a man carrying a "Roving Help Desk" sign. A man with a broom and dustpan is sweeping up, and another scuttles to bring paper towels to wipe up some coffee that's spilled a bit too near some sleeping bags.

Over the weekend, the computers throughout the plaza (at the media station as well as the "Internet cafe" and phone charging station) were powered not by the generators that have kept them going most of the time, but by a solar panel-laden truck brought up by Greenpeace.

Robert Gardner, whose business card describes him as a "Coal Campaigner" for the organization, explains, "It's a two-kilowatt array on the truck, which rolls down. I'd take up the whole street if I could," gesturing to the panels. It provides 50 kilowatt-hours of storage and can provide for the energy use of an average American home—or for several laptop computers and cell phones as well as a few lights that stay on as the late-night crowd works. Gardner says Greenpeace normally uses the truck as a campaign tool to demonstrate clean energy, but they heard the occupation was using gas generators and came up to donate clean power and lend their support.

That's not the only way the occupation is modeling more earth-friendly technologies. The kitchen, which now has several racks of dishes and supplies, has created a gray-water system to filter the water used to wash the dishes before using it to water the plaza's flowers. And after the gas generators were taken away by the city, new bicycle-powered batteries have replaced them—tourists passing by are invited to take a spin on the bikes to help power the media tent and the kitchen.

It's not just the New York occupation that is creating institutions to provide care. Jamieson Robbins, who has been involved with Occupy Dallas and Occupy Fort Worth in Texas, tells me:

> *The experience that I've had with my 3-year-old daughter out at Occupy Dallas and now Occupy Fort Worth has been nothing short of fantastic. Several days before our first march, discussion began on OccupyDallas.org about children being involved. Many people felt that having children present at our march was a liability and many were waiting to see how it goes before bringing out their young ones.*
>
> *I, and many others, thought about it a little differently. I think people should involve their families, their friends, their co-workers, their neighbors, but most of all their children. What are we fighting for if not for the chance to one day answer the question, 'Grandma, what was Occupy Wall Street?' with 'It was the beginning of change, my love. The country wasn't always the way it is now.' Not only that, but what a fantastic statement to onlookers to see not just hippies and anarchists, but families with their children's futures at stake.*
>
> *Now, I'm proud to say that Occupy Dallas, even under threat from city council to either buy a million-dollar insurance policy or face eviction, has set up a permanent 'Occuplay' child center within Pioneer Park.*

The shifting, growing infrastructure at the occupations around the country is taking shape differently in different places, but in nearly all of them, there's been priority placed on providing services that people often can't get anywhere else.

Street medic Red says, "It really restores your faith that there's some level of decency left in our culture."

JOURNALIST-PARTICIPANT DESCRIBES WHAT LIFE IS REALLY LIKE AT LIBERTY PLAZA

BY KRISTEN GWYNNE

HUNDREDS OF CHARACTERS buzz through Liberty Plaza, weaving through makeshift campsites of tarps and sleeping bags, park tables, meetings, and circles of music or chatting. There are arts and crafts, guitar groups, meditation circles, nap time, and hang-outs. At the west end of the park, a loud drum group beats the pulse of the movement, playing late into the night. But stitched throughout the fun is serious hard work. All through the day and into the night, working groups (and there are dozens) hold meetings to carve out their responsibilities in the movement. On the north side is the media center, the nucleus of the whole operation, where tech-friendly activists edit video, update the Web site and manage social networking 24/7. A generator's hum blends with the helicopters buzzing overhead.

Occupy Wall Street is actually far more organized than the mainstream media and critics might suggest. The lack of one common goal is not disorganization, but freedom. I've been on the ground at OWS, sleeping, marching, getting arrested, and reporting almost daily, and I can tell you that most of the media have the story all wrong. Here is what's really happening. People are living, and thriving. Using donations, demonstrators have set up their own society, with free books, food and healthcare. When I slept there Sunday night, I found I had almost everything I needed to survive. There was plenty of food—baked ziti, fruit and cookies—laid out in the buffet-style line. Between meals and late at night, there is always something to munch on, usually healthy foods like apples and bananas.

After I finished eating, my friends and I searched for a place to set up camp. By 8 p.m., just finding an unoccupied spot was difficult. After we finally posted up by the steps at Broadway, we wandered off to socialize. About 9 p.m., an organizer texted me, "Wall St. and Broad. Now!" I hurried over to find a sight much more peaceful than I'd expected.

About 10 people stood on the sidewalk with their backs to a barrier, talking quietly as one man slept on the street-side of the sidewalk next to another barrier. Another couple seemed ready to sleep as well. They started to lie down, and as the police started talking, the rules kept changing. First, the police moved the street-side barrier inward so that one of the legs wasn't "on the street." Then, it was OK to sit up, but not lie down, on the sidewalk. Then, half the sidewalk had to be open. Then, we had to be moving. A group of protesters walked back and forth on the block, teasing the police with lines like "I don't mean to be a stickler, officer, but they're not moving" and "Officer! Officer! I can't walk!" Next thing you know, white-shirted cops were putting up barriers to block off Wall Street and demanding IDs. Then all entrances to Wall Street were blocked. Suddenly, cops shouted, "This is a frozen zone!" and we all had to leave. Notably, amid all the overreaction from the police, there were only a handful of demonstrators still pacing on the sidewalk.

Back at camp, I was wide awake for hours. People were skateboarding, quietly strumming guitars, discussing, debating, and arguing with the press for photographing people who were asleep. It was just loud enough to keep me awake. When I finally did fall asleep, I slept hard. I rolled over at the crack of dawn to witness an ironic scene, blurry without my contacts, of suits surrounding the park and walking to work. When I woke up again, it was to a mic-check announcement that a girl was being arrested for writing on the sidewalk with chalk.

Although it may appear chaotic to the outside observer, the decision-making process in Liberty Plaza is incredibly organized. The working groups ensure that no ideas are lost, while the general assembly (GA) assures that none becomes tyrannical. That all opinions are considered is perhaps the best rebuttal to offer people who have yet to understand OWS. If you are part of the 99 percent exploited by corporations and their government, but dislike Occupy Wall Street, don't write off the demonstrators; join them and ask questions—create your own change. But the GAs and working groups are not the only times ideas are expressed. All day long, enthusiasts show up and exchange pertinent information. Some, like Naomi Klein, Slavoj Zizek and Jeffrey Sachs, have been more influential than others. But aside from celebrity voices, regular people continually express their opinions as well.

But as crowds gather in growing numbers at Liberty Plaza, the visibility and egalitarianism of OWS is being challenged. Some working groups have moved off-site; not far, but a few blocks away on Wall Street. As organizer Scott Simpson, 22, said, "Some people are worried that it raises visibility issues. Because it's not in the park, it's more difficult for people to know when and where a meeting is being held."

The influx of people at Liberty Plaza has generated a few more concerns. The communal movement has attracted people from all walks of life, and as people with personal issues and various types of self-promoters squeeze in, the ecosystem shows some fragility. Organizers are scrambling to deal with homelessness, and the complicated issues that accompany this vulnerable, yet important population. But they must also confront the few who use the space as a hang-out, and not always respectfully. Marginal personalities—perhaps those with emotional issues or using drugs—will inevitably turn up at a space offering free food and mass camp-outs.

Further complicating the issue is the recent emergence of tents and camp sites where sleeping bags once unrolled. The additional privacy the tents offer is a complex force in the movement. While they give organizers personal space, they complicate transparency and chip away at community. Creating private spaces also facilitates shady behaviors more easily executed behind closed doors or zipped-up tents. Adding to the trouble is the possibility that the tents themselves, or the behaviors they make possible, are potential excuses for police intervention, and ultimately eviction.

Still, the community has hung together despite unavoidable pressures from both outside and inside the movement. Organizers do not accept belligerence. Not too long ago in Liberty Plaza, a long mic-checked announcement declared "This is not a dive bar...This is not Bonnaroo [a music festival]."

This is the homebase for a global movement.

FINDING OUR VOICES AND CREATING SAFE SPACES AT OCCUPY WALL STREET

BY MELANIE BUTLER

IF WEEK I OF Occupy Wall Street was about surviving, Week II has been about finding our voices. This protest is about the 99 percent of people in America who have been on the short end of the economic stick, but it appears the media believes it's 90 percent made up of men. Some of the organizing and facilitation processes we've developed to make our movement inclusive and participatory have proven not to be enough, and we are constantly adapting and regrouping to ensure that everyone's voice in this broad and vibrant coalition is heard.

During Monday's general assembly I announce through the call-and-response system of people's microphone that CodePink's Medea Benjamin will be leading a media training session for women and gender queer/non-male identifying members of the demonstration.

This morning I watched / *This morning I watched*
News coverage of this protest / *News coverage of this protest*
10 people were interviewed / *10 people were interviewed*
1 of them / *1 of them*
Was a woman / *Was a woman*
The 99 percent / *The 99 percent*
Is not 90 percent men / *Is not 90 percent men*

The message is received enthusiastically. When we do our introductions in the training, we realize many people are not only finding it difficult to speak to press but also during the general assembly (GA). CodePink members following from across the country via livestream have expressed similar concern that women's participation in the GA seems limited to logistical report-backs from working groups that run the encampment at Liberty Plaza rather than more weighty discussions about our principles of solidarity and declaration. As these important discussions have intensified, so have women's insistence on meaningful inclusion and representation in the drafting of our "living documents."

Since the demonstration began two weeks ago, I've been coordinating with members of CodePink, the Granny Peace Brigade and the Speak-Easy Caucus looking to take the demonstration to the "next level" by staying overnight, and wanting to generate a critical mass of trusted friends to create a safe encampment for the night. On Friday we gear up for our first Occupy Wall Street sleep-out. After last Friday's was rained out, this time we are ready. At least most of us are—I still don't have a sleeping bag.

I receive an email from Eve Ensler. She wants to pay a visit and is wondering if there's anything we need that she can bring. Problem solved. I notify one of the founding members of the Speak-Easy Caucus. Her eyes well up. "Omigosh! Are you serious? Here? When?" She tells me about how her closest group of friends formed around a high school production of *The Vagina Monologues* and still lovingly refer to each other as "the Vaginas." When Ensler arrives, she tells her, "I wouldn't be here if it weren't for you."

Eve and Alicia (one of the V-girls) have brought bags of supplies, including a wonderful sleeping bag that I gratefully accept. Ensler tours the grounds, interviewing people, and says she will return tomorrow night with the rest of the V-girls. For now, she just wants to take it all in. Her face glows with awe, praise and curiosity: "A second wind is coming."

CodePinkers come and go from the square throughout the day and gather for the march against police brutality at 5:30. After the march, more members stop by to offer support and delicious home-baked chocolate chip cookies. As night falls, I go to the nearby fast-food restaurant that has become our bathroom. It is packed with young women from Occupy Wall Street. Nicole, 20, watches me take out my toothbrush and nods knowingly. I ask her how long she's been staying in the plaza. She says since last Saturday. She tells me she wasn't planning on staying, she just came down one day to check out the scene, met some cool people and didn't want to leave. "You can't capture that on camera, that sense of community. I've never felt so close to the people around me."

A woman I recognize from the encampment's medic committee reminds us that our cell phones will be the first thing taken by the police and instructs us to take down the National Lawyers Guild number in case of emergency. We obediently pen the number on our forearms in pink Sharpie and wish each other luck.

As I consult with the Safer Spaces committee—identifiable by their pink armbands—about where to set up camp, it begins to rain. I run over to where the general assembly is meeting and duck under a big red umbrella with Sara Beth, a member of the Speak-Easy caucus. We reminisce over how the umbrella originally brought us together in a moment that seems years ago but was probably last week, when I asked to trade my red umbrella for her pink one. The rain gets harder and louder. A young woman in a poncho tours the plaza with a cardboard sign shouting like a newsboy: "FREE HUGS!" People huddle under tarps and shout jokes across the plaza to keep spirits up: "Two fish are swimming in a river. One slams into a concrete wall. Dam!"

I ask Sara Beth what she wants to do if the rain continues. We decide to stick it out. I duck from tarp to tarp trying to cover my belongings and rally together other Speak-Easies. Eventually we seek refuge in the WikiLeaks truck, owned by fellow Bradley Manning supporter Clark Stoeckley. Referring to our Occupy Wall Street-induced evolution from Twitter-following to friendship, I joke that I'll thank the bejesus out of him on Twitter.

There's about seven people in the van already, only one of whom is a woman. They welcome us in, joking that it'll make her feel better. This is not exactly the "safe-space" we were envisioning, but it is warm, cozy and most importantly, dry. Someone pokes her head in asking if anyone would like a pair of clean, dry socks. A few of us hold back out of politeness before accepting. Wiggling our toes with glee in the too-large white tennis socks, we all agree: they are the best socks we have ever worn in our lives.

Around 11 p.m. I receive a text from my husband asking where I am. I reply, "Still in Liberty," expecting him to text back that I should come home because it's pouring. Instead, he arrives about half an hour later with a huge Tupperware container of freshly baked brownies. More people stop by the truck as the night progresses, including members of the security committee, who leave us with one of their yellow walkie-talkies in case we should need it. Like many of the committees, they mention they are looking for more women members.

People returning from bathroom runs report back: "We have occupied McDonald's!" "They're singing 'This Little Light of Mine.'" And, eventually "We have been evicted! Need to find a new bathroom!" We keep a running tally of the number of people in the truck, joking that we should adapt the restaurant's slogan: 17 served. Everything is funny to us. One of the served says he wants to make a big sign that says, "For the first time in my life I finally feel at home."

At 5 a.m. I return to the 24-hour fast-food bathroom. It is as hot as a sauna, and we pack in, taking turns using the hand drier. Some are changing, some cutting each other's hair, some just sitting on the floor to get some warmth into their soaked bones. People tell each other they're beautiful, reunite, hug and compare horror stories of the rough night we just survived. One woman jokes that tonight we should all just sleep here in the bathroom where it's safe and dry. "Let the guys figure out their own thing."

OCCUPY YOUR MIND: THE PEOPLE'S LIBRARY

BY JENNIFER SACKS

HOWARD ZINN IS here. Dominick Dunne and Tom Wolfe, too. Ernest Hemingway and Barbara Ehrenreich and Dr. Who and *Beowulf.* All here, and all free. Barnes & Noble may be endangered and the Borders across the street closed months ago, but the People's Library at Liberty Plaza is open for business and thriving.

That a lending library would spring up fully operational on Day One of an occupation makes sense when you consider that the exchange of ideas is paramount here, at a new crossroads of the world. Just as occupiers young and old mingle with Africans, Jews, Algonquins and Latinas, de Tocqueville rubs elbows with Nicholas Evans and Noam Chomsky.

Mandy Henk, 32, saw *Adbusters'* call to occupy Wall Street and drove in from Greencastle, Indiana, on her fall break to work in the library. A librarian at DePaul University, she'd been waiting for "an actual movement" for years when she saw a photo of the library and a poster beside it that read, "Things the library needs: Librarians."

"And here I am," she said cheerfully, as she shelved books into clear plastic bins, dozens of which line the northeastern edge of Liberty Plaza. Henk isn't surprised that a library was erected so quickly. "Any time you have a movement like this, people are going to bring books to it. People are going to have information needs. And historically, the printed word has played an extraordinarily important role."

Younger readers can find a wealth of age-appropriate material, like A.A. Milne's *When We Were Very Young, Oliver Twist* and *The Hobbit,* as well as more offbeat titles like *Tales For Little Rebels.*

Another volunteer librarian, Steve Syrek, 33, is earning his master's degree in English at Rutgers University. He has commuted to Liberty Plaza from his Washington Heights apartment every day since October 7. A sign he made for the library was snapped up by the Smithsonian Institution: "Literacy, Legitimacy and Moral Authority: The People's Library," it read.

"More people arrived, more books appeared, and it's just been growing ever since," Syrek said. "And then everyone in New York City just has to clean out their basement," he quipped, which would explain how inventory has ballooned to nearly 1,800. Authors like Naomi Klein, Eve Ensler and Katrina vanden Heuvel have donated signed editions, and vanden Heuvel has pledged hundreds of copies of *The Nation*, past and present. As a result of the influx, the library has become something of a clearinghouse for books. "People are shipping us stuff from all over the country and we just give them out," Syrek said. "We don't need them to be returned."

Volunteers log each book on LibraryThing, an online cataloging site, by scanning the ISBN number using an iPhone app. This just in: *Wicked*, *Eat Pray Love* and *Get Rich Cheating: The Crooked Path to Easy Street*. A blog and a Facebook page chronicle visits from literary luminaries and the formation of libraries at Occupy sites across the country.

On a recent Tuesday, a few people sat on the granite benches facing the bookshelves, so absorbed in their reading they didn't look up, despite the din around them. Henk, for one, appreciates the role of escapism, especially when you consider the weighty issues that drew everyone to Liberty Plaza.

"Stories are incredibly important for helping people to understand the world," she said. "And so this is a place to come to understand the world."

This story first appeared in the Occupied Wall Street Journal, *the print publication of the Liberty Plaza occupation in New York City.*

WHO ARE THE BLACK WOMEN OCCUPYING WALL STREET?

BY MIKKI BRUNNER

THEY CAME FROM New Jersey, Harlem, the Bronx and as far away as Seattle. The small, but diverse group of black women we met at Occupy Wall Street at the end of October included students, a member of the Board of Ed, community organizers and church elders. Ranging in age from 19 to 62 years old, they gathered in New York's Zuccotti Park with a common goal: to lend their voices to the swelling demand for social and economic change.

Althea, a retired schoolteacher, remembered marching on Washington with Dr. King 48 years ago. She applauded the political message of "We are the 99 percent," a slogan intended to highlight disparity between economic classes, but questioned the focus of the occupiers. To Althea, the event seemed "more like a celebration than a sit-in."

Protesting in the '60s meant risking life and limb to participate in the democratic process. Still, she said, we must bring the message of economic equality for all back to our own communities. As churches and schools get involved, she predicted, the movement will become more visibly diverse. For many black women long used to struggling against the twin tides of institutionalized racism and wealth disparity, survival despite crushing poverty is nothing new.

"We *are* the 99 percent," April said as she sold $2 political buttons emblazoned with the Wall Street bronze bull. "We've been doing this for years."

If image is everything, however, the organized chaos of Zuccotti Park does little to dispel the media representation of a movement without a unified cause.

A mother and daughter visiting New York from Los Angeles knew little about the protests, but took photographs of the makeshift city teeming with food lines and dogs, huddled blue tents and worn sleeping bags. Some media outlets have likened Occupy Wall Street to a drug-fueled, free-for-all for privileged kids, a parasitic movement lacking the sound goals and ideology to affect social change.

Is Occupy Wall Street overwhelmingly white? Yes and no. The women we spoke to maintained that women of color were working behind the scenes in their own communities. Plus, they said, media reports of a mostly white crowd failed to acknowledge the presence of lighter-skinned women of color.

The issue of the poverty gap affects black women directly, but how, when and where they rise against it differs. After all, Rosa Parks helped launch the civil rights movement after a 10-hour day at work. Fifty-six years after Rosa's history-making refusal to give up her seat on the bus, the economic picture for black women remains startling grim:

- 43 percent of black women with children live in poverty
- Single black women have median wealth of $100 while their white counterparts have $41,000
- Half of all black single women have zero or negative wealth; this occurs when debts exceed assets

These statistics, writes Mariko Chang, PhD, are vital to understanding the current economic crisis and its impact on working families. Her 2010 report, "Lifting As We Climb: Women of Color, Wealth, and America's Future" warns that the success of our nation in the changing global marketplace depends directly upon the long-term prosperity of women of color.

THE EYE OF THE STORM FOR CHANGE
BY NELINI STAMP

Stamp is a community organizer with the Working Families Party who has been involved with Occupy Wall Street since September 17. This is edited from an interview with AlterNet.

I CAMPED OUT THE first couple of weeks and I've been there pretty much every day since. I think the nature of the park has changed a little bit, with the tents, it's harder to walk through the space, but it is also nice to see that we can actually have people there feeling that they have a little bit of privacy.

When I first got there, I thought it was another protest, but I did see something that was different. I saw dedicated people who had been so disenfranchised their entire lives, finally feeling like they had a voice. That's why I slept there the first night with cardboard, because I wasn't expecting to stay.

We had a needs list the first night. And then we started getting lots of donations, we didn't know what to do with all the donations. But things grew on their own. At first we had a food area, then we had a food table, then we had a food kitchen. The comfort station was where there were sleeping bags and other things, then we said, "Oh, we should have a station for comfort."

You see what's going on right now in New York as far as schools, how this public-private battle is going within them, it is really important that we make that connection. All the schools they are trying to privatize, public housing that doesn't really exist in the city anymore. Private-public is what the city is becoming now.

I think it's really symbolic that we are in a public-private space, we don't always make that connection, the media never makes that connection. I think it's really important that we continue to highlight that, the importance of public space—we've opened this space for imagination for folks to think big, to think large, to have dreams. But we have to talk more about the connection of the banks to the state; we've talked about corporations and so forth but we haven't really talked about the state as is. Our mayor is a corporation, he is the 1 percent and he is our mayor. Our governor is letting the tax surcharge on millionaires expire in December, he's protecting the 1 percent.

I think the space has been liberated, we've liberated it for other folks who have decided to come there just out of curiosity. The space has created an environment that's like the eye of the storm for change. I think that's what has drawn so many people there, to observe, but also to participate, because it is about participatory democracy. You feel comfortable because it is an all-inclusive environment but you also feel empowered to participate further.

A lot of people are saying that it is a carnival environment, that it's all about the plaza. I think that the plaza is important because it's near Wall Street, because we are disrupting business as usual at Wall Street, but I don't think the plaza is the be-all and end-all. A lot of the planning of the future of the movement is going on outside of the plaza. The working group meetings are at 60 Wall Street now.

We need both. We need the physical protest but we also need to organize. I think people need to start participating, going on the Web site and finding working groups, going to meetings, submitting themselves to the process. That is the way that we can get things done, to organize things together as a whole.

The difference between this and other efforts was that we used social networking and we used the idea of the unknown to open it up to folks. We said, "This is a new movement, this is a new time, this is a new space."

It's not just occupation. At least in the Western world, Argentina occupied factories, last year students in Puerto Rico barricaded themselves in the university for two months. Occupation has been a form of tactic since the early 1900s. I think it was the jolt of Wisconsin and the whole world watching Tahrir Square and then us taking a square, it reinforced that opening up of the imagination, and not only opening up but remembering it, too, remembering where we were in the 1930s, the Flint factory sit-in, those protests.

There's a lot of factors that are going to go into winter; we need to expand to indoor spaces, claim some buildings. I think we might lose the narrative for the winter, but that we have to build up for an enormous spring. There's a lot of things we can do on a local level, really bringing people out to spring where we should have thousands of people in thousands of public spaces. That's when maybe we decide to bring out some demands.

WHERE ARE THE WOMEN AT OCCUPY WALL STREET? THEY'RE EVERYWHERE

BY SARAH SELTZER

ARIEL FEDEROW HAS a pithy phrase for a problem many at Occupy Wall Street are trying to avoid. "There's a 'manarchist' problem in a lot of left-wing spaces," says Federow, a young New York-based artist and activist who has been active in Occupy Judaism and has regularly volunteered downtown. "By that I mean a small group of white guys take up space and make de facto choices for a larger group of people."

But what's surprised her so far about Zuccotti Park is that this concentration of power hasn't happened. "There's a strong current of actively saying no to that element when it does pop up," she says, "of people doing work around safer spaces and speaking out against sexual assault. And while women are leading, there are also other men involved."

A number of other women echoed Federow's sentiment. Jackie DiSalvo, a CUNY professor and member of the OWS labor working group, says that while she's heard younger women report issues like unwanted attention, her veteran eyes see a huge difference between mass movements of the '60s and the culture of Occupy Wall Street. "I was in SDS—we had all these ego-tripping superstars. There was very macho leadership, and very aggressive sectarian fighting," she says. Now, thanks to decades of work by the women's movement and other kinds of consciousness-raising, within OWS, "there's really a big effort to avoid domination."

Part of the reason Occupy Wall Street has evolved this way, says Shaista Husain, an activist from the CUNY media and culture studies department, is that women, people of color and working-class people have been part of the occupation from the beginning. "It wasn't just *Adbusters* and Anonymous calling this occupation from out of nowhere," she says. "It came from Bloombergville and CUNY students: working-class, multicultural students with a connection to labor history."

At Bloombergville, a group of students, union workers and others camped out in front of City Hall to protest Mayor Bloomberg's teacher firings, firehouse closings and education and service cuts. Sound familiar? Many of these people are the same people who are at Zuccotti Park—and the "code of conduct" they had in their tent city has helped determine the culture of the new occupation.

"One of the things we didn't want, which has always been the history of the Left, is to start splintering among ourselves," Husain says. "So how do we create a movement that allows us to swim with one another?" She notes that this includes an effort to discourage anti-Semitism and Islamophobia as well as racism, sexism and homophobia.

The solution, for her and others, lies in the essence of Occupy Wall Street: its leaderless, non-hierarchical nature, which allows any participant to have a say in the movement's direction. The casual observer, unaccustomed to organizations without hierarchy, might mistake leaderlessness for structurelessness. But in fact OWS is governed by a highly structured, constantly evolving series of processes, with checks and balances to make sure no one voice or faction takes over.

Here's an example: Early in the occupation, the general assembly—an all-inclusive decision-making body that convenes nightly in the park—was voting on a mission statement that referred to all people being a "human race" "formerly divided" along ethnic lines. A group of South Asian women "blocked" the resolution, using the human microphone to share their concerns that the proposal would erase centuries of historical racism. (Participants may "block" proposals that raise ethical concerns for them. As a rule, people are reluctant both to block or to overrule blocks.) Despite their discomfort, the women said the act of blocking symbolizes something unique about the movement; it allows anyone to voice concerns. "When we looked up and saw all those faces looking back at us, we realized it's a really big moment," said Hena Ashraf, one of the women who participated in the block.

Another check on structurelessness comes in the form of the "progressive stack," in which the "stack-keeper," who is in charge of taking questions and concerns from the audiences at general assemblies, is given the ability to privilege voices from "traditionally marginalized groups." In other words: women and minorities go to the front of the line. Yesenia Barragan, 25, a Columbia student and longtime activist, notes that in reality, progressive stack often means, "my partner, who's a white man, has to wait 20 minutes or more to say his piece." That's how it should work, she says. "We need to address those power relations."

A "step up, step back" policy ensures that a diversity of voices are foregrounded by encouraging those who have spoken to let others speak, and prompting those who have been quiet to share their thoughts. Finally, the movement arrives at decisions by consensus; that is, by more than 90 percent agreement in the group.

This highly structured process seeks to avoid what Jo Freeman called "the tyranny of structurelessness" in an essay of the same name critiquing the women's movement: "Structurelessness becomes a way of masking power, and ... is usually most strongly advocated by those who are the most powerful."

In consensus models, that "tyranny" looks like this: white men and other loud voices facilitating too often and dismissing concerns they say aren't germane—while other voices raise objections again and again. At OWS, since the onset of the GAs, organizers have taken it upon themselves to make sure that more and more women, people of color and new voices are part of the facilitation team, holding trainings and keeping facilitators accountable.

Working groups also use consensus. None of the women I interviewed had major complaints about gender politics in their individual working groups. When I observed about 10 working groups sitting in serious, focused circles in an atrium on Wall Street hashing out ideas, at least half of the speakers at any given time were women.

Many women involved in the protests say the process of direct democracy directly counteracts the experiences of their lives. They have come to this protest because they've seen their families, neighbors and friends lose homes, jobs and healthcare, and they haven't been heard when they try to register their concerns.

"We all come from disenfranchised communities," says Nelini Stamp, a young activist who has been working with people of color and labor working groups. The feeling of agency and power that's created by "having a voice, having a say in your day-to-day life" can't be measured, she says—and that's what leads to people being invested in the movement. "These are people that have been pushed and shoved. They just really want to see something work for them, unlike before."

For many of the women I interviewed in New York, frustrations arise not from direct slurs or insults but from a lingering feeling that at times they're not heard in discussions, or not respected when they try to explain their perspective. For other women, it's more about interaction.

Protest participant Ashwini Hardikar wrote a powerful blog post about two such experiences that occurred within an hour: a male protester gave her an unwanted hug and then expressed shock when she loudly told him she found his hug unwelcome and intrusive; and a young man who chanted "Lady Liberty is a whore," and then defended himself when she questioned his language. This kind of explaining and educating can be exhausting.

But Hardikar, a health educator, was not deterred. In fact, she sat in on a "Safer Spaces OWS" meeting and watched the group try to deal with and prevent incidents like the ones she experienced. "People within Safer Spaces OWS are trying to be point people to address these kinds of concerns, without involving the police or the court system unless the person wants that," Hardikar says. The point people wear pink armbands to identify themselves to protesters who need assistance. Early on, a serial groper in the park was turned over to police by the protesters after their interventions failed.

Hardikar says she finds it inspiring that there are people trying to "envision a world that is different." She says, "A movement like Occupy Wall Street isn't created in a vacuum. We live in a racist, sexist and homophobic society."

Several New York-based activists say their position as the "flagship" occupation has prompted them to try even harder to create a model society, to be an example to others who are just starting their movements. The Safer Spaces OWS initiative and a corner of the park devoted to a women's sleeping area have attracted notice; I met several groups of young college women who had come to the park for sleepovers and praised these efforts.

And the size and scope of the occupation in New York is, for many women, an advantage that smaller occupations may not offer. Many women have joined smaller subgroups to find an emotional "safer space" with like-minded people. That participation shores up their commitment to the larger group.

These new spaces for critique and examination exist online too. Hena Ashraf and others have started a blog called "In Front and Center" to spotlight writing about the movement around issues of inclusiveness. "Solidarity with critique. That's the framework," she says. "You can do both—and it makes sense to do both."

What's exciting about OWS is that its openness allows for this kind of input, they say.

"If there's one thing I could tell everyone at the park and around the country, it's that a critique isn't an attack. It's really healthy," Suzahn Ebrahimian says. There's pushback from the privileged, sometimes, the assertion that "we're just dividing the movement, but the reality is we want to make it a viable movement for everyone."

On the ground, women worry that the media and onlookers are eager to find "leaders" and that those leaders won't look like them. "As we started to grow, and started to be taken seriously, there was a concerted effort to bring in diverse voices and faces to reporters," says Yesenia Barragan, a Latina woman who is a member of the press team. "In the beginning it was really exhausting because I noticed that reporters didn't take me seriously. My job is to go up to them—and often I would be ignored. I'm not used to that," she says.

Still, their persistence has paid off. "Since then we've made an effort so that even if they say 'I want John, a white dude,' we say, 'No, we're going to bring you to someone else,'" she says.

And there's a payoff for those who commit to this work. Educating people at Zuccotti Park about privilege "means a lot of work," says Manissa Maharawal, and it's not always easy. "But it's worth it."

Stamp has had a similar experience. The slow process of reaching consensus, the focus on anti-oppression, the support offered by the caucuses and working groups, she says, means "I've gotten to learn how to talk to people again. I've really felt a sense not just of solidarity but of kindness and compassion and all of these things that when you're busy and on the go, you don't stop to think about."

A version of this story originally appeared in the October 26, 2011 issue of The Nation.

EXPERIMENTS IN DEMOCRACY AT LIBERTY PLAZA

BY MANISSA MCCLEAVE MAHARAWAL

MONDAY NIGHT AT a bar in Brooklyn, my friend Alex and I looked through pictures on his phone of the "early days" of Occupy Wall Street. He had pictures of the general assembly from Day 5 and we laughed together about how empty it looked, how ramshackle and tenuous almost, how we could still see the pavement and there was still space between the people. We had just biked back from Occupy Wall Street and we were commenting, again, on how different the space seems every time we are down there. This time I had been surprised to see tents everywhere, something I hadn't seen before and honestly, between the tents, the problems with the drumming in the past week and the debate about moving to a spokes-council structure, it felt like the movement was in a moment in which it was trying to deal with its own internal dynamics. Growing pains almost.

It makes sense for a movement like Occupy Wall Street to be having growing pains. It is still a surprise to most people, those inside the movement and those observing, whether in solidarity or not, that it is still there and that it is growing. It's still a surprise that in places like Occupy Oakland, where their tents were torn down in the middle of the night and they were tear-gassed the next evening, they came back the next day in even stronger numbers and called for a general strike. It has become clear in the past month that the political discourse has shifted and it has become clear in the past month that this thing isn't going away. But some mornings I still wake up surprised about it all.

These are Occupy Wall Street's experiments in democracy. They are our experiments in a new form of power. Last Sunday I facilitated the largest meeting I have ever facilitated, a 100-person meeting of the people-of-color working group and it was really tough work to make sure that the process of this meeting went smoothly. I know I alienated someone when I told them not to speak out of turn. I know I was personally frustrated that the meeting ran an hour over. I found out how really, really hard it is to say to people: "You've spoken a lot, let's hear a voice we haven't heard yet this meeting." But while I was saying these things I was also imagining how my classes in graduate school would look if I could say these sorts of things to the many men who monopolize them, how different my work meetings would feel if there was this sort of awareness.

And so Occupy Wall Street has been having growing pains in the past week. There were fears that not being able to work with the community board about the drumming would shut down the whole thing. There was a divisive and hard spokes-council decision that we made on Friday night. A decision in which we could not reach consensus and instead had to vote on using a modified 9/10 consensus model.

The creation of a spokes-council is a move away from making all of our decisions at the nightly general assemblies. Instead there will also be a spokes-council where "clusters" of people from the various working groups (of which there are now upwards of 50, encompassing everything from sustainability to media to education and empowerment) will meet together every day and connect with each other and make day-to-day decisions.

This was a hard decision because many people were worried about a spokes-council creating a de facto power structure, creating a hierarchy of decision-making or creating more bureaucracy. I understood these concerns— a spokes-council can look a lot like the sort of representative governing we are trying to move away from, but also from working in the movement I think we need a better way to communicate across working groups and a better way to make day-to-day decisions. To put it simply: 300 people at the general assembly do not need to make a decision about whether or not the comfort working group should buy recycled plastic trash bags or not.

I also think that a spokes-council structure, in which working groups meet together every day and discuss issues is a great way to communicate across working groups that issues of racism, patriarchy, oppression and inclusivity are not just something for the people-of-color working group (and women and people of color themselves) to take on but for all working groups to be thinking about. So I was in support of the spokes-council.

And so I spent my Friday night standing outside for hours listening to the discussion and finally at around 10 p.m. voting in favor of it. The vote was needed because, like I said, we couldn't reach consensus. There were two "blocks," both for ideological reasons—that in this movement we should not have any sort of body that acts as if it is representing others and that could be mistaken for a power structure or a "leader." I think these concerns and these blocks are completely valid and necessary critiques. Standing outside in the cold on Friday night, listening to people passionately express these views, I was so glad that the process forced everyone to hear, and attempt to deal with, dissent before we made our decision.

I was glad to be reminded that we should proceed with how we structure ourselves with care. With immense care. And I was glad that when we couldn't reach consensus fully on this decision, we voted knowing that we needed a 9/10th majority for this to go through. In the end there was a 95 percent majority that voted for the spokes-council. Not full consensus, but close enough. As we carefully counted the votes (17 noes and 300-something yeses) I thought about voting and consensus and democracy. It felt good to know that this structure allowed for people to block things, but it also felt good to think that a 95 percent consensus was still a victory for the process and for everyone who took part in it.

On Thursday I went to a community watch meeting at 60 Wall Street, or the Atrium, as it has been called. The Atrium is another one of these "density bonuses" like Zuccotti Park: a privately owned but publicly accessible space. This one seems like a cross between a corporate lobby (it is indoors) and a bizarre, sandy park. There are fake palms. There are white plastic chairs and marble benches. The ceiling and walls are weirdly textured and mirrored. To get from Zuccotti Park to the Atrium you have to walk south on Broadway for two blocks. You can either enter the Atrium from Wall Street or one block closer on Pine Street. Even though Pine Street is closer I like to enter from the Wall Street side because there is something about running past the Stock Exchange, around the barricades they have put up, through the crowds of tourists and businesspeople, past Tiffany's and past the Trump building to finally duck into the Atrium for a working group meeting that makes me feel powerful and excited about the world.

In the past two weeks there have been multiple working groups meeting here at all times. Last night the community watch meeting met next to a media training, which was next to the demands working group, which was next to the security meeting, across from the sustainability meeting, which was next to the anti-racism group. On a Thursday night there were over 100 people in that strange corporate public space, meeting and working together on various different aspects of the movement.

As I looked around on Thursday I realized that we are also occupying this space now, that by being assembled together in this space we are occupying it and by learning how to work together in doing this we are making this occupation, this political shift, this chance at a new way of being in the world, possible. Of course this process has growing pains, it wouldn't be revolutionary if it didn't. It wouldn't be revolutionary if it wasn't complicated and messy, but also inspirational. The facilitator at the community watch training I attended last night said something that struck me as she was outlining the steps of response for how to deal with unsafe situations at Zuccotti Park. She said: "This process isn't perfect yet and we know that, but this is what setting up a town, a movement in four weeks, using direct democracy looks like."

III.

NEW YORK:
KEY EVENTS
THAT GREW THE
MOVEMENT

INTRODUCTION

THE OCCUPATION NEVER ends in the city that never sleeps. New York is the place that sparked the "American Autumn," and as a result events in the Big Apple have proven to be a rallying cry for the Occupy movement worldwide. New York is occupied territory: Every time the intrepid campers in Zuccotti Park have needed help, New Yorkers have rallied to their sides. And every time the movement has grown stronger downtown, it has branched out: to neighborhoods poor and rich, touristy and forgotten, to make its presence felt all over town.

You've already read about the pioneering first days of the occupation in New York; here's what happened next. From the mass arrests on the Brooklyn Bridge to the cold October dawn when bystanders linked arms with occupiers to block a potential eviction; from the neon spectacle of Times Square to the streets of Harlem; the movement is sustaining itself and maturing.

Here is our first-hand coverage of some of the biggest events in occupied New York City. You know what they say: If OWS can make it here, it can make it anywhere.

I WAS ARRESTED WITH 700 OTHER PROTESTERS, IN FRONT OF THE ENTIRE WORLD

BY KRISTEN GWYNNE

ON SATURDAY AFTERNOON, October 1, we lined up peacefully. There was no rush or chaos, just a steady stream of people exiting the park onto Broadway and heading north. We chanted "We are the 99 percent—and so are you!" the classic, "This is what democracy looks like!" and "All day, all week, occupy Wall Street!" I looked behind me to see an incredible mesh of people. We were teenagers, college graduates, grandparents and children. We were peaceful, marching down the sidewalk with a list of guidelines passed out to us before we left.

As we closed in on the bridge's entrance, some people marched right onto the roadway as police appeared to block traffic; others took the pedestrian walkway. Confused, I heard a demonstrator yell, "Go this way if you don't want to get arrested!" Some people turned to take the safer route, while the statement encouraged more fearless demonstrators to walk on the street. Still, the majority of people must not have heard anything.

Because thousands of people marching down the narrow walkway seemed implausible, I opted for the street. At the same time, I expected us to be treated with some selectivity. Only the hardcores, I thought, would be arrested. We walked alongside a single lane of cars, crawling up the bridge. There was an element of danger, a small fear that someone might trip or get pushed and fall in front of a car. At the same time, there were a suspiciously low number of police officers. I expected them to swarm, but saw only one white-shirted police officer before we were trapped, and even he seemed calm and said nothing.

Twice, we stopped moving. The first time seemed like a pause to soak it all in, hundreds of people cheering in loud exhilaration, "We took the bridge!" It was a moment of pride and courage.

When we paused again a few moments later, there were still no police in sight. Stationary, people sang and danced, "Get up! get down! There's a revolution in this town!" Then, suddenly, people started to turn around. Groups of protesters were pushing back against others. "Sit down!" people chanted, and we complied though there was barely enough room. As those in front of me bent down, I saw what was happening up front: Police had formed a barrier in front of us. They were shoving, pushing what was now the front line of protesters back toward us, and they were filming the crowd.

We got to our feet again, and the arrests began. One police officer in a now notorious white shirt was red in the face, literally huffing and puffing. Then people started screaming "Fall back!" The police kept pushing, and suddenly we were crushed, slammed up against each other and corralled on both sides by police. Some people screamed, "sit down!" but we were crammed in too tight to reach the ground. Men and women climbed up the guardrails to the pedestrian parkway above, where other protesters pulled them over the railing. My heart dropped as I watched people climb, often as many as four at at a time, to safety. With our elbows bent at our sides, we used our forearms to pass around water bottles and dried pineapple. Some people complained it was hard to breathe. Others said they had to pee. After about 10 minutes as sardines, the spaces between us widened, but not by much.

As I scanned the front, I saw a cop's hat fly from his head as he made an arrest. A girl screamed and cried that her cuffs were too tight. "Shame!" the crowd chanted, and "Who do you protect?" Some police officers grabbed people, often forcibly, and locked their hands. Others were more gentle. Some made no arrests at all. We were all confused; no one had any idea what was happening. We hoisted a small girl in the air so she could look back. "They're arresting people there too," she said. There was an orange net. It became clear we were trapped, locked in on both sides.

People were shouting at us to stay calm. Incredibly, most of us were. And still, the cops plucked people out of the crowd, one by one, seemingly arbitrarily, with minutes passing in between arrests. Even though this was only the first hour of an ordeal that would end 10 hours later with a late-night release from jail, we knew the whole world was watching, had been watching, and much of it was ready to join us. Our spirits soared despite the discomfort. *This is the beginning of something big*, I thought.

WHEN THE PROGRESSIVE COMMUNITY EMBRACED THE OCCUPATION

BY SARAH JAFFE

AFTER THE OUTCRY responding to the arrests at the Brooklyn Bridge, it was clear that people would come to a community and labor march in solidarity with the occupation. But they came in numbers surpassing expectations, jamming streets and making spirits soar.

On Wednesday, October 5, over 20,000 protesters packed Foley Square near New York City Hall and marched to Liberty Plaza to support the occupiers on Day 19 of their protest. Colorful union signs dotted the crowd as well as the handmade kind, showing delegations from the United Auto Workers, Amalgamated Transit Union, Teamsters, City University of New York faculty, and many more. All of the protesters I spoke with knew exactly why they were there.

"When someone's looking for a job, they're not visible," Jesse LaGreca, a blogger at Daily Kos who recently became an Internet celebrity for his smackdown of Fox News in an interview leaked to the Web, told me. The occupation, and the massive march in support, made those problems visible. LaGreca's takedown of Griff Jenkins, whom he called "one of the biggest cheerleaders for the Tea Party movement," resonated with activists tired of not being taken seriously. He pointed out, "The last thing they want is someone who can clearly state why we're here. It's called Occupy Wall Street, not Big Bake Sale, for god's sake."

"Naturally we would join," said Lisanne McTerran, a New York City teacher wearing her United Federation of Teachers hat. She pointed out that the unions have been in this fight for a while, noting that UFT had marched down Wall Street back in May to protest continued banker power. McTerran is an art teacher by trade, but has been working as a substitute since New York's school budget cuts.

"Arts are the first thing they cut," she said, handing out a flyer pointing out that budget cuts have led directly to the loss of over 100,000 jobs.

The permitted rally began at 4 p.m. and it seemed strange to hear the sound of a loudspeaker broadcasting speeches as we approached in a crowd from Liberty Plaza. The crowd of occupiers communicated on the move using the people's mic, repeating each other's words back, and it did seem that the union leaders who spoke took a page from the activists in the plaza, keeping their words brief and powerful, stoking the crowd's excitement at the popular support they were receiving. The organizers at Occupy Wall Street have been reaching out to labor from the beginning, and their efforts were paying off.

Stuart Appelbaum, president of the United Food and Commercial Workers International Union (UFCW) New York City local RWDSU, told the crowd he had a message for Mayor Bloomberg. "If your police department overreacts again like it did last Saturday, stifling dissent and limiting free speech, New Yorkers will not stand for it!"

Héctor Figueroa of SEIU's 32BJ, the building service workers' union, made the connection between the occupiers in Liberty Plaza and the international protests that have echoed around the world in recent months, declaring, "*Nosotros somos los indignados del Nueva York, los indignados del Estados Unidos, los indignados del mundo!*"

It was a sentiment heard at my first visit to the occupation, when I met Spanish activist Monica Lopez, who had been part of Spain's *Indignados* movement. Lopez has been back to Spain and is now back again at the Liberty Plaza occupation, taking photos and working the media table.

"It's the right thing at the right time after so many mistakes," Thomas Blewitt told me when I asked why he was involved in the movement. Blewitt, a former member of ACT UP in a trim shirt and tie, was one of the many defying the popular image of the protesters as all young hippies. He explained that he'd cared for his mother until her death and between Medicare and AARP, "That system works." Everyone, he said, deserves the same access to healthcare.

Healthcare was also on the minds of the National Nurses United, which came out in force with signs declaring support for Occupy Wall Street on one side and calling for a financial transactions tax on the other, as the union has been for months. "It's catching on like wildfire," Pam Merriman, a nurse from the University of Chicago, told me.

"The hardest pill to swallow," her colleague Talisa Hardin said, "is America is hurting, and when you look at how well corporations are doing, it doesn't seem fair."

The nurses' president, Karen Higgins, spoke at the rally as well. "We're sick of the greed!" she told the crowd. "As nurses, we can fix that."

Lindsay Personett, a recent graduate in dance performance from Oklahoma City University, was handing out flyers that read "I Owe Sallie Mae," and offering a marker to fellow grads who've found themselves in debt to the loan giant. "Kids are told to get this expensive degree and you'll get a job," she said. "You end up owing too much and owning nothing."

As the march moved off slowly through the financial district, I ducked into a cafe and struck up a conversation with Joel Wise, a tall, burly member of Operating Engineers Local 68 from New Jersey. Wise noted that his union had yet to express an opinion on the occupation, but told me, "I'm here as an American, proud to be a union member." He told me that the sign he'd been carrying earlier, which he'd given away, had read "The Tea Party is Owned By Big Business."

Wise's friend commented, "If they keep monetizing debt, it's gonna be ugly," and Wise continued, "Most people are outraged that white-collar criminals weren't prosecuted. If you steal a loaf of bread, or a kid sells some weed, they go to jail for five years, but these guys stole millions."

Back at Liberty Plaza, as scuffles with cops break out around lower Manhattan, I am struck once again at the ease with which the organization here falls back into its duties. The medics treat the injured or sick, the food team hands out pizza, rumors are quashed with a quick mic check and the legal team works to keep people out of jail—or get them out quickly.

I walk out past the barricades, hearing a round of cheers erupt behind me from something going on in the plaza.

An uneasy truce at Liberty Plaza holds, but the protesters inside remember the feeling of elation, of support from the huge crowds earlier. It's not just rhetoric; they know they are the 99 percent.

PROTESTERS VISIT THE 1 PERCENT AT THEIR HOMES

BY LYNN PARRAMORE

IT WAS LIKE an alien invasion. In fact, it *was* an alien invasion. On Tuesday, October 11 thousands of regular people—the kind without homes in the Hamptons, yachts or private planes—marched past some of the country's most privileged addresses.

If there's a neighborhood the 1 percent call home, it's New York City's Upper East side, where fatcats like Chase CEO Jamie Dimon, billionaire financier David Koch, media mogul Rupert Murdoch, and hedge funder John Paulson hang their hats. And they got paid a visit, from the rest of America.

The Millionaire's March, dedicated to the radical idea of asking the rich to pay their fair share of taxes during a time of economic hardship, included Occupy Wall Street protestors from Zuccotti Park, along with community groups, labor unions and people who just wanted to show their solidarity. The marchers were young, old, black, white, and certainly weren't dominated by what David Brooks contemptuously called "pierced anarchists" in a *New York Times* smear piece.

Their plan was simple: Expose the actors who work to produce and maintain gross inequality and demand real economic change. No more, no less.

The march kicked off at 59th Street and 5th Avenue. I followed the trail of police officers strewn like breadcrumbs along the sidewalk over to Park Avenue, where I noticed a young man wearing a Wisconsin cheese hat trying to give an interview to a TV reporter. He found himself accosted by a well-coifed, gym-toned woman in her 50s, presumably a resident, who lectured the young man in high decibels: "We have to give Obama the Congress he deserves! OK? It's not the president's fault! OK? He doesn't want the economy to look like this! Stop blaming Obama!" When she stopped for a breath, the bewildered Wisconsinite asked, "Who said anything about Obama?"

This moment spoke volumes. A wealthy New York liberal talked without listening and assumed she knew why the protesters were there. She reeked of defensiveness and clearly felt the sign-carrying crowds were a personal affront.

I made my way to the crowd, past Upper East Siders staring out of the windows and grand entrances of their posh abodes. They looked bemused, curious, shocked, a little frightened and sometimes even supportive of the protesters who had the temerity to suggest that they, too, deserved to share in the nation's vast wealth.

A chic young mother turned to her puzzled daughter clad in a tony school uniform, "People don't have jobs right now," she explained. Whether Mom connected this fact to the actions of any of her neighbors was anyone's guess.

Blessed by perfect weather, the march was upbeat, accompanied by a marching band that did a lively rendition of Twisted Sister's "We're Not Going to Take It!" In between songs, protestors chanted "What happens on Wall Street won't stay on Wall Street!" and "How do we end this de-fi-cit? End the wars and tax the rich!"

I kept trying to figure out whose houses we were passing, but I was too far away to hear the announcer. Until we got to Jamie Dimon's pad at 1185 Park Avenue: at that point, the crowd began to shout the name of the person who seemed to raise the most ire. "No more tax breaks for Jamie Dimon!" they yelled. "Want to leave the country because of regulations? We'll help you pack!"

Protestors called for the big-mouthed banker—who recently called bank regulations "un-American"—to come out and show his face, but unsurprisingly Mr. Dimon, despite his $4.6 billion donation to the NYPD Police Foundation last spring, did not make an appearance. One protester claimed to have the number of Dimon's secretary, which she urged marchers to call.

And did Dimon's neighbors come to his defense? Not really. One or two opened their windows to take pictures, but most laid low. Only one blonde woman stood up for the banker-next-door, shouting abuse on the protesters from her lofty perch.

A girl in the crowd had an answer for her: "There's more of us than there are of you!"

LINKING ARMS AND KEEPING THE OCCUPATION ALIVE

BY SARAH JAFFE

IT WAS ABOUT 5:45 a.m. on Friday, October 14th at Liberty Plaza, and the unions had just arrived. (Richard Kim of *The Nation* would later compare the moment to the one in *Lord of the Rings* when the elves arrived at the last battle.) It felt like war—but we weren't armed except with the number of the National Lawyers Guild scrawled somewhere on our bodies in Sharpie.

The barrier between journalist, observer and participant was completely gone that morning in the park. Everyone I spoke to later said the same thing: "I knew I had to be there when it went down."

"It" was the proposal from Brookfield Properties, the owners of the occupation site, and Mayor Bloomberg to clear the park, supposedly for cleaning. They claimed that protesters would be allowed back in, but reporters and occupiers alike smelled a rat and spent Thursday trying to get better information. Slowly, word trickled out that the plan was to clear protesters out, then let them back in—but not with sleeping gear or any of the extensive infrastructure they'd built over a month in the park.

On Thursday at noon, an emergency general assembly decided to authorize spending $3,000 from the funds donated to the occupiers on cleaning supplies. The human mic echoed, "We are now creating a society that we envision for the world. Being responsible for ourselves is at the heart of that," and even as they talked, the sanitation team and its new temporary volunteers hustled around us, sweeping, scrubbing and picking up cigarette butts and broken glass by rubber-gloved hand.

I left the park on Thursday wondering if it would be my last time reporting from Liberty Plaza. Thursday afternoon, my email inbox was ablaze with "All hands on deck" calls from progressive organizations from MoveOn to the Working Families Party to the AFL-CIO, calling for everyone who could make it to be at Liberty Plaza at 7 a.m.

I didn't sleep much that night. On the train at 5 a.m. I crossed paths with an acquaintance. Rubbing sleepy eyes, he answered the question I hadn't asked: "We're going to the same place you are."

New York had answered the call.

I circled the edge of the park, spotting colleagues, friends and former students from my graduate school days, and choked down a dry bagel with egg and cheese from a food truck. The park was packed. Behind me in the food truck line were a man in a clerical collar, another man in a keffiyeh, and a man dressed as Santa Claus.

The plan, formed Thursday evening by wiggly-fingered consensus at the general assembly, was that protesters would encircle the park, holding hands and allow one section of the park to be cleaned. If they were not allowed to rebuild camp in that section, they would not move aside again. The line of people holding hands were prepared to be arrested, and the consensus was that those who were not arrested would be protected or leave. But even those of us in the press expected that if it came to a face-off, we would be penned up and plastic-cuffed the way the 700 on the Brooklyn Bridge had been.

Passing cars honked their support, and even in the jam-packed space the cleanup continued. As more people rolled in, I clung to a friend's backpack and thought of lines from Chris Hayes' 2005 essay on solidarity:

> *Sublime solidarity, on the other hand, embodies a powerful moral aspiration to realize the fundamental fellowship of humankind. The human subject imbued with full solidarity would treat each person the same way she would treat the interests of her closest kin ... you are propelled to do something for your fellow human beings, to act as if their interests were your own.*

The roar that went up from the crowd as union workers marched in with signs—United Auto Workers, National Nurses United, the New York Laborers' Union and more—nearly drowned out the people's mic, where the words of a now-hoarse young woman were being repeated in three waves across the crowd of thousands (estimates were 2,000 to 3,000).

I saw the announcement on Twitter first, from my friend Phillip Anderson, also in the park: "Looks like @MikeBloomberg just blinked.*Hard*. Brookfield postpones cleaning of #LibertyPlaza."

Nelini Stamp was at the center of the park, reading the announcement. "Late last night, we received a message from the owners of Zuccotti Park, Brookfield Properties, that they are postponing their cleaning!" The park erupted. "The people, united, will never be defeated!" When the chants died down, she continued, "The reason why is they believe they can work out an arrangement with us, but also—because we have a lot of people here!"

Wiggly fingers had been used for weeks to signal agreement, happiness, to stand in for applause, but there was no containing the reaction in that moment. People shrieked and cried. A burly, rough-voiced man in a bright orange laborer's union T-shirt called his aging mother to let her in on the celebration. He told us, "This is power. My mother, she's from the '60s, I called her on the phone so she could hear."

The celebration faded; the moment couldn't last. But as the sun came up, as the crowd dispersed and people made their way to their offices, as the financial district opened for business, we knew Phillip was right—Bloomberg had blinked. The power of the people in that space, the willingness of thousands of New Yorkers to show up before dawn in a crowded little park to defend the rights of a few hundred people to camp out in protest had beaten, at least for the moment, the mayor's power and the power of his allies.

IN GLOBAL SOLIDARITY, WE JAMMED THE STREETS THAT ARE THE WORLD'S MOST JAMMED

BY SARAH SELTZER

AFTER THE CRUSHING excitement of the 20,000-strong labor march, momentum was building for the occupation party in Times Square on Saturday, October 15. The planned twilight celebration and occupation was at the jam-packed center of tourism, commerce and kitsch—a place most New Yorkers avoid.

It turned out to be one of those parties that are so successful everyone you know shows up—and then so do the cops.

We took the train downtown, fielding eager questions based on our signs ("Tax the Rich" and "Fund Schools") from fellow travelers, and entered a crush of people the second we emerged, moving at a snail's pace into barricaded protest pens in the middle of the pulsing lights of marquees and stores.

Native New Yorker though I am, I'd never seen Times Square bustling with that kind of energy. It was like the celebratory crush of New Year's Eve or a local sports franchise winning it all, plus an added measure of defiance, radical politics and tension. The reverberation of the human mic from our penned-in free-speech zones ricocheted across the streets, where the sidewalks were overflowing with more of us than they'd ever expected. We chanted, we cheered every time the ABC news ticker declared that today, on a global day of action, "The Occupy Movement Goes Worldwide." We shivered with apprehension, bristled with anger, as cops trotted back and forth in riot gear. We stayed as night fell and the lights grew brighter.

Later, many people went down to Washington Square Park where clashes with police were frightening, ominous. The energy and anger from this day would spill over into the weeks to come. But so would the conversations. After my companions and I left a still-occupied Times Square and headed to the subway at Rockefeller Center, having more interactions along the way with antagonists, supporters and friends, I realized the Fox News ticker we passed actually put it even more poetically: These were indeed "twilight protests that jammed the streets" of Manhattan's symbolic center.

A sign that had been held aloft near me all evening was true: "The movement is the message." And we'd sent a powerful message with our presence— the warning that we'd be back.

OWS TAKES A TRIP UPTOWN TO STOP 'STOP-AND-FRISK'

BY ANNA LEKAS MILLER

ON FRIDAY, OCTOBER 21, an historic movement to combat the New York Police Department policy of "stop and frisk" began in the heart of Harlem.

"I'm a former military officer," a young man named Marvin told the crowd assembled at the corner of 125th Street and Adam Clayton Powell Boulevard. "One night, me and some of my friends were minding our own business, just going out to pick up some Chinese food. We got stopped by a police officer. He demanded that we show him identification and handcuffed us to the sidewalk while he searched our car for a warrant. After searching our car and finding nothing the officer turned to us and said, 'Can you do the chicken noodle soup dance?' Even though he had found nothing, he told us that the only way he would let us go without a record was if we sang and danced for him.

"I hate that people see me on the street and automatically think that I am a criminal. I don't have any police record—but I will after today," he concluded.

The New York Police Department is on track to "stop and frisk" over 700,000 people in 2011 alone. That is over 1,900 people stopped and searched without a warrant per day; 85 percent of them are black or Latino and more than 90 percent were doing nothing wrong.

In July, a few weeks before *Adbusters* released the call to Occupy Wall Street, professor and civil rights activist Dr. Cornel West and Carl Dix, a spokesman for the Revolutionary Communist Party, held a strategy session to discuss how to take action against the New York Police Department's policies of racial profiling, police brutality and mass incarceration of young blacks and Latinos. At the commemoration of the 50th anniversary of the Attica riots, they announced the day, October 21, as the beginning of the Stop Stop-and-Frisk movement, beginning with a march and action of nonviolent civil disobedience at the 28th Precinct in Harlem, and hopefully gathering momentum and spreading throughout New York City and communities of color around the United States.

Coincidentally, October 21 in New York City happened to fall during the time Occupy Wall Street was surging—and its participants have experienced their own bitter taste of police brutality. Almost 1,000 protesters have been arrested in New York City. They are often thrown to the ground, belittled and arrested on charges such as "resisting arrest" when their only crime is exercising their First Amendment rights. Protesters have been penned in, surrounded by orange nets, unaware that they are under arrest until it is too late. NYPD officer Anthony Bologna is being penalized 10 vacation days and may face charges of assault for pepper-spraying five women, inadvertently turning public attention toward the New York Police Department's policing practices.

What many of the predominantly white protesters in Liberty Plaza didn't realize until recently is that their experiences are only a small taste of the police brutality that communities of color experience on a daily basis.

"My first thoughts after seeing five white women get pepper-sprayed in the face was, what would they have done to a black man?" a man at the Harlem rally wondered.

If a black or Latino man is arrested at a demonstration of civil disobedience, it will affect his life far more than if he were white. Many young blacks and Latinos—due to racial profiling in common police practices such as stop-and-frisk—already have a police record, and can't afford to risk being put through the system again. As it is, one in 15 black adults is behind bars, and the statistic climbs to one in nine for black males between the ages of 20 and 34. To many communities of color, the New York Police Department is not a force that maintains order, but one that institutionalizes racial inequalities, segregating blacks and Latinos into a pipeline toward mass incarceration and criminalization.

"I don't fault people for not knowing that this happens," Carl Dix told me. "That's a conspicuous policy on the part of the people who run this country—blacks are the problem and we have to devise a solution, while keeping the white middle-class unaware. I want to bring Occupy Wall Street to what is actually happening. I want to challenge them: now that you know, are you going to act?"

Earlier in the week, activists at Occupy Wall Street began to pass around "Stop Stop-and-Frisk" flyers during the general assembly. Dix made several guest appearances at Liberty Plaza to harness Occupy Wall Street's energy to combat police brutality. The people-of-color Occupy Wall Street working group pushed to endorse the action, discussing the urgency of the issue. Occupy Wall Street decided to endorse it, asking, "How can we truly stand as the 99 percent, if we don't stand with the people of Harlem?"

On the day of the action, several protesters—a mix of black, brown and white—from Occupy Wall Street assembled, joining the Stop Stop-and-Frisk rally in both solidarity and civil disobedience. Though they were met with curious stares while marching through Zuccotti Park, upon reaching the streets of Harlem they were greeted with cheers and messages of support and gratitude from street vendors, shopkeepers and passersby.

Cornel West addressed the crowd at the Harlem State Office Building on the corner of 125th Street and Adam Clayton Powell Boulevard. "This corner has been consecrated by giants like Malcolm X, Ella Baker, Marcus Garvey, Martin King and Fannie Lou Hamer," began Dr. West. "We are here today because we have come to terms with arbitrary police power to ensure that the rights of poor young people, disproportionately black and brown, are acknowledged and affirmed."

After marching to the precinct, those who were willing to get arrested—many of them young black and Latino men who have spent their lives trying to avoid a police record—linked arms in front of the precinct, chanting until they were hauled away in plastic cuffs. Cornel West, who was arrested only a few days ago in Washington DC, Carl Dix, Reverend Stephen Phelps and several other organizers and activists were among the 33 arrested outside of the 28th Precinct.

Stop Stop-and-Frisk held multiple other actions around the city. Strategy meetings are being planned, both separate from and in conjunction with Occupy Wall Street. Though the movements were originally organized separately, they occurred at a progressive nexus in history that is too coincidental to be ignored. Both movements have demonstrated that this is only the beginning of a continuous and persistent battle. Creating a permanent alliance between the two movements could mean diversifying and expanding Occupy Wall Street and spreading the call to stop stop-and-frisk beyond communities of color as a collective force against police brutality of all kinds, and in all communities.

POLICE RAID ZUCCOTI PARK, OCCUPIERS RESPOND WITH MASSIVE ACTION

BY SARAH SELTZER AND SARAH JAFFE

"WE'RE BEING EVICTED!" the text message went out to Occupy Wall Street supporters around 1 a.m. on November 15.

"The park has been cleared," the text message read a few hours later, as bedraggled, pepper-sprayed protesters, having lost their home in Zuccotti Park, reconvened for a GA in Foley Square and vowed to keep going. Over 200 had been arrested, including city council member Ydanis Rodriguez. Blocks away, Mayor Michael Bloomberg held a press conference, announcing that police would be now able to search all people entering the park.

Pictures taken after sunrise showed that the park was stripped bare—ugly and undamaged, as it was before.

The raid cleared the protests' two-month-long "model society" of its infrastructure, including the women's safe space tent, the medical tent, and thousands of books from the "People's Library"—which were seen in the back of a dumpster and only partially recovered a day later.

Some downtown subways and the Brooklyn Bridge had been shut down, airspace was blocked off, and supporters who were alerted by text—and came to help—were prevented from entering, violently. "There was a funny smell and something in my eyes that was making them burn..." wrote Anna Lekas Miller, who arrived after she got the text. "I was shoved against a wall by a cop."

"This is crazy: pepper spray, pushing us, beating and arresting peaceful protestors," tweeted Kristen Gwynne, who also raced down to the park, but was unable to get in.

Later in the morning, some marched back to Zuccotti, others took over a small lot owned by Trinity Church and were arrested.

Meanwhile, a tense day of legal wrangling resulted in this court decision: protesters could come back, but without sleeping gear.

They finally re-entered the park, with a police search in place that evening to hold a boisterous general assembly and begin the process of planning their moves for the days after, particularly the 17th.

That day, the two-month anniversary of the occupation, had been the center of plans for weeks, and the crackdown in the early morning hours of the 15th had only given new determination to the organizers and activists. They were uncowed.

"Everyone as of last night was totally exhausted and drained," Olivia Leirer of New York Communities for Change said, "But ready to put their energy into the 17th and to make sure the energy ... is not about the police crackdown, but about the message of the movement."

That message will be heard across New York's five boroughs, from morning til evening, from an early gathering at Liberty Plaza to "exchange stories rather than stocks" to a student strike. The centerpiece of the day? A massive rally at Foley Square, capped off with a "'musical" march to "the bridges." Leirer pointed out that the day's actions will remind everyone of the core truth: "I think that the Occupy movement is so much bigger than the park," she said.

IV.

THE

POLICE

REACTION

INTRODUCTION

IN THE EARLY morning hours of November 15, the NYPD stormed Liberty Plaza, laying waste to the sophisticated, lively space OWS had built over two months. Reporters were essentially barred from the scene by police. But videos and accounts of the day show police in riot gear wielding batons, dragging out resistors, and making liberal use of pepper spray.

Since the start of the occupation, lower Manhattan has often been under what Tom Engelhardt calls a second occupation—an overwhelming police presence evidenced by the stacks of metal barricades, by the police cars, vans and buses that stretch endlessly down city blocks, by helicopters that hover over peaceful marches, and by the hundreds to thousands of police, often in riot gear, shadowing every protest. Beyond the physical police presence, the electronic eye of the force is at work, too, with surveillance cameras blanketing the area and a two-story-tall police watchtower hovering above Liberty Plaza.

And that's just in New York. Police forces across the country have reacted in a similar, or more brutal, manner to their local occupations. Predictably, as the Occupy movement has grown, so have the number of violent police clashes. Former Marine Scott Olsen is still recovering, his skull split open by a police projectile during clashes following the forced eviction of the Oakland, California encampment.

Oakland occupiers regrouped, only to be evicted on November 14. In what appears to be a somewhat coordinated campaign, police also busted up encampments in Portland, Denver, and Salt Lake City.

To be sure, many individual police officers may be sympathetic to the Occupy movement. But the volume of arrests—thousands worldwide—and of unprovoked violent encounters with demonstrators suggests a deep-seated discomfort by law enforcement authorities with the aims of the occupiers: an impulse to protect the interests of the 1 percent by the higher-ups.

Aggressive tactics have not worked. Hundreds of protesters massed in Liberty Plaza the night after the brutal bust, chanting "We are home."

In the following pages, you'll read accounts from several of those protesters as well as some sharp analysis of the police reaction to the Occupy movement.

The 99%

POLICE v. OCCUPY MOVEMENT

September 24:
NYPD Senior Officer Anthony Bologna pepper-sprays two female OWS protesters in the face.

October 1:
NYPD officers allow OWS marchers to flood onto the Brooklyn Bridge, but then block them and arrest some 700 people.

October 14:
New York cancels a previously-planned eviction of OWS. During a victory march, several protesters are injured by NYPD officers and 10 are arrested.

October 25:
Police officers in riot gear descend on Occupy Oakland, throwing tear gas and detonating flash-bang grenades. Several protesters are injured, one of them critically.

October 28:
Officers evict Occupy Nashville protesters and arrest some 3 dozen occupiers who don't leave. Night court officials refuse to issue arrest warrants for the protesters. Additional protesters are arrested over the next several nights.

November 11-14:
There is a rash of eviction attempts, arrests, and police violence in Salt Lake City, Albany, Denver, San Francisco, Oakland, and Portland, Oregon

October 16 / October 23:
175 and then 130 protesters are arrested in Chicago when they resist eviction from Grant Park.

October 26:
At least 10 protesters are arrested in New York City during a solidarity march for Oakland.

October 29:
Denver police use pepper spray and pepper bullets on protesters as they attempt to retake their occupation site.

November 3:
Oakland police clash with a group of protesters occupying an abandoned building. A protester allegedly sets a barrier on fire, and the police spend several hours deploying tear gas and projectiles.

November 15:
Police storm OWS under the cover of darkness, demolishing the encampment and carting resisters to jail. Reporters are restricted from the scene. After a day of protests, OWS returns to Zuccotti, chanting, "We are home."

Artwork by Cristian Fleming for The Public Society

WALL STREET'S SECOND OCCUPATION: THE RISE OF THE NYPD'S HOMELAND SECURITY STATE

BY TOM ENGELHARDT

OVER THE PAST few months, there have been two "occupations" in lower Manhattan. One has been getting almost all the coverage—the demonstrators camping out in Zuccotti Park. The other occupation, in the shadows, has been hardly less massive, sustained, or in its own way impressive—the police occupation of the Wall Street area.

On a recent visit to the park, I found the streets around the Stock Exchange barricaded and blocked off to traffic, and police everywhere in every form (in and out of uniform)—on foot, on scooters, on motorcycles, in squad cars with lights flashing, on horses, in paddy wagons or minivans, you name it. At the park's edge, there is a police observation tower capable of being raised and lowered hydraulically and literally hundreds of police are stationed in the vicinity. I counted more than 50 of them on just one of its sides at a moment when next to nothing was going on. Many more can be seen almost anywhere in the Wall Street area, lolling in doorways, idling in the subway, ambling in the plazas of banks, and chatting in the middle of traffic-less streets.

At one level, this is all mystifying. The daily crowds in the park remain remarkably, even startlingly, peaceable. (Any violence has generally been the product of police action.) On an everyday basis, a squad of 10 or 15 friendly police officers could easily handle the situation. There is another possibility suggested to me by one of the policemen loitering at the park's edge doing nothing in particular: "Maybe they're peaceable because we're here." And here's a second possibility: as my friend Steve Fraser, author of *Wall Street: America's Dream Palace*, said to me, "This is the most important piece of real estate on the planet and they're scared. Look how amazed we are. Imagine how they feel, especially after so many decades of seeing nothing like it."

And then there's a third possibility: that two quite separate universes are simply located in the vicinity of each other and of what, since Sept. 12, 2001, we've been calling Ground Zero. Think of it as Ground Zero Doubled, or think of it as the militarized recent American past and the unknown, potentially inspiring American future occupying something like the same space. (You can, of course, come up with your own pairings, some far less optimistic.) In their present state, New York's finest represent a local version of

The 99%

the way this country has been militarized to its bones in these last years and, since 9/11, transformed into a full-scale surveillance-intelligence-homeland-security state.

Their stakeout in Zuccotti Park is geared to extreme acts, suicide bombers, and terrorism, as well as to a conception of protest and opposition as alien and enemy-like. They are trying to herd, lock in and possibly strangle a phenomenon that bears no relation to any of this. They are, that is, policing the wrong thing, which is why every act of pepper spraying or swinging of the truncheon, every aggressive act (as in the recent eviction threat to "clean" the park) blows back on them and only increases the size and coverage of the movement.

Though much of the time they are just a few feet apart, the armed state backing that famed 1 percent, or Wall Street, and the unarmed protesters claiming the other 99 percent might as well be in two different times in two different universes connected by a Star-Trekkian wormhole and meeting only where pepper spray hits eyes. Which means anyone visiting the Occupy Wall Street site is also watching a strange dance of phantoms. Still, we do know one thing. This massive semi-militarized force we continue to call "the police" will, in the coming years, only grow more so. After all, they only know one way to operate.

Right now, for instance, the police hover in helicopters with high-tech cameras and sensors over crowds of protesters, but in the future there can be little question that in the skies of cities like New York, the police will be operating advanced drone aircraft. Already, as Nick Turse indicated in a groundbreaking report, "America's Secret Empire of Drone Bases," the U.S. military and the CIA are filling the global skies with missile-armed drones and the clamor for domestic drones is growing. The first attack on an American neighborhood, not one in Iraq, Afghanistan, Pakistan, Somalia, Yemen, or Libya, surely lurks somewhere in our future. Empires, after all, have a way of coming home to roost.

This story first appeared on TomDispatch.com.

'WRAPPED IN ORANGE NETS, SEPARATED, TRAPPED:' ONE WOMAN'S ARREST STORY

CHRISTINA GONZALEZ

On September 24, Christina Gonzalez, 25, who lives in Far Rockaway, Queens marched with Occupy Wall Street to Union Square. That march, which became known for the iconic "pepper-sprayed girls" footage, was a turning point for OWS, helping the movement gain support and media attention. This is her account of that day, beginning with the march on Union Square.

THE NYPD FOLLOWED us the entire time, but got aggressive once we reached 14th Street. I remember tears coming down my cheeks as the officers forcefully pushed us back with large orange nets. I felt like an animal. People were taking pictures, yelling at the cops. Finding your way through this orange maze was almost impossible; you would see people being arrested, pushed, pulled, thrown to the floor, slammed on walls, on cars, wrapped in orange nets, separated, trapped. I saw a woman in a wheelchair struggle out of a tangle of nets and white shirts. I saw a young man on the floor being pulled in all directions. I tried to film but an officer blocked my camera with his body.

When I confronted him, we started arguing, until he yelled "Get her!" I didn't know what was happening and I started to run. I only got a few yards before I felt a bunch of hands grab my shoulders and my arms. I was swung around and then there were hands pushing my back, feet kicking my legs from underneath me. I was screaming, "Please don't throw me down! Just cuff me!" They zipped those plastic cuffs so tight, that as I write this I still have limited feeling in my thumbs. I screamed and cried for 10 minutes before they cut them from my wrists, only to replace them with a new pair, which were slightly less painful. When the doors to that police truck opened, the heat hit my face as if there were a fire in there. I was held in the van with doors closed, no windows, for over four hours, with 15 other people—no water, no fresh air.

What got me through that experience was thinking of those who came before me who have been through so much worse. In my thoughts was my best friend who has been sitting in solitary confinement in a maximum-security prison for several years.

I'm a survivor of intimate partner violence, so maltreatment by the police was really nothing compared to that. The police and courts in that situation blamed, demeaned, ignored and re-victimized me. When the opportunity came to express my frustration at the feelings of powerlessness I had experienced and join other brave young people, I was glad to finally be doing something. But on September 24th, we were all treated like criminals.

AN EYEWITNESS ACCOUNT OF POLICE CRACKDOWN ON PEACEFUL DEMONSTRATORS

BY J.A. MYERSON

DEEP IN THE belly of the beast, among the financial district's skyscrapers, next to derivatives traders in business suits and Rolex watches, you will find a one-block-large democratic society, governed by consensus, whose features include free food, free professional childcare, an arts and culture area, medical and legal teams, a media center, constant music, a library and a stand with refreshments for the many police stationed to supervise the area. This is the week-old occupation of Wall Street, located at Liberty Plaza Park.

A group of protesters from the camp ventured outside the park and marched on Union Square Saturday morning, and around 100 of them were arrested. Police sprayed peaceful protestors in the face with pepper spray, threw them to the ground and assaulted them with elbows, dragged a woman around by the hair and jumped over barricades to grab and rough up young people. This is exactly the sort of violence and brutality American authorities routinely condemn when perpetrated against nonviolent civilians demonstrating for democracy in Middle Eastern dictatorships, even as they employ horrifying cruelty right here.

Filmmaker Marisa Holmes was recently in Egypt, documenting the revolutionary movement there in its attempt to transform the ouster of Hosni Mubarak into a democratic society. Inspired by the Egyptians, she became involved with the group organizing the Wall Street occupation, hoping to emulate the Egyptians' success in mobilizing the public to wrest their country from the brutal forces in power. Video shows police abusing her, confiscating her belongings and falsely alleging that she had resisted arrest.

In the aftermath of the mass arrests, Liberty Plaza was gripped by an agitated nervousness. Would the cops move in on us in an attempt to seize the square? What was in store for our comrades? Some of them texted people back at camp, giving brief glimpses of the fates they were meeting: a marcher with a concussion denied access to medical attention: a group locked in a van parked at Police Plaza; people clubbed about the head and chest with police batons.

As the reports came in and people in the camp began to see video and photos of the violence, nervousness turned to anger. These were our friends who had been brutalized for no reason apart from their earnest desire to avail themselves of their First Amendment rights in order to call for a more just, more humane, more equal America. One young man implored those assembled, "There are people right now bleeding in handcuffs! Let's march!"

As tempers rose, the NYPD let us know that they were, as one friend put it, "playing for keeps," standing shoulder to shoulder and occupying every inch of the block of Broadway adjacent to the square, displaying the orange nets the same police force had used to corral demonstrators at 2004's Republican National Convention. During a shift change, as the sun dropped behind the buildings to the west, dozens of cop cars, sirens and lights blazing, began to circle the plaza, intimidating its denizens. Rumors began to circulate that the cops were waiting for cover of dark to invade the square and avoid the watchful eye of the media.

After all, they had targeted the internal media team in the arrests, capturing, among others, Marisa Holmes. That would have been bad enough, but the cops stationed at Liberty Plaza were also spotted harassing the mainstream media and prohibiting news vans from parking in convenient locations. As of today, most of those arrested have been released; the rest, including Holmes, await arraignment. But the mood back at camp is defiantly jovial. The occupation will not be intimidated by state violence, will not be suppressed by a hostile police force and will not be discouraged by snarky hack journalism.

This group remembers that Tea Party dissenters were allowed to bring guns brazenly to town hall meetings, without being subjected to mace and arrest. Similarly, the crooked Wall Street thugs who obliterated the economy and then extorted the country for staggering sums of money have never faced police brutality or even justice. And the Congress (a subsidiary of Wall Street), as it proposes huge budget cuts, is even jeopardizing the pensions of those cops whose batons bloodied my friends' face.

If only they knew what really needs to be smashed.

OCCUPY WALL STREET PROTESTER, ARRESTED AND JAILED FOR 30 HOURS, TELLS HER STORY

BY BARBARA SCHNEIDER REILLY

I SPENT A WEEKEND in jail.

On Saturday, October 15, I went to Washington Square Park to take a closer look at the Occupy Wall Street movement. There were many young people who could be my children or rather grandchildren, but many older people, too, all generations united, it seemed, under the banner, "We are the 99 percent."

Different groups decided to go to a bank. I joined one that went to Citibank at La Guardia Place and Bleecker Street. As we entered, there were a couple of customers and a few banktellers inside. A teach-in ensued. The story the students told, surprisingly calmly and politely, was shocking.

"I am $100,000 in debt. The costs Citibank charges me go up and up. I don't know how I can repay it. I find it deeply irresponsible that Citibank makes the kind of profit they do from our indebtedness." Another student said, "I'm not $100,000 in debt, only $30,000 so far. And I still have two years to go. This kind of profit-taking cannot go on. We are here to say we will not tolerate it. We need fundamental change."

And so it went. After we were told to take our action outside, some people stayed and continued to tell their stories.

I, by far the oldest, had not come to get arrested, but as we tried to leave, several enormous undercover cops in sweatshirts and jeans appeared, blocked the exits and quite literally pushed us back into the bank. One giant in particular seemed to have it in for me, saying, "Oh no, you're not leaving!" his right arm shoving me. Ready to pounce on us, they made leaving the bank impossible. Two of the student participants had come to close their bank accounts; customers in every sense. They, too, were to be arrested. Police officers in white shirts seemed to swarm from everywhere. They rushed into the bank and told us we were being arrested. At no point was there a warning from anyone in authority offering a chance to leave without being arrested. As they handcuffed us, we did not anticipate the next 30 hours that were in store for us.

The ride to Central Booking in the "paddy wagon" was an ominous beginning. Either New York's potholes are beyond repair or the shock absorbers of that vehicle were non-existent. With our wrists handcuffed behind our backs, there was no way to hold on to anything as we were thrown off our seats into the air during that ride in hell. After hours of "booking procedures"—standing in line, being handcuffed, getting uncuffed, our backpacks, wallets, phones and any other object, even a single tissue, taken from us, our names shouted as we were inspected and lined up spread-eagled across a wall—we were finally led into three cells, allowed for the first time to sit down. It was early evening by now but we were not allowed an extra piece of clothing for the cold, just a T-shirt or whatever first layer of clothing we wore.

During an inordinately lengthy fingerprinting procedure, with the male officers operating the machines and the female officers locking and unlocking our cells as we were called out one by one, it sometimes seemed the police outnumbered us. But still, it took what seemed like hours.

Barely back in our cells, we were taken out again, handcuffed again, this time with a chain between our cuffs, and led "upstairs." But there had been some mistake. A female officer told "our" officer that, no, she couldn't process us. Some paperwork was missing, some order, some stamp. Time to cuff us again and go down the stairs back into our cells. How many more instances of handcuffing, uncuffing, leading us up and down stairs and long hallways, waiting, returning, repeating what seemed nonsensical procedures and reversals then followed I do not know and did not count. But a deep sense of disorganization, competence fighting incompetence, if not chaos, reigned. It seemed as if, in the name of bureaucratic rules and regulations, in the name of "security," we were witnessing a dysfunctional institution and people not used to daylight shining in; people generally accountable to no one but themselves.

Finally, we were driven to "the Tombs" (the nickname for a lower-Manhattan jail complex). We landed in a large collective prison cell; there were 11 of us plus an Indian woman with her own sad story and two run-down black women on some sort of drug who occupied the only three mattresses in that medieval cell, and whose intermittent yells, shouting and appalling screams made rest, let alone sleep impossible. We spent many hours on extremely narrow, hard benches, no blankets, with pieces of dry bread and a dry piece of cheese or peanut butter for food. The young women, all in their early 20s, somehow managed to bend themselves into shape to catch an hour of sleep here and there. For my 70-plus-years bones and for K., a 68-year-old lifelong environmental activist, it was tough going.

The experience was depressing in every way. All of us could see the irrationality, the nearly obscene bureaucratic time, energy and money spent on our (probably illegal) arrest. During that constant cycle of being cuffed and uncuffed at every step and during each transfer, some of us couldn't help feeling that the 9/11 terrorists had indeed won. The culture in this institution seemed a noxious mix of breathtaking incompetence, disorganization and open or just-beneath-the-surface-always-present brutality. Hardly a verbal communication without harsh and loud shouting and orders to stand here, move there, stop doing this or that.

Searching our bags and moving our belongings somewhere else took an inordinate amount of time. Then everyone's ID had to be returned for the next step in the "arresting process." Which meant a new search by the female officers for everyone's ID; all the bags and wallets had to be painstakingly searched a second or third time. As it turned out, my ID had somehow been overlooked. Or rather, the officer responsible for it couldn't be found. Again, everyone had to be uncuffed, led down the stairs, locked into their cells until the officer who had my ID was found. Low-level chaos is the only word to describe it.

During the long, cold night in the Tombs, at some point we asked a female officer if we could have some blankets. "We have no blankets." Some mattresses, since we were 12 or so people? "We have no more mattresses." Some change in exchange for dollar bills so we could call parents and loved ones? (The one public telephone in the cell would only take coins.) "It's against regulations." Some soap? "Maybe we'll come up with some soap." After no, no, no to every reasonable request, we wound up with a small jar of soap. Distressing is hardly the word for a culture of willful neglect and the exercise of what power those officers held over us for those 30 hours.

But there were a few, mostly black cops, who, as we were transferred from point A to point B, told us openly, "We support you. If I could, I'd participate in what you're doing."

The initial charges of criminal trespass were finally reduced by the district attorney to disorderly conduct, with the invaluable help of our lawyers from the National Lawyers Guild. When we were finally released, we were greeted like heroes from people in the Occupy Wall Street movement standing in front of the huge 100 Center Street Building. They offered us hats against the cold, dried apricots, chocolate bars, tampons, water, self-rolled cigarettes. It was really touching.

But even the young women were seriously exhausted, physically and mentally burnt out. Perhaps I and my older compatriot were better prepared, at least psychologically. But by and large these young women were very impressive. After this dismal experience no one even considered leaving the movement. No hues and cries. Society must be changed. They insist on it, and I hope, will continue to insist—and, not withstanding the difficulties ahead, fight for it.

WALL STREET FIRMS SPY ON PROTESTERS IN TAX-FUNDED CENTER

BY PAM MARTENS

WALL STREET'S AUDACITY to corrupt knows no bounds and the co-option of government by the 1 percent knows no limits. How else to explain $150 million of taxpayer money going to equip a government facility in lower Manhattan where Wall Street firms, serially charged with corruption, get to sit alongside the New York Police Department and spy on law-abiding citizens?

According to newly unearthed documents, the planning for this high-tech facility on lower Broadway dates back six years. In correspondence from 2005 that rests quietly in the Securities and Exchange Commission's archives, NYPD Commissioner Raymond Kelly promised Edward Forst, a Goldman Sachs executive vice-president at the time, that the NYPD "is committed to the development and implementation of a comprehensive security plan for Lower Manhattan ... One component of the plan will be a centralized coordination center that will provide space for full-time, on-site representation from Goldman Sachs and other stakeholders."

At the time, Goldman Sachs was in the process of extracting concessions from New York City just short of the mayor's firstborn in exchange for constructing its new headquarters at 200 West Street, adjacent to the World Financial Center and in the general area of where the new World Trade Center complex would be built. According to the 2005 documents, Goldman's deal included $1.65 billion in Liberty Bonds, up to $160 million in sales tax abatements for construction materials and tenant furnishings, and the dealbreaker requirement that a security plan giving it a seat at the NYPD's Coordination Center would be in place by no later than Dec. 31, 2009.

The surveillance plan became known as the Lower Manhattan Security Initiative and the facility was eventually dubbed the Lower Manhattan Security Coordination Center. It operates round-the-clock. Under the imprimatur of the largest police department in the United States, 2,000 private spy cameras owned by Wall Street firms, together with approximately 1,000 more owned by the NYPD, relay live video feeds of people on the streets in lower Manhattan to the center. Once at the center, they can be integrated for analysis. At least 700 cameras scour the midtown area and also relay their live feeds into the downtown center where low-wage NYPD, MTA and Port Authority crime-stoppers sit alongside high-wage personnel from Wall Street firms that are currently under at least 51 federal and state corruption probes for mortgage securitization fraud and other matters.

In addition to video analytics that can, for example, track a person based on the color of their hat or jacket, insiders say the NYPD either has or is working on face recognition software that could track individuals based on facial features. The center is also equipped with live feeds from license plate readers.

According to one person who has toured the center, there are three rows of computer workstations, with approximately two-thirds operated by non-NYPD personnel. The *Chief-Leader*, the weekly civil service newspaper, identified some of the outside entities that share the space: Goldman Sachs, Citigroup, the Federal Reserve, the New York Stock Exchange. Others say most of the major Wall Street firms have an on-site representative. Two calls and an email to Paul Browne, NYPD deputy commissioner of public information, seeking the names of the other Wall Street firms at the center were not returned. An email to city council member, Peter Vallone, who chairs the Public Safety Committee, seeking the same information, was not returned.

In a press release dated October 4, 2009 announcing the expansion of the surveillance territory, Mayor Michael Bloomberg and Police Commissioner Kelly had this to say:

> *The Midtown Manhattan Security Initiative will add additional cameras and license plate readers installed at key locations between 30th and 60th Streets from river to river. It will also identify additional private organizations who will work alongside NYPD personnel in the Lower Manhattan Security Coordination Center, where corporate and other security representatives from Lower Manhattan have been co-located with police since June 2009. The Lower Manhattan Security Coordination Center is the central hub for both initiatives, where all the collected data are analyzed.*

The project has been funded by New York City taxpayers as well as all U.S. taxpayers through grants from the Federal Department of Homeland Security. On March 26, 2009, the New York Civil Liberties Union (NYCLU) wrote a letter to Commissioner Kelly, noting that even though the system involves "massive expenditures of public money, there have been no public hearings about any aspect of the system … we reject the Department's assertion of 'plenary power' over all matters touching on public safety…the Department is of course subject to the laws and Constitution of the United States and of the State of New York as well as to regulation by the New York City Council."

The NYCLU also noted in its letter that it rejected the privacy guidelines for the surveillance operation the NYPD had posted on its Web site for public comment, since there had been no public hearings to formulate these guidelines. It noted further that "the guidelines do not limit police surveillance and databases to suspicious activity ... there is no independent oversight or monitoring of compliance with the guidelines."

According to Commissioner Kelly in public remarks, the privacy guidelines were written by Jessica Tisch, the director of counterterrorism policy and planning for the NYPD who has played a significant role in developing the Lower Manhattan Security Coordination Center. In 2006, Tisch was 25 years old and still working on her law degree and MBA at Harvard, according to a wedding announcement in the *New York Times*. Tisch is a friend to the mayor's daughter, Emma; her mother, Meryl, is a family friend to the mayor.

Tisch is the granddaughter and one of the heirs to the now-deceased billionaire Laurence Tisch who built Loews Corporation. Her father, James Tisch, is now the CEO of Loews Corporation and was elected by Wall Street banks to sit on the Federal Reserve Bank of New York until 2013 representing the public's interest. The Federal Reserve Bank of New York is the entity that doled out the bulk of the $16 trillion in bailout loans to the U.S. and foreign financial community. Members of Tisch's family work for Wall Street firms or hedge funds that have prime broker relationships with them. A division of Loews Corporation has a banking relationship with Citigroup.

The Tisch family stands to directly benefit from the surveillance program. In June of this year, Continental Casualty Company, the primary unit of the giant CNA Financial which is owned by Loew's Corp., signed a 19-year lease for 81,296 square feet at 125 Broad Street—an area under surveillance by the downtown surveillance center.

Loews Corporation also owns the Loews Regency Hotel on Park Avenue in midtown, an area that is also now under round-the-clock surveillance on the taxpayer's dime.

Wall Street is infamous for perverting everything it touches: from the Nasdaq stock market, to stock research issued to the public, to auction rate securities, mortgages sold to Fannie Mae and Freddie Mac, credit default swaps with AIG, and mortgage securitizations. Had a public hearing been held on this massive surveillance sweep of Manhattan by potential felons, hopefully someone might have pondered what was to prevent Wall Street from tracking its employee whistleblowers heading off to the FBI offices or meeting with reporters.

One puzzle has at least been solved. Wall Street's criminals have not been indicted or sent to jail, because they have effectively become the police.

This story first appeared on CounterPunch.

CHAOS IN OAKLAND: WHY DID POLICE CRACK DOWN ON PEACEFUL PROTESTERS?

BY JOSHUA HOLLAND

ON OCTOBER 26, I watched as police in Oakland tear-gassed and threw "flash-bang" grenades into crowds of largely peaceful protestors. That's the night Iraq veteran Scott Olsen had his head torn open by a tear-gas canister fired by police. Here are some observations from that night.

AGAIN AND AGAIN

I heard this spiel blasted over loudspeakers so many times that I have it memorized:

> *This is Sgt. Somebody with the Oakland Police Department. I hereby declare this to be an unlawful assembly. You must leave the area of such-and-such (mostly 14th Street and Broadway) immediately. You can disperse via X street, heading in X direction (mostly 14th Street heading east). If you do not disperse immediately, you will be subject to arrest, regardless of your purpose. If you do not disperse immediately, chemical agents will be used. If you do not disperse immediately, you will be subject to forcible removal, which may result in serious injury.*

We're taught from an early age that we have a right to peaceably assemble and protest, that this is guaranteed by the U.S. Constitution and can't be overridden. So protesters did not acknowledge that they were assembling unlawfully, remained, and the tear gas came flying. And this happened again and again for much of the night.

MISSING THE POINT

That's not to say that a few idiots in the crowd didn't throw some objects at police. But that's not the point. Long before any act of violence occurs on the streets, a series of command decisions are made, and those decisions ultimately determine whether a protest will be largely peaceful or descend into chaos. Smart crowd control requires letting protesters protest—giving them an outlet. That night in Oakland, long before anything bad happened, police decided to deny Occupy Oakland that outlet. A peaceful, if rowdy march was headed from the main library towards Frank Ogawa Plaza—the location from which they'd been forcefully evicted the night before. They were headed off by a hastily assembled line of police clad in riot gear. The protesters decided to change course and head towards the jail where, according to a National Lawyers Guild legal observer on the scene, 105 protesters were being detained.

Again, the police blocked their route. They made another turn—I don't know what the objective was at that point—and were again blocked. The police did not have the manpower to actually block the many cross-streets we crossed, but somewhere a commander decided to put five or six cops on every side street. This was a stupid move. Officers cannot keep 500 protesters, now angrier than they were at the onset, at bay.

It was only then that I witnessed the first violence. As protesters swarmed around these five officers they started swinging batons, made two arrests and then found themselves completely surrounded. I'm certain it was a scary moment for the officers. There was another, thicker line of riot police a block away. At some point they realized their comrades were in a jam, and maybe two dozen came running and responded with extreme force. (It was at this point that a flash-bang grenade came flying towards me, going off about three feet away and leaving me shaking for about an hour.)

One officer, at the front, was firing projectiles wildly at the crowd—which, at that point, was in full retreat—until he was physically restrained by another (maybe a supervisor). There were injuries and arrests. I think none of it would have happened had they decided to let the protesters chant, "Let them go!" for a while in front of the jail instead of forcing them, seemingly arbitrarily, to walk around in circles facing off against line after line of police blocking their way.

You could of course take this a step further: the entire exercise was unnecessary. One can only guess how much resources the cash-strapped city devoted to evicting Occupy Oakland in the first place. And not just Oakland. Various reports have suggested that 10 or 15 different law enforcement agencies were involved—I saw officers from at least five agencies. And then there's the opportunity cost—police clad in riot gear standing a line against protesters aren't out catching bad guys, writing speeding tickets, etc.

SELF-POLICING

That night in Oakland I saw both law enforcement and protesters policing themselves. It's all but guaranteed that in any crowd—be it a group of protesters or a PTA meeting—there will be a few hotheads. I saw a number of self-appointed "marshals" among the protesters physically intervening to prevent damage to property or acts that might provoke the police. These folks, I imagine, are sophisticated enough to understand that the media are never on the side of protesters, and can only get a semblance of a fair shake by remaining peaceful.

"You see all these people here?" one protester asked as we rinsed the residue of tear gas out of our eyes a few blocks from Frank Ogawa Plaza. "They're all going home more radicalized than when they arrived." He was right—this kind of crowd control doesn't deter protesters, it steels them.

TENS OF THOUSANDS OF PROTESTORS MARCH THROUGH LOWER MAN-
HATTAN IN SUPPORT OF OCCUPY WALL STREET, WHICH HAS TAKEN OVER
ZUCCOTTI PARK IN NYC, AND SPAWNED MOVEMENTS WORLDWIDE.
PHOTO: NINA BERMAN/NOOR

A MEMBER OF OCCUPY WALL STREET LOOKS OVER THE QUICKLY GROWING
ZUCCOTTI PARK LIBRARY IN THE EARLY WEEKS OF THE OCCUPATION.
PHOTO: ZACH D ROBERTS

TWO OCCUPY WALL STREET PARTICI-
PANTS AT AN OCTOBER 25 EVENT.
PHOTO: JOAN LIPKIN

AN OCCUPY PROTESTOR DURING
AN OCTOBER 14 ACTION.
PHOTO: MICHAEL GOULD-
WARTOFSKY

OCCUPY WALL STREET DIGS IN,
WITH THE CONSTRUCTION OF
MORE PERMANENT INFRASTRUC-
TURE AND SERVICES. EVENTS/
SPECTACLES HAPPEN DAILY
INCLUDING THIS HAIR CUT.
PHOTO: NINA BERMAN/NOOR

TWO OCCUPY KNITTERS SITTING AT CAMP ON NOVEMBER 1.
PHOTO: MICHAEL GOULD-WARTOFSKY

NATIONAL NURSES UNITED JOINS THE OCTOBER 5 MARCH
OF UNIONS IN SOLIDARITY WITH OCCUPY WALL STREET.
PHOTO: DAVID SHANKBONE/ WIKIMEDIA COMMONS

OPPOSITE: PROTESTORS MARCH ON THE PORT OF OAKLAND TO SHUT IT DOWN AT
THE GENERAL STRIKE IN OAKLAND, CALIF. ON WEDNESDAY, NOVEMBER 2 AS PART
OF THE OCCUPY WALL STREET MOVEMENT.
PHOTO: LANE HARTWELL

OCCUPY WALL STREET CAMP ON OCTOBER 29
DURING AN EARLY SNOW STORM.
PHOTO: DAVID SHANKBONE/ WIKIMEDIA COMMONS

A GROUP GATHERS IN ZUCCOTTI PARK
FOR A MEETING ON OCTOBER 13.
PHOTO: MICHAEL GOULD-WARTOFSKY

A MEMBER OF THE NYPD COMES INTO
A CROWD OF PROTESTORS WIELDING
A NIGHTSTICK, AFTER A STANDOFF ON
WALL STREET ON OCTOBER 5.
PHOTO: ZACH D ROBERTS

AN OCCUPY PROTESTOR TAKES TO THE STREET ON SEPTEMBER 30.
PHOTO: MICHAEL GOULD-WARTOFSKY

AFTER DAYS OF PIZZAS SENT
FROM ANONYMOUS, SUPPORTERS
START BRINGING FOOD AROUND
THE CLOCK AND THE OCCUPY
WALL STREET KITCHEN BEGINS.
PHOTO: ZACH D ROBERTS

POLICE PEPPER SPRAY STUDENTS WHO WERE SITTING WITH THEIR ARMS LINKED AROUND
THEIR OCCUPY ENCAMPMENT AT THE UNIVERSITY OF CALIFORNIA AT DAVIS.
PHOTO: LOUISE MACABITAS/CREATIVE COMMONS

AN OCCUPY WALL STREET PROTESTOR ON OCTOBER 5.
PHOTO: NINA BERMAN/NOOR

WHY IS OWS BLANKETED WITH NYPD CAMERAS—AND ARE POLICE BREAKING THE LAW?

BY TANA GANEVA

ON OCTOBER 15, the day OWS solidarity protests broke out as far away as Australia and Japan, and thousands of people poured into Times Square, a line of NYPD Technical Assistance Response Unit (TARU) officers stood on the street, pointing handheld digital cameras at the protestors jammed behind metal barricades. The SkyWatch tactical platform unit—a watchtower with tinted windows like the one that's loomed over Zuccotti Park for most of the occupation—stood at one corner, its four cameras roving across the crowd. The whole scene unfolded under the NYPD security cameras stationed all over Times Square and in most parts of the city.

Like the massive crowd control arsenal unleashed on OWS—riot gear, smoke bombs, rubber bullets, pepper spray, horses, metal blockades, helicopters, plastic cuffs, and the police motorcycles, cars and vans that clog the streets—the three-tiered surveillance seemed like overkill for an overwhelmingly peaceful movement, where the occasional slur thrown at police is usually shouted down with reminders not to goad cops because they're part of the 99 percent.

It's unclear what the NYPD plans to do with footage obtained by TARU. But recording legal protest activity violates the Handschu decree, a set of legal guidelines designed to check the NYPD's historic tendency to steamroll First Amendment rights. The order emerged from a class-action lawsuit prompted by revelations that the NYPD had spent much of the 20th century and millions of dollars monitoring legal protest activity, an endeavor that generated up to a million files on such dangerous radicals as education reform groups and housing advocates. The Handschu decree prohibits investigations of legal political activity and the collection of data, including images and video of protests, unless a crime has been committed.

The ruling has had a complicated life post-9/11, mutating in response to terrorism fears and authorities' willingness to exploit them. A judge relaxed the order in 2003 after the NYPD argued it needed more flexibility to deal with terror threats. The department promptly proved its trustworthiness by secretively shooting hundreds of hours of footage of protesters at the Republican National Convention. In 2007 the court ruled that the NYPD had repeatedly violated Handschu and tightened the guidelines, limiting videotaping to cases where there's specific evidence that a crime has taken place.

An internal department memo sent out in 2007 instructs police to comply with the new order by only rolling the tape when "it reasonably appears that unlawful conduct is about to occur, is occurring, or has occurred during the demonstration." But Franklin Siegal, a lawyer who has spent years fighting for Handschu in court, tells AlterNet he's received multiple complaints about police videotaping OWS protesters for no good reason.

"Your photo shouldn't be taken and made into a record if you're not engaged in anything illegal. At demonstrations with no illegal activity taking place, cameras shouldn't be on," Siegal says.

The NYCLU has called on police commissioner Raymond Kelly to stop surveillance of the protests, citing the cameras pointed at Zuccotti Park and an incident where NYCLU representatives observed TARU members filming a peaceful march.

"This type of surveillance substantially chills protest activity and is unlawful. In light of the mayor's recognition of the peaceful nature of these protests, we call on you to stop the videotaping of lawful protest," read the letter.

Another camera has more recently been hoisted above Zuccotti Park, joining the four sitting on top of the tactical platform unit (police claim the cameras are only transmitting a live feed and do not record video). Those cameras are visible, at least. Donna Lieberman, executive director of NYCLU, told AlterNet over the phone that Zuccotti can be seen from any number of NYPD security cameras in the area, both by private cameras attached to businesses that are accessible to police and NYPD security cameras.

A 2005 NYCLU survey found over 4,000 cameras below 14th Street in Manhattan; five times more than they'd tallied in 1998. Lieberman says that number was a lowball because there are so many cameras that the NYCLU didn't have the manpower or the time to count all of them.

Authors of the report warned at the time about a "massive surveillance infrastructure" creeping across the city, unattended by adequate public oversight or outside regulation. Five years later, there's no exact count of all the cameras in New York, but Lieberman says, "We believe if we were to try to repeat the survey today, we would find that there are so many more cameras. Way beyond our wildest imagination."

Today that task would be complicated by the rollout of the Lower Manhattan Security Initiative, a plan launched in 2005 to cover the area below Canal Street in video cameras constantly streaming footage that's analyzed at a centralized location. In 2009 police commissioner Raymond Kelly announced that the Initiative would be expanded to midtown. (Pam Martens explains in this book how the law enforcement center where much of the camera footage is examined can be accessed by high-level Wall Street employees.)

The surveillance gadgetry available to the NYPD, and apparently to the very finance industry forces that OWS is protesting, is sophisticated. There are license plate readers that can capture license plate numbers and match them to a database. The cameras can be programmed to alert officers to activities like loitering, and people can be followed as they move from camera to camera.

Over the past year, reports have come out suggesting that the NYPD has plans to integrate face recognition technology into the operation.

As the AP reported, "New facial-recognition technologies will soon make it possible to track exactly who is walking down the street," [Bloomberg] said, adding that he believes "we're going in that direction."

The mayor then opined, "As the world gets more dangerous, people are willing to have infringements on their personal freedoms that they would not before."

At the beginning of the year, local outlets reported that the NYPD was recruiting officers for a new face recognition unit. The NYPD has not replied to repeated requests for comment, so it's not clear if the face recognition technology is in use, and if so, in what cameras, but a representative of ICX Technologies, the company that builds tactical platform towers like the one stationed at Zuccotti Park, told AlterNet that the cameras on the tower are compatible with face recognition software.

That would mean an image can be matched up to a mugshot in any criminal database, or any non-criminal database for that matter, including one of the largest public identity databases in the world: Facebook.

Right after 9/11, when airports and cities enthusiastically embraced face recognition, the technology was fairly crude and a lot of the programs were dropped. But in the past 10 years advances in the software—including 3-D imaging and "skinmetrics," which maps marks and imperfections in the skin of the face—have revived the interest of law enforcement and Homeland Security.

Sophisticated face recognition software, combined with cameras that can track activity all over the city, would be a useful tool if police wished to collect dossiers on people involved in OWS, as they so casually did pre-Handschu.

Whatever the advances in technology, Siegal says that core principals should remain. "Police should not be keeping records about the legal, political, non-criminal activities of anyone."

OCCUPY OAKLAND FACES A TROUBLED POLICE DEPARTMENT

BY ROBERTO LOVATO

WHILE PRESIDENT OBAMA was telling the small crowd at a $7,500-a-plate fundraiser in San Francisco that "Change is possible," Pooda Miller was across the bay trying to get her plate back from the Oakland Police Department. "They came, pulled out rifles, shot us up with tear gas and took all our stuff," said Miller, at an afternoon rally condemning the violent evacuation on October 25 of more than 170 peaceful, unarmed Occupy Oaklanders by 500 heavily armed members of the Oakland Police Department and other local departments.

With a long, metal police fence separating Miller and other members of Occupy Oakland from their confiscated items—tents, water, food, clothes, medicine, plates—Miller grabbed a big blue-and-white bullhorn that looked half as large as her 4-foot, 5-inch frame. "Give us our stuff back! It don't belong to you!" she yelled, later expressing relief that her baby was not camped out with her that morning.

The sound of Pooda Miller's ire shot across the protective masks of the officers standing at alert on the other side of the metal police fence, but her loudest, most acidic anger was directed at a young, female African-American officer.

"Who are you serving?" Miller screamed at the top of her high-pitched voice, turned raspy from hours of denouncing. "You're being used. You're getting paid with our tax money to put down your own people! Why are you doing this to your own people?"

Miller's questions about the role of race in the policing of Occupy Oakland points to what is and will continue to be the larger question in Oakland and other U.S. cities where former "minorities" are becoming majorities. What does it mean when those charged with defending elite interests against multi-racial and increasingly non-white activists are themselves multiracial and non-white? The ongoing protests, mayor recall, phone calls, emails and other pressure and pushback of Occupy Oakland are no longer aimed at cigar-smoking white men. They are aimed at a power structure in Oakland whose public face looks more like Miller and other non-white protesters.

Miller and others are calling for the recall of Jean Quan, who made history as Oakland's first Asian-American mayor (full disclosure: Quan's daughter is my Facebook friend); and they are complaining about the use of excessive police violence authorized by Interim Chief Howard Jordan, an African American. Such conflicts between former minorities are becoming the norm in what more conservative commentators call the "post-racial" era ushered in by the election of Barack Obama.

Quan and Jordan are in the throes of dealing with a police department plagued by officer-involved shootings and killings, corruption and other crimes—crimes that have forced a federal consent decree to reform the department, after officers were convicted of planting evidence and beating suspects in West Oakland. Taking her cue from the 2008 Obama campaign, Mayor Quan announced Jordan's appointment at a public safety forum titled "Creating Hope in the Community."

Many like Miller and other Occupy Oaklanders are having second thoughts about what feels like the affirmative actioning of policing and state violence. Others, like Ofelia Cuevas of the University of California's Center for New Racial Studies, see the workings of a not-so-21st-century pattern of policing and power.

"Having people of color policing people of color is not new," said Cuevas. "This was part of policing history in California from the beginning. In the 1940s, while the federal government was interning Japanese Americans in camps, officials in Los Angeles were starting to recruit black police officers as a way to decrease police brutality."

Cuevas noted that big-city mayors like Quan or Los Angeles Mayor Antonio Villaraigosa are, by electoral and structural necessity, required to act like any of their predecessors, who headed up police forces that attacked, surveilled and even killed those perceived as a threat to the establishment. The Bay Area police's violent modern history stretches from OPD's assault on the Black Panther Party—which was founded just blocks from the center of Occupy Oakland—to the shooting of Oscar Grant, a young black man shot in the back by a transit police officer at a nearby train station. (The officer claimed he intended to use his Taser but mistakenly shot Grant with his pistol; he was found guilty of involuntary manslaughter.) "Being mayor is being pro-police. They perceive that it's their job to crush what they consider threats to the status quo," said Cuevas.

Regardless of who is mayor or police chief, keeping the status quo is the last thing that Gaston Lau, a 21-year-old English major at the University of California, Berkeley, sees as an option. "[Quan's] support for this amount of police brutality here is ridiculous," said Lau, who held a placard that said "Down, Down with Jean Quan."

"The future power struggles are not just going to be about fights between one race and another," said Lau. "They're mostly going to be about class, which is a big part about what the whole Occupy movement is about."

Lau is hopeful that the movement will inspire younger Asian Pacific Islanders to engage with the issues of the Occupy moment, but worries about the generational conflict such a political engagement entails. "Some older Chinese might see having one of our own as mayor as a source of pride, but we need to help them understand how Quan and police act against us."

Despite the internal and external challenges posed by multicultural powers putting down multicultural movements, Lau is, like his Occupy Oakland peers, undeterred. Clashes between occupiers and Oakland police continued after the eviction as protesters tried to reclaim the park and police met them with tear gas. "Whether or not the mayor is Asian," Lau said, "when she acts against the people, then we will respond as the people."

This story first appeared on Of América.

V.

THE

MOVEMENT

SPREADS

INTRODUCTION

WHAT BEGAN IN New York City's financial district has since sparked a wave of occupations in hundreds of U.S. cities and thousands worldwide. From Chicago, DC, and Nashville to Europe, Australia and Africa, people have joined forces in solidarity with Occupy Wall Street to demand an end to corporate dominance of the world's economic and political system that has left the poor and working class to suffer under the weight of massive debt, joblessness, homelessness and an uncertain future.

Amidst an economic crisis caused by the world's financial and political elites, or "the 1 percent," tens of thousands of people in all corners of the globe have been rising up, in places like Italy, Greece, France and Madison, Wisconsin, refusing to succumb to the massive push for austerity by the very elites responsible the crisis. OWS has simply taken that message to the scene of the crime—Wall Street—where so much of the blame for the crisis lies.

The Occupy movement isn't simply a call for economic justice, but also a demand for democracy, inclusiveness, and a culture that respects the rights of the many over the profits of the few. This is why it's impossible to separate OWS from the self-immolation of Mohamed Bouazizi whose desperate act ignited the Arab Spring in Tunisia, or the brave demand for human rights and democracy in Tahrir Square that overthrew a brutal dictator.

While the global reach of OWS is phenomenal, its roots lie in worldwide struggles for justice, equality, and democracy. And as OWS continues that struggle, the support for the occupy movement is only growing.

The 99%

GLOBALIZING DISSENT, FROM TAHRIR SQUARE TO LIBERTY PLAZA

BY AMY GOODMAN

THE WINDS OF CHANGE are blowing across the globe. What triggers such change, and when it will strike, is something that no one can predict.

Last January 18, a courageous young woman in Egypt took a dangerous step. Asmaa Mahfouz was 25 years old, part of the April 6 Youth Movement, with thousands of young people engaging online on the future of their country. They formed in 2008 to demonstrate solidarity with workers in the industrial city of Mahalla, Egypt. Then, in December 2010, a young man in Tunisia, Mohamed Bouazizi, set himself on fire to express the frustration of a generation. His death sparked the uprising in Tunisia that toppled the long-reigning dictator, President Zine el-Abidine Ben Ali.

Similar acts of protest spread to Egypt, where at least four men attempted self-immolation. One, Ahmed Hashem el-Sayed of Alexandria, died. Asmaa Mahfouz was outraged and posted a video online, staring directly into the camera, her head covered, but not her face. She identified herself and called for people to join her on January 25 in Tahrir Square. She said (translated from Arabic):

> *I'm making this video to give you one simple message: We want to go down to Tahrir Square on January 25. If we still have honor and want to live in dignity on this land, we have to go down on January 25. We'll go down and demand our rights, our fundamental human rights ... I won't even talk about any political rights. We just want our human rights and nothing else. This entire government is corrupt—a corrupt president and a corrupt security force. These self-immolators were not afraid of death but were afraid of security forces. Can you imagine that?*

Nine months later, Asmaa Mahfouz was giving a teach-in at Occupy Wall Street. Standing on steps above the crowd that Monday night, she had a huge smile on her face as she looked out on a sea of faces. After she finished, I asked her what gave her strength. She answered with characteristic humility, speaking English: "I can't believe it when I saw a million people join in the Tahrir Square. I'm not more brave, because I saw my colleagues, Egyptian, were going towards the policemen, when they just pushing us, and they died for all of us. So they are the one who are really brave and really strong ... I saw people, really, died in front of me, because they were protecting me and protecting others. So, they were the most brave, bravest men."

I asked how it felt to be in the United States, which had for so long supported the Mubarak regime in Egypt. She replied: "While they giving money and power and support to Mubarak regime, our people, Egyptian people, can succeed against all of this, against the U.S. power. So, the power to the people, not for U.S. bullets or bombs or money or anything. The power to the people. So that I am here to be in solidarity and support the Occupy Wall Street protesters, to say to them 'the power to the people,' and to keep it on and on, and they will succeed in the end."

The Egyptian revolution has not been without consequences for her. Last August, she was arrested by the Egyptian military. As my colleague Sharif Abdel Kouddous reported from Cairo, Asmaa sent two controversial tweets that prompted the arrest by the Supreme Council of the Armed Forces, the military government that has ruled Egypt since Mubarak's fall. Her arrest provoked a worldwide response, with groups ranging from the Muslim Brotherhood to Amnesty International condemning it. She was released, but, as Sharif noted at the time, Asmaa was only one of 12,000 civilians arrested since the revolution.

The arrests are happening here in the U.S. now, at many of the protest sites across the country. As Asmaa was preparing to head back to Egypt, hundreds of riot police descended on Occupy Oakland, firing beanbag rounds and tear gas. The University of New Mexico is threatening to evict the encampment there, which is called (Un)occupy Albuquerque to highlight that the land there is occupied native land.

Asmaa Mahfouz is running for a seat in the Egyptian Parliament, and maybe someday, she says, the presidency. When I asked her what she had to say to President Barack Obama, who had given his speech to the Muslim world in Cairo, she replied: "You promised the people that you are the change and 'yes, we can.' So we are here from the Occupy Wall Street, and we are saying the same word: 'yes, we can.' We can make the freedom, and we can get our freedom, even if it's from you."

Denis Moynihan contributed research to this column.

THREE REMARKABLE OCCUPATIONS YOU HAVEN'T HEARD ENOUGH ABOUT

BY RANIA KHALEK

OCCUPY WALL STREET has spread to all corners of the globe. No matter the distance between them, the protests bear a striking resemblance to one another in spirit, courage and resolve. The non-hierarchical decentralized structure, the inclusiveness and cooperation are staples of the occupations. The authoritarian response that accompanies any powerful uprising is also a constant among the protests, with little exception. As the eyes of the country are glued to Zuccotti Park, the epicenter of Occupy Wall Street, and to Oakland, where the violent police response has ignited a historical series of protests, OWS offshoots in over 900 cities worldwide are building communities and transforming the world despite all the obstacles.

OCCUPY TUCSON (ARIZONA)

The city of Tucson has avoided attention-grabbing police raids. They're trying to quell protests using a quieter approach.

Occupy Tucson has been camped out at Armory Park, just two blocks from the city's financial district, since October 15. Every night since, police enter the park at the 10:30 p.m. curfew armed, not with riot gear and paddy wagons, but with a pad of citations or written arrests. Each citation amounts to a class one misdemeanor that carries up to $1,000 in fines, up to six months in jail, and up to three years probation. Occupy Tucson activists refer to these tactics as "financial and legal attrition to kill the movement."

Craig Barber, 28, an Occupy Tucson protester who describes himself as an "underemployed professional with unaffordable student debt," says the Tucson Police Department has issued over 400 criminal citations so far. This includes protesters in the two nearby satellite camps at Veinte de Agosto Park and Library Park. There is a permanent presence of roughly 100 protesters every night, many of whom have received multiple citations.

"I think that the city of Tucson has been watching the national theater and has noticed that the physical reaction does in fact galvanize more support, so they're using the more insidious tactic of legally intimidating the occupiers as well as financially bleeding the movement and also overwhelming our legal support," said Barber, adding that the handful of attorneys volunteering their time to support the cause are swamped by the sheer volume of citations.

There is a growing concern that the potential for criminal charges is stifling participation. "If you're a teacher or somebody who needs to pass a criminal background check for your employment, a criminal misdemeanor charge is a real concern," said Barber. "There is also the chilling effect that it has on people who would want to come and participate in the occupation, but can't necessarily afford a $1,000 fine per night or afford to have a misdemeanor charge on their record."

The citation protocol has also distracted the movement by diverting energy away from their original goals. "We started out wanting to protest the issues of economic inequality and disenfranchisement in our democracy because of corporate financing of politicians, but now because of the city of Tucson's response to the movement, our priorities have shifted to defending our First Amendment-protected activities."

Despite phone call and email campaigns demanding that city council members change the citation policy, and marches to city council meetings, Tucson representatives have remained silent on the issue. Having given up on swaying the city government to step up, members of the legal working group are in the process of filing a lawsuit against the city.

Occupy Tucson is trying to get the word out to the community that sleeping overnight is not required. "You don't have to get a misdemeanor charge in the Occupy Tucson movement. During the day we don't have any problem with the police; it's only when the 10:30 curfew rolls around," Barber says.

This message is particularly significant to the surrounding Hispanic community. "The broader implication," Barber says, "is that it has caused the Latino community to be fearful of law enforcement in general and I think it's a further chilling effect which is discouraging people of Hispanic descent in our community from participating, because if they come out and they get a citation, the officer could then ask them for their papers. And we also have a large undocumented population that could be deported if faced with a citation. It's very accurate to say that Arizona's immigration policies are having a chilling effect on First Amendment activities." Occupy Tucson's PR and outreach working groups are teaming up with Latino community activist groups to encourage more participation to accurately represent the people of Tucson.

Even in the face of such complications, Occupy Tucson has flourished, creating its own library, medical tent, a food station (that consists of four different tents in order to comply with Pima County health codes), a garden and solar panels with rechargeable batteries that are used at night for lighting. Barber refers to the encampment as a "micro-city." Moving forward, Occupy Tucson hopes to continue growing and get back to protesting the corporate greed and political disenfranchisement that inspired them to camp out in the first place.

OCCUPY RICHMOND (VIRGINIA)

Occupy Richmond was launched on October 15 in Kanawha Plaza, a public park in front of the city's Federal Reserve Bank. After just two weeks of building what became a vibrant and thriving movement against corporate greed, the Kanawha encampment was torn down by police in an unannounced late-night raid that shocked protesters.

Despite being employed and in school full-time, 34-year-old Alex Pagliuca has committed himself to the movement. He told AlterNet, "I'm doing this with whatever time I can scrape together. It's the first time I've seen a protest movement in my lifetime where people are willing to actually sacrifice something, their comfort and convenience. They're even willing to go to jail."

Richmond law prohibits camping in public parks overnight, but according to Pagliuca, the city often directs its sizable homeless population to take shelter in Kanawha, making it the only public space where the homeless are safe from police harassment, which is partly why the group chose to occupy Kanawha in the first place.

When the city's mayor, Dwight C. Jones, visited the park on Thursday, October 27, he used the people's mic to inform protesters that, "As mayor of this city, I'm going to have to ensure that the laws of the city are enforced," adding he would send city representatives to meet with demonstrators.

On Sunday, Oct 30, protesters received a late-night visit, not from city representatives, but from the Richmond Police Department, first on foot, then horseback, and eventually by air. At a brief point in the raid, a helicopter hovered overhead. Nine people were arrested for failing to follow police warnings to leave the park, four of whom are being held without bail. After allotting the movement 15 minutes to collect their belongings, police spent the next four hours bulldozing the two-week-old encampment.

A post on the Occupy Richmond Facebook page read, "When the Richmond Police raided our camp on Sunday night, they slashed our tents, bulldozed our supplies, and threw countless tents and food stocks into dump trucks." According to Pagliuca, that included a kitchen, library, information center, and media tent as well as a "comfort tent" where extra blankets and gloves were stored. Pagliuca wasn't present when the police arrived, but immediately grabbed his camera and headed to Kanawha after receiving a text. "When I got there, there was 150 to 175 police surrounding the place and probably 100 to 125 protesters," Pagliuca noted.

This was Occupy Richmond's first large-scale confrontation with the police. Pagliuca places the blame on the city government, saying police had been largely cooperative prior to the incident. "I think people are genuinely shocked. We've been nonviolent. We were feeding and clothing the homeless. We were exercising our First Amendment rights and were essentially told we can't do that. This doesn't make any sense," said Pagliuca.

The level of resolve that comes out of these midnight raids is encouraging. A representative from the Occupy Richmond media team had this to say about the police raid: "We're still active, and our numbers have grown exponentially since the raid. The Richmond Police Department made a huge mistake on Sunday night in their attempt to stop the Occupy Movement, and this is a mistake they will fully realize when they see how many new members we've acquired in the past 30 hours."

Meanwhile, Kanawha's homeless population, most of whom have joined the movement, "have nowhere to go," says Pagliuca. Occupy Richmond formed a working group to assist them in finding temporary shelter as the group decides where to occupy next.

(UN)OCCUPY ALBUQUERQUE (NEW MEXICO)

(Un)occupy Albuquerque began October 1 on the University of New Mexico campus. The demonstrators at UNM originally called themselves Occupy Albuquerque, but later voted to change the name to (Un)occupy Albuquerque out of respect for New Mexico's indigenous communities which have suffered under U.S. government occupation for centuries.

Cody Jo, an undergraduate student studying creative writing and philosophy at UNM, said he and his classmates were encouraged to observe and participate in (Un)occupy Albuquerque by their professor, Desi Brown. According to Jo, the UNM faculty has been largely supportive of the movement. One exception is UNM president David Schmidly, who refused to renew the movement's permit when it expired last week. Instead, Schmidly ordered campus police to clear Yale Park of any protesters who remained past the permit's 10 p.m. deadline on Tuesday, October 25. The *Digital Journal* called the evening "a face-off ... between some 500 protestors and about 80 police officers" made up of UNM police, the Albuquerque Police Department and New Mexico State Police. As the deadline passed, a helicopter hovered overhead while 20 officers in riot gear stood in the street in "defensive formation." Ultimately, some two dozen protesters who refused to leave were arrested for trespassing.

Jo was a casualty of Schmidly's policy as well, although he wasn't actually involved in the protest when he was arrested. The day after the police raid, the campus police busied themselves with keeping the park clear of occupiers. That evening, as the general assembly was pushed out of Yale Park, protesters took refuge in the coffee shop across the street, at which point Jo decided to relax on a bench on the perimeter of Yale Park away from the protest. Twenty minutes later he was approached by 10 campus police officers and ordered to vacate the bench. Jo stood his ground, exchanging words with the officers for about five minutes about his right, as a student, to sit where he pleased at a school he pays to attend. The campus police said they were required to follow the university president's orders, but Jo remained resolute, even replying, "He [the president] might be your boss, but he's not mine, so I don't have to do what he says." Ultimately, the police became impatient, at which point Jo was lifted from the bench by two officers, thrown to the ground, handcuffed and arrested.

Meanwhile, the ACLU filed an injunction and the movement's permit was reinstated with conditions. According to an ACLU press release:

> *The new permit is valid through November 6, and allows for the use of the park as a forum for protest on weekdays from 5:00 PM to 10:00 PM and Saturday and Sunday from 11:00 AM to 5:00 PM. The American Civil Liberties Union (ACLU) of New Mexico was involved in facilitating the balancing of protesters' First Amendment rights with the university's desire to impose reasonable restrictions on the time, place and manner of the protest.*

The various Occupy movements across the country highlight the remarkable level of courage and commitment that protesters have devoted to this cause. Whether it's New York City, Oakland, Tucson, Richmond or Albuquerque, the 99 percent have shown that, against all odds, they are here to stay.

Occupy America

The spark from New York's Occupy Wall Street has ignited the revolutionary fire in hundreds of cities across the country.

● = Occupation location

Artwork by Cristian Fleming for The Public Society

DAVID KOCH MEETS THE 99 PERCENT
BY ADELE M. STAN

TIME WAS WHEN David Koch could bring his Americans for Prosperity Foundation convention to our nation's capital and conventioneers could feel pretty secure in the notion that Washington, DC was theirs for the taking. No longer.

The triumphant glow of hagiography that usually marks the convention's annual Ronald Reagan tribute dinner on Friday, November 4 gave way to the heat of confrontation with the Occupy DC movement. Apparently, the AFP Foundation was prepared for shenanigans, as there seemed to be a readily available cadre of Metropolitan Police throughout the Walter E. Washington Convention Center where the event took place, a sprawling complex of glass and stone that takes up a full city block.

As the dinner began, one group of demonstrators convened outdoors for a peaceful film festival featuring a series of short documentaries about the Koch brothers, the billionaire executives of Koch Industries, the conglomerate founded by their father, Fred, who was also a founding member of the John Birch Society.

But others, from the Occupy DC and Occupy K Street movements, were more aggressive, shutting down streets around the convention center, and holding their ground at intersections with the forbearance of the police.

But not all the occupiers were out in the cold. Hijinks began inside the convention center as the Tea Partiers picked at their salads during a speech by Andrew Napolitano, the retired Superior Court (N.J.) judge who is now a talker on Fox News Channel. A young white man began shouting—I couldn't quite hear what he said—and was poised to unfurl a banner when he was grabbed by police and escorted from the hall.

"God bless the First Amendment," Napolitano said, as the crowd jeered the young man. "I disagree with what you say, but I will defend to the death your right to say it."

I followed the cops and their quarry out of the hall, watching as the officers pressed the protester to the floor just outside the entrance to the ballroom.

As police went through his pockets, he kept repeating, "I did not consent to this search. I am not resisting. But I did not consent to this search." He said his phone and his wallet were the only things he cared about being taken from him. After the cops were satisfied that he had nothing worth confiscating on his person, the wallet, phone and all his effects were returned to him. When a cop handed back his conference pass, an AFPF staff person said, "Officer, you need to take his credentials away from him." The officer obliged, handing the pass to the staffer. Then he and another cop took the protester by the arms and down an escalator.

I tailed them and got his name: Ricky Lehner, from Florida.

I returned to the hall for the rest of Napolitano's speech, and afterward exited the ballroom to head toward the ladies room. But once outside the banquet hall, I saw a small cluster of people facing one of the giant glass panes at the front of the building. Among them was a very tall man. It was David Koch, surveying the hundreds of protesters who had gathered outside the building.

Soon protesters were at the entrance, chanting and holding signs. Later reports said they had surrounded every entrance to the building.

Back in the hall. AFP Foundation executive vice-president Tracy Henke introduced David Koch to the crowd, which gave him a standing ovation. Along with the other dignitaries present from the AFP Foundation board, she also got a warm round of applause for her shout-out to Art Pope, chairman of the foundation's sibling organization, simply known as Americans for Prosperity. Pope is the North Carolina political powerhouse who is behind the attempts to re-segregate the public schools of Wake County.

Then Henke warned the audience that if they left the building during the program, they would not be able to return, because of the occupiers.

"We are so incredibly successful at what we do," she said, "[that] there are 500 protesters that have set up outside." She then directed the audience to look at the giant video screens used to magnify the speakers. Photos flashed of the view of protesters David Koch had seen from the building's south-facing window. "That's success," she added. "That's prosperity."

Before the program concluded, Phil Kerpen, the foundation's vice president for policy, would make a complaint about the Left's "racial grievance groups," as part of his rant on how President Barack Obama is, through regulation, usurping the powers of Congress.

Author Dinesh D'Souza was the evening's big-ticket speaker. Before he launched into his shopworn theory about how Obama is redistributing America's wealth to "third-world nations" in an effort to vindicate his father's anti-colonial activism, D'Souza noted one wonderful thing about America: that an American can belong to any racial group, and be born to parents of any nation.

Dessert was not served after the dinner; guests were herded instead into a hallway for D'Souza's book signing, where they could pick up some cookies, petits fours and coffee along the way. As the Tea Partiers mingled, plucking sugary treats from white porcelain trays, a young, brown-skinned woman stood on a chair. "This is a message from the 99 percent," she yelled. The crowd began to boo.

"We are not Democrats," she said. "We are not Republicans. We are you."

But the "We are you" part was drowned out by the chants of a group of young white people: "U-S-A, U-S-A, U-S-A," they roared—until an AFPF staff member told them to stop.

The woman was escorted from the premises. I spoke to her later, outside the building. She told me her name was Rooj Alwazar; she's an American of Middle Eastern descent. She said she felt the chants of the young people who surrounded her had something to do with her appearance. "Didn't that guy just say that anybody can be an American?" she asked, referring to D'Souza's remarks. "Obviously, that's not true."

After the dessert incident, I packed up my notebook and recorder, ready to call it a night. But as I made my way toward the one exit the police had directed me to, protesters sat down on the ground, with their backs against the door.

I left through the center doors instead, only to be encircled by a human chain of chanting people who were determined not to let me pass. I talked a young woman at one end of the chain into letting me by. "We are the 99 percent," they chanted. Somehow they had missed the point that most of the people in that hall were also part of the 99 percent. It was a stupid and threatening move on the part of protesters. It's one thing to make people take an inconvenient detour; it's quite another to trap people in a building. I don't like having my rights violated by anybody, especially by those whose cause I'm sympathetic to. And from a strategic point of view, this is hardly a way to win hearts and minds.

A standoff of sorts ensued, with police calling in reinforcements—still small in number, compared to the protesters. When the protesters refused to budge and the cops directed the exiting Tea Partiers down a long wheelchair ramp that runs across part of the building, some protesters scurried to block their path, as well. I saw one scuffle ensue between an older conference-goer and a younger protester.

Then came word that a protester had been hit by a car at a different entrance. According to one protester, a car plowed into a group of 99-percenters who were blocking an intersection at the rear of the convention center. The total number of people struck was three, apparently in two incidents involving the same driver, who was not charged.

For all the tension, it was managed with a minimal number of police—no riot gear, no pepper spray. Protesters' accounts about the incident with the car differ substantially from those of the police. Protesters dispute police assertions that demonstrators jumped in front of the car. Protester Heidi Sippel, who was among those struck, told the *Washington Post* that police refused to take her statement. The driver was let go without citation, but Sippel said she received two police citations.

OCCUPYING THE RUST BELT
BY ARUN GUPTA

THE SUREFIRE METHOD to find occupations in small cities is to head for the center of town. After leaving Philadelphia on our Occupy America tour, we drive an hour north to Allentown. Pennsylvania's third-largest city at 118,000 residents, Allentown has been weathered by years of deindustrialization in the steel, cement and textile industries that once made it an economic powerhouse.

Along MacArthur Boulevard, one of Allentown's main drags, tidy but weary brick row homes line outlying neighborhoods. Close to Center Square, site of the requisite Civil War monument, the neighborhoods are heavily Latino and buildings exhibit signs of disrepair. Occupy Allentown has taken up residence in Center Square, inhabiting one of the four red-brick plazas on each corner. There are a handful of tents, a well-supplied kitchen pavilion and an information desk. A large blue and gray nylon tent, which 12 people crammed into the first night of the occupation, has laundry hanging off a clothesline in back and a cardboard sign on the front that reads "Zuccotti Arms," in reference to the original Wall Street occupation.

We've come in search of Adam Santo, said to be the local leader of a leaderless movement. A handsome, boxy-glassed youth a few years out of college, Santo says he knew about the planning for Occupy Wall Street prior to Sept. 17.

"I wanted to go to New York, but I've been unemployed and finances were tight, so I thought wouldn't it be cool to have an occupation in the Lehigh Valley," where Allentown is nestled. Eight months earlier he and three coworkers were laid off from their jobs at a local bank because of a "lack of work."

Santo says when Occupy Wall Street "really took off. I thought, I'm going to make this take off in the Lehigh Valley, gather support, get people into the streets." Santo set up a Facebook page on September 30, the day before the 700 arrests on the Brooklyn Bridge, and "harassed my friends to join." Next, he designed, photocopied and handed out thousands of flyers to spread the word.

I mention Asmaa Mahfouz, the woman who helped ignite Egypt's uprising with powerful video blogs and by handing out thousands of flyers in the Cairene slums. He wasn't familiar with her story but he does take Egypt's revolution as inspiration.

Occupy Allentown is very much defined by the local. According to Davina DeLor, a 39-year-old freelance artist who is painting slogans on her tent when we encounter her, residents initially assumed the occupation was in protest of a planned hockey arena, which she says "they are using our tax money for."

It's one of those familiar enterprises of our time: socialism for the well-to-do. Allentown is using eminent domain to buy up businesses next to the encampment, including a Wells Fargo branch, that will be demolished to build an 8,500-seat arena for the Phantoms, a minor league hockey team. The city has authorized borrowing up to $175 million to pay for the multi-use facility, while the Phantoms' team owners are willing to throw in perhaps 10 percent of the cost. While anger is widespread over what is seen as shady political dealings for a taxpayer-funded stadium that will displace dozens of local businesses, many residents are more consumed just trying to survive the grinding economic crisis. Allentown's official poverty level in 2009 was 24 percent, twice the state average.

In a departure from big-city occupations like the one in New York, beat cops are openly supportive, Santo says. "They drive by, they wave, they honk. They give us handshakes and hugs … because they realize they are part of the 99 percent." Local clergy are encouraging their congregations to donate goods and "[supply] us with warm bodies, which we definitely need," says Santo.

At the same time, local conditions have limited the growth of the occupation. DeLor says many supporters have to juggle multiple part-time jobs, which limits the time they can spend protesting. During the week the number of campers and occupiers dwindles. This also may be why the day we were there, October 18, the occupiers were mostly unemployed or retired. Despite a Latino community that comprises 41 percent of Allentown residents, few appear to be involved in the occupation. Santo speculates that newer Latino communities aren't as active due to fears of immigration status and cultural divides, while younger Latinos are not involved simply because "it's just not the cool thing to do."

OCCUPATION WITH AN EXPIRATION DATE

Youngstown, Ohio, is an elegiac city a few hundred miles west of Allentown. What was once the manufacturing district is a mausoleum of industry. A brick smokestack stands sentinel over acres of cavernous shells that once poured out streams of goods. Crumbling brick buildings sprout trees two stories up, while inside pancakes of concrete drip toward the ground, suspended precariously by a bramble of rusted rebar.

Demolition is one of the few signs of economic life. Starting in 2006, the city tripled its budget for razing abandoned buildings. In an open-air yard in the industrial quarter, heavy machines whine and billow exhaust as they pound large concrete slabs, surrounded by small mountains of rubble sorted according to size. With more than 43 percent of the land vacant, Youngstown is slowly being erased. In some neighborhoods boarded-up houses and empty lots surround the remaining inhabited homes, which shrink behind spreading foliage lest they be next.

Since 1950, the population has declined from a high of 218,000 to less than 67,000 today. The poverty rate is a stratospheric 32 percent, and the median value of owner-occupied homes is a paltry $52,900. Manufacturing dropped from 50 percent of the workforce in 1950 to 16 percent in 2007. This includes a staggering loss of 31 percent of manufacturing jobs in the region from 2000 to 2007—and that was *before* the economy fell off the cliff.

At the downtown crossroads, Occupy Youngstown has taken up position in the shadow of three different banks, including a Chase branch. The occupation is a latecomer, having started on October 15, with a rally more than 400-strong at its peak, according to Chuck Kettering Jr., an aspiring actor who has been unemployed for a year after his previous position as an HVAC technician.

"We were once a huge steel city for America," says 27-year-old Kettering. "In the 1970s they started closing up all our steel mills, taking all the jobs and shipping them down south and overseas where labor is cheaper. Youngstown's been a city that has been going through this economic struggle for almost 40 years now, and I think we have a valid voice of addressing these issues on a national scale."

His family is living proof of the toll of deindustrialization. In a phone interview, Chuck Kettering Sr. calls himself "the poster boy for the Rust Belt." A Youngstown native, he went to work in 1973 at age 19 and worked at two local U.S. Steel plants that shuttered, one in 1979, the other in 1982. Next, he landed a position with Packard Electronics in 1985 making electrical components for GM cars. After GM spun off Delphi in 1999, Packard was subsumed by the auto-parts maker. The company started moving jobs overseas.

"Local operations were pressured by wages, and most operations moved south of the border" because of NAFTA, he says. Following Delphi's bankruptcy in 2008, Kettering and some coworkers were given a one-time chance to work for GM itself and keep their wages, benefits and pensions.

"It was a no-brainer," he says, but their seniority did not transfer to plant assignments. Despite nearly 25 years at Packard and Delphi, Kettering says, "I found myself at the age of 54 starting at the bottom, working alongside 21-year-olds trying to keep up on the line. Many of us who transferred were not spring chickens and it was hard to keep up." Today, he's on disability. His wife, hired by Packard in 1979, worked her way into management and was forced to retire after 30 years with a monthly pension that was slashed in half to $1,600, with expectations of further cuts.

"I'm really proud of our local guys," Kettering says. "The police and the firefighters really support the Occupy movement. Our mayor supports it. We have a united front here in Ohio."

Unlike the seven other occupations I have visited, Occupy Youngstown embraces electoral issues. Kettering and other occupiers wave signs and wear buttons opposing Issue 2, which would strip some 350,000 public sector workers of collective bargaining rights.

Karen Joseph, a softspoken 59-year-old mother of two whose family spends one-third of its household income on health insurance, is by no means the only one who is against Issue 3, which would exempt Ohio from the incoming national healthcare law.

Everyone is against privatizing the Ohio Turnpike, which is being pushed by Republican Gov. John Kasich. All the occupiers we talk to express dismay at the prospect of hydrofracking in Mill Creek Park, which Kettering describes as "the jewel of the area with waterfalls, streams and lots of wildlife."

This occupation comes with an expiration date. The city asked the occupiers to "take down the tents before business hours on Monday, October 17, when the banks were opening," according to Chuck Kettering, Jr. He says they complied, but Occupy Youngstown still maintains a 24-hour presence and has pledged to do so until November 8, Election Day.

TOLEDO BLUES

In Toledo, Ohio, occupiers are struggling with trying to live outdoors in a harsh climate because the city is making life difficult for them. Christopher Metchis, an energetic 19-year-old student who will be attending the Musicians Institute in L.A. next spring, explains that City Hall has denied them use of tents and generators, and dispatched city crews to cut off their access to electricity. He has just spent the last two nights outdoors in a rainy windstorm, huddling under tarps with a few hardy souls on a grass plaza in the downtown business district near the baseball stadium for the AAA Toledo Mud Hens.

While we talk, a few people come by to help with consolidating supplies, folding tarps, stuffing blankets into a crib and kitchen work. A local pastor has also stopped by with words of support. Candice Milligan, a 30-year-old trans woman, says the living conditions make it "difficult for people who aren't able-bodied." She also admits that concrete support is not as forthcoming because much of the public does not know what Occupy Toledo is trying to accomplish. And they have to contend with a police force that is indifferent at best and a local media that is hostile at times.

Awareness of the occupation movement coexists with despair. During dinner one evening at an Italian restaurant in Toldeo, our waitress, Dawn, tells us she supports it because "the people need a voice, not just the corporations and politicians." A few minutes earlier, she lit up in excitement when she found out we were from New York, but her face crumpled instantly, exclaiming quizzically, "But now you're *here?*"

It has been a common sentiment on the trip so far. After decades of economic decline, Americans in this part of the country are beaten down. Their prospects are limited. Civic embarrassment is more prevalent than pride. They lament the end of the "American Dream," the notion that hard work and sacrifice would be rewarded with a comfortable retirement and a better life for their children and grandkids. But in the hundreds of occupations around the country they have found a space where they can speak of their struggles, burdens and aspiration. People listen and they hear similar stories, creating a genuine sense of community. They say it is giving them dignity. And perhaps most important, it is giving them hope.

THREE WAYS BEN & JERRY'S AND OTHER COMPANIES ARE SUPPORTING OCCUPY WALL STREET

BY LAUREN KELLEY

THE OCCUPY MOVEMENT has garnered the support of labor unions, celebrities and thousands of individuals participating in solidarity actions around the globe, all combating the brand of capitalism that allows the nation's wealthiest 1 percent to thrive at the expense of the poor and the middle-class. But the movement has also started drawing some support from a more unlikely source: for-profit companies. It's not as if hoards of Fortune 500 companies are tripping over themselves to get on the Occupy Wall Street bandwagon. Still, there have been some small but significant displays of support from the business world.

1. BEN & JERRY'S BOARD OF DIRECTORS: 'WE STAND WITH YOU'

Ben & Jerry's is far and away the biggest company to explicitly endorse Occupy Wall Street. The company, a subsidiary of Unilever that brings in hundreds of millions of dollars in annual revenue, issued a statement from its board of directors in October:

> *We, the Ben & Jerry's Board of Directors, compelled by our personal convictions and our Company's mission and values, wish to express our deepest admiration to all of you who have initiated the nonviolent Occupy Wall Street Movement and to those around the country who have joined in solidarity. The issues raised are of fundamental importance to all of us.*

Ben & Jerry's is known for having maintained its social and environmental standards even as it "sold out" to Unilever. Still, the letter is surprisingly candid, noting that "corporate profits continue to soar and millionaires whine about paying a bit more in taxes."

The following month, Ben & Jerry's put at least a symbolic amount of its considerable money where its mouth is, donating ice cream to hundreds of Occupy DC protesters.

2. LOCAL BUSINESSES DONATE GOODS

A number of small local businesses have also been inspired by the message of the Occupy Wall Street crowd. After all, small business owners have felt the effects of Wall Street greed as much as anyone. To show solidarity, some of them have donated food and supplies to the protesters at Zuccotti Park.

Contrary to reports from Fox News that businesses in lower Manhattan roundly despise the protesters, many local businesses have been supportive of the occupation. Local design shop and consultancy FearLess sent food and a megaphone down to the park, while Brooklyn-based craft brewery Sixpoint delivered kegs of water to the occupiers and released a statement of solidarity. Some are even finding a business opportunity in Occupy Wall Street. Local pizzeria Liberatos is advertising the "Occu-Pie," which supporters can purchase and have sent to Zuccotti Park for $15.

And some activists are trying to show some love back to these small businesses. When it became clear that Occupy Wall Street had negatively impacted several lower Manhattan street vendors, the Street Vendor Project launched a Web site where people can donate money that will be used to buy food for protesters from the vendors, thus helping both the occupiers and the local vendors.

3. THE 'PEOPLE'S MCDONALD'S'

McDonald's is probably the last company you'd think would support Occupy Wall Street. And as far as Micky D's corporate headquarters is concerned, it isn't. However, occupiers have dubbed one McDonald's near Zuccotti Park the "people's McDonald's." Staffers at the location have been generally friendly to the Occupy Wall Street protesters, letting them use their restrooms and free wireless Internet.

Meanwhile, the local UPS Store is accepting packages on behalf of the occupiers. While hardly an explicit endorsement of the movement, the company could easily have chosen to distance itself from the action. You can find the address for that UPS Store, and a list of items that the occupiers need, at nycga.net/how-to-help.

The 99%

OCCUPY WALL STREET TRADES 'THE WHOLE WORLD IS WATCHING' FOR WATCHING THE WHOLE WORLD

BY NICK TURSE

MORE THAN 40 years ago, he was in the thick of protests here in New York City. And here he was again, joining in the Occupy Wall Street protests in Lower Manhattan—marching a pre-approved route inside a police cordon from the heart of the movement in Zuccotti Park to a pre-approved rally in a city square, where traditional activist speakers said traditional activist things to a crowd that, while it wasn't lacking energy, did nothing that wasn't traditional for city protests of the last 15 years.

An aging radical, his heyday was a time when, as the police beat them in the streets of Chicago during the 1968 Democratic National Convention under the glare of television cameras, American youth chanted in unison: "The whole world is watching." (A phrase today's New York City protesters resurrected recently when set upon by police on the Brooklyn Bridge.) He mentioned his thoughts to a group of them: the Wall Street protests would have erupted years sooner, if not for the election of President Obama. On the face of it, the analysis seemed credible. Earnest young Americans had put their faith in an dashing young president who seemed to promise hope and change, only to have their dreams dashed on the hard realities of expanding wars, moral compromises and policies that cater to the rich at the expense of the "other 99 percent," as the protesters term themselves.

As public intellectual Tom Engelhardt, who attended that same rally, has noted, the protests have almost nothing to do with President Obama. He might as well be a non-entity. Engelhardt wrote:

> *Amid the kaleidoscopic range of topics on those signs and in those chants and cries, one thing, one name, was largely missing: the president's. In those hours marching and at Foley Square amid the din of so many thousands of massed people, I saw one sign that said 'Obama = Bush' and another that went something like 'The Barack Obama we elected would be out here with us.' That was it. Sayonara.*

The Occupy Wall Street movement has so much more to do with Mohamed Bouazizi, Bradley Manning and Mona Seif—all of them in their 20s, all
of them breaking new ground—than it does Barack Obama. (And none of them
was influenced by the American president in anything but the most indirect
ways.) The nascent Occupy Wall Street movement, by most accounts, wasn't
watching and waiting for Obama to save them, although plenty of Americans
no doubt were—it was watching similarly young activists in Tunisia, Egypt,
Libya, Bahrain, Iraq, Yemen, Syria, Greece, Syria, Spain, Belarus and elsewhere.
Back in the '60s, Americans said the whole world was watching; today Occupy
Wall Street activists are watching the whole world for ideas and inspiration.

If the Occupy Wall Street movement succeeds, whatever success means,
it will be because of their youth, inexperience and ability to fend off co-
optation and the sure-to-be-destructive advice of aging activists, political
opportunists and liberal commentators with their failed prescriptions, faulty
analysis and hopeless notions of "proper" protests. It will be because of a
worldwide movement of action-oriented young people to whom Barack
Obama is less than an afterthought.

For 26-year-old Tunisian fruit peddler Mohammed Bouazizi, harassment
by the police was the final straw in a short life filled with economic privation
and few opportunities. Angry at having been mistreated by the local security
forces, Bouazizi marched to the local governor's office in his hometown of
Sidi Bouzid to air his grievances. "If you don't see me, I'll burn myself," he
reportedly declared upon being rebuffed. Within an hour of his humiliation
at the hands of the security forces, he had doused himself with gasoline and
set himself aflame in protest.

"What kind of repression do you imagine it takes for a young man to do
this?" his sister asked, after her brother died of his injuries. "A man who has to
feed his family by buying goods on credit when they fine him ... and take his
goods. In Sidi Bouzid, those with no connections and no money for bribes are
humiliated and insulted and not allowed to live."

Bouazizi's actions sparked grassroots protests that spread from his dusty
town to the capital, taking aim not just at the local repressive arms of the state,
but the corrupt regime running the country, specifically Tunisia's longtime
strongman Zine al-Abidine Ben Ali. The protests were also fueled, in part,
by a trove of secret U.S. State Department documents allegedly leaked by
then 22-year-old Army private Bradley Manning. "Whether it's cash, services,
land, property, or yes, even your yacht, President Ben Ali's family is rumored
to covet it and reportedly gets what it wants," one 2008 cable from the U.S.
embassy in Tunis explained, offering confirmation of what Tunisians instinc-

tively knew about their dictator and his family. As one Tunisian praising the "youth revolution" put it:

> And then, WikiLeaks reveals what everyone was whispering. And then, a young man immolates himself. And then, 20 Tunisians are killed in one day.
>
> And for the first time, we see the opportunity to rebel, to take revenge on the "royal" family who has taken everything, to overturn the established order that has accompanied our youth. An educated youth, which is tired and ready to sacrifice all the symbols of the former autocratic Tunisia with a new revolution ...

That revolt quickly spread to neighboring Egypt where another longtime dictator was soon in the crosshairs of disaffected youth with big dreams and faith in street protest predicated on holding the capital's great public space, Tahrir Square, running an alternative society there and speaking out in ways their elders hadn't dared in the face of drawn weapons and live ammunition. It was something new, something they had to do for themselves.

"I was angry about the corruption in the country, [about the police killing of] Khaled Said and the torture of those suspected but never convicted [of being behind] the Alexandria Coptic church [bombing]," 24-year-old Egyptian activist Mona Seif told al Jazeera earlier this year.

"I realized this was going to be bigger than we had anticipated when 20,000 people marched toward Tahrir Square on January 25. That is when we saw a shift; it was not about the minimum wage or emergency law anymore. It became much bigger than this, it turned into a protest against the regime, demanding that Mubarak step down and that parliament be dissolved.

"On the night later dubbed 'the battle of the camels' when pro-Mubarak thugs attacked us, I was terrified. I thought they were going to shoot us all and get it over with. The turning point for me was when I saw the number of people ready to face death for their beliefs."

When *Adbusters* set the Occupy Wall Street protests in motion, an early email proclaimed: "A worldwide shift in revolutionary tactics is underway right now that bodes well for the future. The spirit of this fresh tactic, a fusion of Tahrir with the *acampadas* of Spain, is captured in this quote [from Raimundo Viejo, Pompeu Fabra University, Barcelona, Spain]:

> The antiglobalization movement was the first step on the road. Back then our model was to attack the system like a pack of wolves. There was

an alpha male, a wolf who led the pack, and those who followed behind.
Now the model has evolved. Today we are one big swarm of people.

"Leaderless" movements are nothing new. Ask an aging Yippie if you can find one. But old movements weren't the model. "Tahrir succeeded in large part because the people of Egypt made a straightforward ultimatum—that Mubarak must go—over and over again until they won," read *Adbusters'* missive. Obama was a target for demands, nothing more. He wasn't a fallen messiah, just the guy in office at the moment. He was never one of "them" and I honestly don't think the young women and men camping out down in Zuccotti Park ever thought he was.

"Where the movement falters is in its demands: It doesn't really have any," a commentator from the *New York Times* recently wrote in a column filled with advice that the Occupy Wall Street protesters make conventional, concrete demands, even while calling their slogans "silly" and admitting that he doesn't share their dreams or vision.

For many years, protesters in New York City have marched up and down Manhattan Island in police-approved marches. They have even marched to Foley Square, to be similarly penned in along the way, by similarly clad cops to attend rallies so similar to so many others, that most of them probably couldn't recall the year, the reason, or anything that set one apart from another police-approved march that led nowhere.

Perhaps it's because the geriatric radical fervently supported Obama and was fooled by him that he wants Occupy Wall Street to share in his shame, just as the *New York Times* columnist would be more comfortable if the movement issued professional-looking position papers, and yesterday's activists are content to march around, flanked by cops to attend yesterday's rallies. Why would the Occupy Wall Street protesters listen to any of them when they're so dissatisfied with the world handed down by all of them? And with so many young activists from Tunisia, Egypt, Libya, Yemen and Syria overturning the established order to look to for inspiration, why would they base anything they do on America's floundering, six-war president?

The antiglobilization protesters used to say "Another world is possible." The Occupy Wall Street movement is living it in Zuccotti Park. They don't need to look to yesterday's protesters or to Barack Obama; they're watching the whole world.

FOUR OCCUPATIONS EMBRACING THE HOMELESS

BY RANIA KHALEK

IN JUST UNDER two months, the Occupy movement has managed to turn the country's attention toward social inequality. As many in the movement struggle with unemployment, student debt and unaffordable mortgage payments, words like foreclosure, debt and joblessness have reentered the public discourse. More recently, as the number of homeless people at Occupy encampments climbs, the conversation has shifted toward the growing but often hidden dilemma of homelessness in America.

Prior to a November 13 eviction enforced by Mayor Sam Adams via police raid, one of the country's largest occupations could be found in Portland, Oregon's Chapman and Lownsdale Squares, where an estimated 500 people spent their nights in a sprawling encampment of tents.

Before the eviction, Kip Silverman, an organizer with Occupy Portland, told AlterNet, "The majority of them are homeless or disenfranchised people. We have folks that have just recently lost jobs, lost their homes, and the Occupy encampment is all they have right now. We actually have nine families living there."

During a one-night count in January conducted by Oregon's Housing and Community Services, the state identified 22,116 homeless people, 30 percent of whom were children. In 2010, the city of Portland had the third highest rate of homelessness in the country. With its free medical facilities, health and outreach services and kitchen serving 1,500 meals a day, it's no surprise that Occupy Portland has attracted such a high number of the homeless.

The movement is well aware of the downsides to inclusiveness. "There's been some rowdiness, there's been drinking, there's been some people fighting on occasion," Silverman admitted, adding, "We're trying to self-police as best we can." Silverman insisted that the people causing trouble were in the minority and that fights were a rare occurrence, however Mayor Adams used the issues of health and safety as a pretext for the eviction.

In addition, there was concern that tending to the needs of the homeless could potentially divert energy away from the occupation's initial goals. "There's a handful of people that feed 500 people three meals a day, that's 1,500 meals a day," said Silverman. "It's a huge strain on the occupation movement itself because we have to focus a lot of time and energy on how we manage our encampment's infrastructure and services."

On top of that, the city may have been contributing to the problem. "I have heard from three individual sources that some of the city institutions that help the homeless and disenfranchised are actually sending some people our way because we have services that we're providing that apparently others cannot or will not," Silverman said. Nevertheless, he said the movement would continue to welcome everyone, including the homeless. "This is why we're out here in the first place, and they are also the 99 percent," he said. "These are the least of our brothers and sisters among us."

Others at Occupy Portland had expressed similar sentiments. "This is a movement that is about justice and inequity and overcoming issues of greed," Gina Ronning, an organizer who volunteers on the peace and safety committee, told the *Wall Street Journal*. "If our own movement didn't attempt to live those values I don't think we'd be much of a movement."

Ronning went even further, arguing that the inclusion of the homeless "has helped clarify for us exactly what issues we need to focus on. They're here not just because of the resources. They're here also because for the first time a silent population is here to be given a voice."

Now that Occupy Portland's encampment has been cleared and fenced off by police, Silverman says that the homeless families and individuals that had taken shelter there are likely back on the streets, which is ironic given the Mayor's stated intention of evicting the occupiers because they were creating an unsafe and unhealthy environment.

Among at risk populations at Occupy Portland were a few addicts and individuals with mental health problems. As a result, there were a handful of overdoses in the encampment, which Mayor Adams referenced as proof of the occupation's deficiencies. However, Silverman explained that two of the overdoses occurred outside the encampment by people who came to Occupy Portland for treatment. "The other two happened after the eviction notice," says Silverman. "One social worker explained to me that addicts tend to OD in times of stress. There is nothing more stressful than losing the safety of your home. I'm not saying the eviction is the direct cause, but it makes sense."

Still, the movement has not given up. According to Silverman, working groups are looking for offsite places to meet for General Assemblies and working group meetings. "We have many different churches and union organizations that have offered spaces for us to meet," says Silverman, adding that Occupy Portland would remain as inclusive and welcoming as possible.

According to Buck Gorrell, an organizer with Occupy Nashville, the Tennessee offshoot has a significant homeless population as well. While Gorrell said they have been overwhelmingly helpful, "for a stretch, there was a contingent there to drink and raise hell and have sex in the bushes; not many people at all, but enough to cause a disturbance."

This has forced Occupy Nashville to self-police, which according to Gorrell is no easy task for a movement that values participation from all who attend. At the same time, Gorrell says the homeless population has played a vital role in Occupy Nashville.

"I can't paint the whole homeless community with one brush, because we have a lot of homeless folks that have hunkered down and been there far more days than not and are filling responsible roles within the encampment and helping out a tremendous amount, even to the point of acting as impromptu liaisons with homeless folks who maybe are confused or drunk or mentally not in charge of their faculties," Gorrell said.

At César Chávez Plaza, Occupy Phoenix has proudly embraced the homeless who serve invaluable roles in the movement.

In a blog post at Salon, Amy McMullen, a volunteer medic at Occupy Phoenix, observes, "while this movement started out as a broad representation of our diverse population, those who have stuck around through thick and thin are predominately homeless." One example she gave was a night medic who lost his job as a medical assistant due to illness. The woman who runs the food and water station is a former investment banker who lost her husband and then her home.

McMullen proceeds to paint a sobering reality of homelessness in Phoenix: "According to an October 2011 report by the advocacy group Phoenix Homeless Rising, Arizona has one of the highest poverty rates in the country: 18.6 percent as of 2010. There are approximately 17,000 beds in Phoenix shelters, which is woefully inadequate for a homeless population that ranges between 20,000 to 30,000 on any given day." To make matters worse, sleeping outside in Phoenix is a criminal offense, thanks to the city's anti-camping ordinances, forcing the homeless into unsanitary and "overcrowded shelter campuses" to "keep them out of sight."

Given the dire state of affairs, it's no wonder the homeless population taking refuge at Occupy Phoenix includes some of the most active and committed individuals in the movement. As McMullen points out, "They are the ones who've lost the most: their homes, their livelihoods and their families. And they must battle every day to maintain their self-respect. It is only fitting that they are the ones who have stepped forward and assumed these roles in our own little corner of the Occupy movement."

Arizona's *State Press* details the plight of Brian Faulk, described as "one of the homeless regulars at Occupy Phoenix." Before volunteering at Occupy Phoenix, Faulk spent weeks on the streets after losing his job and then his home, which he could no longer afford. "I think (Occupy Phoenix) provides a voice for people, for the working class," says Faulk, adding, "The organization of this has been like a blessing. I've been able to feel like I'm committed to a cause."

Steve Ross, an organizer with Occupy Philly, told the *Wall Street Journal* that 30 to 40 percent of the people taking shelter in the 450 tents pitched at Dilworth Plaza are homeless. But the movement has not shied away from embracing the homeless. At Occupy Philly the homeless have access to three hot meals a day, blankets to keep warm and a place to sleep free from police harassment. But the homeless are also deeply involved in the movement. According to Ross, "Every working group has at least one homeless member, at this point."

Occupy Wall Street is clearly not a monolith, therefore the debate over how inclusive the movement should be is likely to continue. However, it's impossible to separate homelessness from the occupy movement's struggle for economic justice. As Barbara Ehrenreich recently reminded us, "Homelessness is not a side issue unconnected to plutocracy and greed. It's where we're all eventually headed—the 99 percent, or at least the 70 percent of us, every debt-loaded college grad, out-of-work school teacher, and impoverished senior—unless this revolution succeeds."

VI.

ROOT CAUSES:

WHY THE

99 PERCENT

REBELLED

INTRODUCTION

WHAT MOTIVATED PEOPLE to put their lives on hold and pitch tents in the middle of New York? And what caused a small, quixotic protest to spread like wildfire across the United States and, indeed, the world?

It may well be that the bailouts were an eye-opener for many Americans—highlighting the folly of calling ours a "free-market economy." It may have been the emergence of the Tea Party Caucus in 2010, whose unprecedented obstructionism brought the legislature to a halt, blocking even the most modest, "pro-business" proposals for addressing the unemployment and foreclosure crises. Perhaps it was the Supreme Court's *Citizens United* ruling, which unleashed undisclosed corporate dollars into our electoral process. And it may have been the way Wall Street, having precipitated the crash only to be bailed out by the public, then bounced back, once again earning fat bonuses and profits as millions faced a raging unemployment crisis and slashed safety nets.

A combination of all of those things may have been what finally awoke the sleeping giant that we've come to know as "the 99 percent." But the events of recent years are only the culmination of longer trends in our political economy: the increasing influence of outside money in our elections and proliferation of well-heeled lobbyists writing legislation, the concentration of wealth at the top, a bloated military budget, and increasingly, a two-tiered system of justice for the haves and the have-nots.

The 99%

AVERTING A 'DAGGER IN THE HEART OF THE COUNTRY:' NOAM CHOMSKY SPEAKS TO OCCUPY BOSTON

A philosopher, activist, linguist, and author, Chomsky spoke to Occupy Boston on October 22.

THE OCCUPY MOVEMENT is unprecedented; there's never been anything like it that I can think of. If the bonds and associations that are being established can be sustained through a long, hard period ahead, this could turn out to be a very significant moment in American history.

That the demonstrations are unprecedented is quite appropriate. We are in an unprecedented era that started in the 1970s. For centuries, we've been a developing society with ups and downs. There was a constant expectation that wealth and industrialization and development would go on, even in dark times.

I'm just old enough to remember the Great Depression. Although the situation was objectively much harsher than it is today, the spirit was quite different. Even among unemployed people there was a sense that we'd come out of it. There was a militant labor movement organizing. CIO was organizing. Sit-down strikes were frightening the business world. By the late 1930s unemployed "working people" could anticipate realistically that the jobs are going to come back.

Between the end of the war and the 1970s, there were no financial crises. We saw the largest period of growth in American history, or maybe in economic history. It was egalitarian, so the lowest percentile did as well as the highest percentile. A lot of people moved into the middle class. The seeds of the high-tech economy were planted, substantially in the state sector. The activism of the '60s civilized the country in lasting ways.

But the 1970s set off a vicious cycle that led to a concentration of wealth increasingly in the hands of the rapidly growing financial sector. Concentration of wealth yields concentration of political power, which, in turn, yields legislation that increases and accelerates the cycle. Meanwhile, the general population experienced stagnation or decline. People got by through artificial means like borrowing. The gap between public policy and the public will grew astronomically. You can see it right now in Washington. The public wants higher taxes on the wealthy and to preserve the limited social benefits. But the outcome in Washington will probably be the opposite. The Occupy movements could provide a mass base for trying to avert what amounts to a dagger in the heart of the country.

For the 99 percent, things are harsh and could get worse. But the 1 percent is richer and more powerful than ever in controlling the political system and disregarding the public. The historic reversal that began in the 1970s could become irreversible. The Occupy movements are the first major popular reaction which could avert this. It's going to be a long, hard struggle. You have to form structures that will be sustained through hard times and can win major victories. But there are a lot of things that can be done.

In the 1930s one of the most effective actions was a sit-down strike. The reason was very simple: it's just a step below a takeover of the industry. Through the '70s decline, some very important events took place. In 1977, U.S. Steel decided to close one of its major facilities, Youngstown, Ohio. Instead of just walking away, the workforce and the community got together to buy it from U.S. Steel and hand it over to the workforce to run. They didn't win, but with enough popular support they could have. It was a partial victory because even though they lost, it set off efforts throughout Ohio and other places.

There are perhaps thousands of not-so-small worker-owned or partially worker-owned industries which could become worker-managed. That's the basis for a real revolution. It's happening here. In a Boston suburb, a multi-national shut down a productive and functioning manufacturing company because it was not profitable enough for them. The workforce and union offered to buy it and take it over and run it themselves. The multi-national decided to close it down, but if something like this movement could have gotten involved, the workers might have succeeded.

For the first time in human history, there are real threats to survival of the species. One is the constant nuclear threat, and the other is environmental catastrophe. Every country in the world is taking at least halting steps toward trying to do something about it. But the U.S. is taking steps to accelerate the threat. A huge propaganda system, openly declared by the business world, says that climate change all just a liberal hoax. Why pay attention to these scientists? If that's happening to the most powerful and richest country in history, then this crisis is not going to be averted and all of this we're talking about won't matter in a generation or two. Something has to be done about it very soon and in a dedicated and sustained way.

The road ahead is not going to be easy. There are going to be barriers, hardships and failures along the way. But if the process that's taking place here and around the world continues to grow and becomes a major social force in the world, then we might just have a chance for a decent future.

Q&A

Q: What about corporate personhood and getting the money out of that stream of politics?

A: These are very good things to do, but you can't do any of these things or anything else unless there's a very large and active base. If the Occupy movement was the leading force in the country, then you could move it forward. Most people don't know that this is happening or they may know about it and not know what it is. Among those who do know, the polls show there's a lot of support. But that assigns a task. It's necessary to get out into the country and get people to understand what this is about, and what they can do about it, and what the consequences are of not doing anything about it.

Q: You mentioned earlier that sit down protests are just a precursor to a takeover of industry. Would you advocate a general strike as a tactic moving forward?

A: The question of general strike is like the others. You can think of it as a possible idea at a time when the population is ready for it. We can't sit here and declare a general strike, obviously. But there has to be approval and a willingness to take the risks on the part of a large mass of the population. That takes organization, education and activism. Education doesn't just mean telling people what to believe. It means learning yourself.

There's a familiar Karl Marx quote, "The task is not just to understand the world but to change it." There's a variant of that which should be kept in mind, "If you want to change the world in a certain direction you better try to understand it first." Understanding it doesn't mean listening to a talk or reading a book, though that is helpful. It comes through learning. Learning comes from participation. You learn from others. You learn from the people you're trying to organize. You have to gain the experience and understanding which will make it possible to maybe implement ideas as a tactic. There's a long way to go. This doesn't happen by the flick of a wrist. It happens from a long, dedicated work. I think in many ways the most exciting aspect of the Occupy movements is just the construction of these associations and bonds that are taking place all over. Out of that, if they can be sustained, can come expansion to a large part of the population that doesn't know what's going on. If that can happen, then you can raise questions about tactics like this, which could very well at some point be appropriate.

THE NUMBERS BACK UP OCCUPY WALL STREET'S ANALYSIS OF THE ECONOMIC DAMAGE DONE TO THE 'OTHER 99 PERCENT'

DESPITE A LOT of handwringing in the media about the Occupy movement's supposed lack of focus, it does have a simple-to-understand message that fits neatly on a bumpersticker: "We Are the Other 99 Percent." Contained in that simple message is an implied demand, whether or not people recognize it: to undo several decades of increasing inequality in this country.

Economists Thomas Piketty and Emmanuel Saez sliced and diced America's income going all the way back to 1913, and their results tell us exactly what the Occupy Wall Street movement is about, at least in broad terms. In the post-war era leading up to Ronald Reagan's inauguration, as a large American middle-class emerged, the top 1 percent of households took in 10 percent of the nation's pre-tax income, leaving 90 percent for the "other 99 percent." Their share was very consistent—in only eight of the years between 1946 and 1980 did those at the top grab 11 percent or more, and only in one year—1946—did they consume more than 13 percent of the pie. They took in less than 10 percent in 13 of those years.

After Ronald Reagan arrived on the scene, things began to change. In his final year in office, those in the top 1 percent grabbed 15.5 percent of our pre-tax income. And in the 10 years before the Great Recession hit, households at the top of the pile grabbed 20.3 percent—twice as large a share as they'd enjoyed when the "Greatest Generation" were making their mark on the world.

By 2007, the year before the crash, they were pulling in 23.5 percent of our pre-tax income, leaving the other 99 percent to share just 76.5 percent of the fruits of our output.

But those at the top of the ladder aren't any more virtuous, intelligent or hardworking than they were 30 or 40 years ago, and this didn't happen by accident. It resulted from specific policy changes that the corporate Right fought hard to enact—international trade deals that facilitated offshoring much of our manufacturing base, changes in labor laws and enforcement that cut the unionized share of the American workforce in half, and a shift in priorities at the Federal Reserve that led it to concentrate far more on keeping inflation in check than on keeping working America employed.

The 99%

The Economic Policy Institute put together some graphics, reprinted here, that tell this story visually.

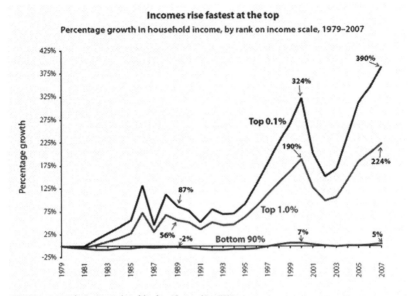

Incomes rise fastest at the top

Percentage growth in household income, by rank on income scale, 1979–2007

SOURCE: Economic Policy Institute analysis of data from Piketty and Saez (2010).

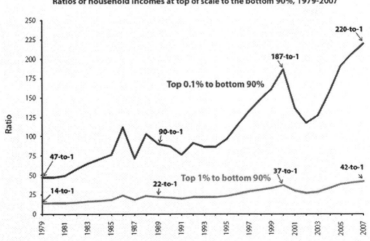

Highest-income groups distance themselves from everyone else

Ratios of household incomes at top of scale to the bottom 90%, 1979-2007

SOURCE: Economic Policy Institute analysis of data from Piketty and Saez (2010).

CEO's distance themselves from the average worker

Ratio of average annual CEO compensation to average worker compensation, 1965–2010

SOURCE: Update of Mishel, Bernstein, and Shierholz (2009).

And it's not just income from work. Wealth has become increasingly concentrated at the top over the past 30 or so years.

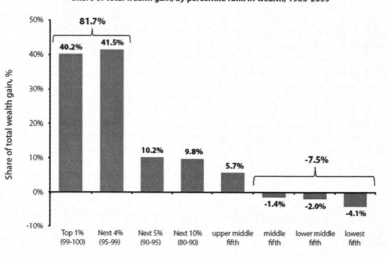

The rich gain most of the growth in wealth

Share of total wealth gain, by percentile rank in wealth, 1983-2009

SOURCE: Economic Policy Institute analysis of Wolff in Allegretto (2010).

Returns on investment income show a similar pattern.

The 99%

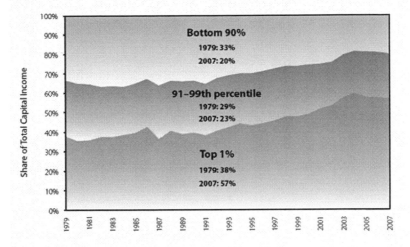

Returns from wealth-holding are rapidly concentrating

Share of total capital incomes claimed by income percentiles, 1979–2007

Bottom 90%
1979: 33%
2007: 20%

91–99th percentile
1979: 29%
2007: 23%

Top 1%
1979: 38%
2007: 57%

SOURCE: Economic Policy Institute analysis of data from the Congressional Budget Office collection of data on effective federal tax rates.

Why look to Wall Street?

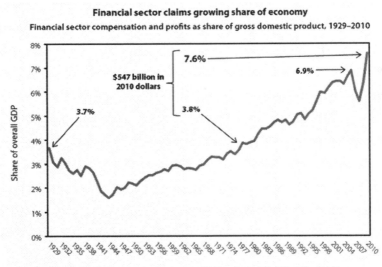

Financial sector claims growing share of economy

Financial sector compensation and profits as share of gross domestic product, 1929–2010

7.6%

6.9%

$547 billion in 2010 dollars

3.7%

3.8%

SOURCE: Bureau of Economic Analysis (BEA) data on National Income and Product Accounts (NIPA), tables 1.1.5 and 1.1.14.

They say a picture is worth a thousand words. These graphs tell a tale of vanishing economic security for the vast majority of American households. They illustrate that even if the occupiers lack a concrete set of demands, they know exactly why they're out there.

CONGRESSIONAL LEADERSHIP POSITIONS FOR SALE TO THE HIGHEST BIDDER

BY THOMAS FERGUSON

THE YEAR IS 1909. The U.S. income distribution is about as lopsided as it is today. J.P. Morgan is fine-tuning a tariff bill by telegraph from his yacht. Morgan and his fellow robber barons have for years reliably tied Congress up in knots whenever anyone proposes regulating trusts, railroad rates, financial speculation or labor disputes. A notoriously corrupt ring of U.S. senators, the so-called Millionaires Club, is on hand to bury in committee any measures that the corporate titans frown upon.

Fast-forward to 2011. Being a millionaire in Congress is nothing special. The legislative process works less operatically, but the result is pretty much the same: gridlock punctuated by occasional blatant special-interest legislation. Banks are rescued; the unemployed ignored. The housing market is in free fall, with the bailed-out banks calling the tune on foreclosures.

As national income stagnates, financiers submerge financial reforms and derivatives regulation under waves of campaign contributions. Meanwhile, a vast array of interested firms and investors dispatch armies of lobbyists to stymie congressional action on everything from climate change to tax increases on the wealthy.

While we hold our breath to see if stalemate will trigger draconian cuts to essential programs like Medicare, popular discussions about Congress have taken a curious turn. Pundits talk nostalgically about the good old days, when representatives from the two parties played golf together and compromised their differences in the name of the larger national interest. What happened?

Political money is an obvious problem. But tired recitations of astronomical campaign-finance spending totals don't tell the full story. Neither does the observation that since the 1990s, Republican leaders both in Congress and out have raised enormous amounts of money from investor blocs that plainly hope to roll back the New Deal as a whole.

Here's the big picture: The tidal wave of cash has structurally transformed Congress. It swept away the old seniority system that used to govern leadership selection and committee assignments. In its place, the major political parties borrowed a practice from Best Buy or Target. You want it, you buy it.

Unique among legislatures in the developed world, U.S. congressional parties now post prices for key slots in the lawmaking process. As Marian

Currinder explained in her book, *Money in the House*, the Democratic congressional campaign following the 2008 cycle asked members "to contribute $125,000 in dues and to raise an additional $75,000 for the party." Senior politicians with committee places were asked to come up with even more cash—up to $500,000. The same expectation of money-raising occurs on the other side, too. But unlike most retailers there are never any sales. Prices only drift up over time.

This destructive practice is perhaps the one case where bipartisanship flourishes in Congress. The Democrats' 2008 price schedules are just variations on themes introduced by the Republicans in the 1990s, when Newt Gingrich brought in the earliest versions of "pay to play" and Tom DeLay consulted computer printouts of members' contributions at meetings to decide on committee chairs. Everyone in DC is in on the game. Only the public is still in the dark.

THE NEW NORMAL

Posting prices does more than energize members of Congress to hunt up new sources of cash in hope of advancing their careers and winning reelection. It makes cashflow the basic determinant of lawmaking. Instead of buffering at least some outside forces, congressional committees and party leadership posts reflect the shape of political money—and in our New Gilded Age, it is obvious where most of that comes from.

The whole is far more sinister than the parts. Big interest groups (think finance, oil, utilities or healthcare) can control the membership of the committees that write the legislation that regulates them. Outside investors and interest groups also become decisive in resolving leadership struggles within the parties in Congress. You want your man or woman in the leadership? Just send money. Lots of it.

On the edges, factors besides money still play some role, especially in ordinary committee assignments. But the New Normal looks like this: In 2009, when the Democrats controlled the House, their leadership slotted many junior representatives on the Financial Services Committee so they could haul in cash to enhance their prospects for reelection. All the money talked; today, despite the passage of the Dodd-Frank financial reforms, U.S. regulators can't even tell which American financial houses are exposed to what risk.

But the real rub is the way the system centralizes power in the hands of top congressional leaders. In the new pay-to-play system, individual representatives dole out contributions to their colleagues to gain support for their bids for key positions within each chamber. But the system also requires them to make large contributions to the House and Senate national campaign committees. These are normally controlled by congressional leaders in each chamber (along with, perhaps, the White House when the president comes from the same party).

MONEY TALKS

When cash is king, access to it determines who rules. The congressional party leadership controls the swelling coffers of the national campaign committees, and the huge fixed investments in polling, research and media capabilities that these committees maintain—resources the leaders use to bribe, cajole or threaten candidates to toe the party line. This is especially true of "open-seat" races, where no incumbent is running; or in contests where an obscure challenger vies to upset an incumbent of the other party. Candidates rely on the national campaign committees not only for money, but for message, consultants and polling they need to be competitive but can rarely afford on their own.

Congressional campaigns thus acquire a more national flavor. They endlessly repeat a handful of slogans that have been battle-tested for their appeal to the national investor blocs and interest groups the leadership relies on for resources. And crossing party lines becomes dangerous indeed.

This concentration of power also allows party leaders to shift tactics to serve their own ends. They grandstand by trying to hold up legislation. They push hot-button legislative issues that have no chance of passage, just to win plaudits and money from donor blocs and special-interest supporters. When they are in the minority, they obstruct legislation, playing to the gallery and hoping to make a splash in the media, aware that most Americans pay little attention.

Congress has become a jungle where individual members compete frantically for donations. Top-heavy, cash-rich leadership structures ensure that national party campaigns rest heavily on slogan-filled, fabulously expensive appeals to collections of affluent special interests. But the Congress of our New Gilded Age is far from the best Congress money can buy; it is a coin-operated stalemate machine that threatens the good name of representative democracy itself.

A longer version of this essay appeared in the Washington Spectator.

The 99%

WALL STREET BLAMES VICTIMS TO AVOID RESPONSIBILITY FOR FINANCIAL MELTDOWN

BY NOMI PRINS

THE SECOND GREAT Bank Depression has spawned so many lies, it's hard to keep track of which is the biggest. Possibly the most irksome class of lies, usually spouted by Wall Street hacks and conservative pundits, is that we're all victims to a bunch of poor people who bought McMansions, or at least homes they had no business living in. But so you know, it wasn't the tiny loan's fault. It was everyone and everything that piled on top, using a plethora of shady financial techniques and overzealous sales pitches.

Here are some numbers for you. There were approximately $1.4 trillion worth of subprime loans outstanding in the United States by the end of 2007. By May 2009, there were foreclosure filings against approximately 5.1 million properties. If it was only the subprime market's fault, $1.4 trillion would have covered the entire problem, right? But there was much more to it than that: Wall Street was engaged in a very dangerous practice called leveraging. Leverage is when you borrow a lot of money in order to place a big bet. It makes the payoff that much bigger. You may not be able to cover the bet if you're wrong. It's a high-risk, high-reward way to make money—as long as you're not wrong.

The Second Great Bank Depression wouldn't have been as tragic without a 30-to-one leverage ratio for investment banks, and according to the *New York Times*, a ratio that ranged from 11 to one to 15 to one for the major commercial banks. Banks would have taken a hit on their mortgage and consumer credit portfolios, but the systemic credit crisis and the bailout bonanza would have been avoided. Leverage included, we're looking at a possible $140 trillion problem.

For $1.4 trillion in subprime loans to become $140 trillion in potential losses, you need two steps in between. The most significant is a healthy dose of leverage, but leverage would not have had a platform without the help of a wondrous financial feat called securitization. Financial firms run economic models that select and package loans into new securities according to criteria such as geographic diversity, the size of the loans and the length of the mortgages. A bunch of loans are then repackaged into an asset-backed security (ABS). This new security is backed, or collateralized, by a small number of original home loans related to the size of the security.

During the lead-up to the Second Great Bank Depression, the securities themselves were a much bigger problem than the loans. Between 2002 and 2007, banks in the United States created nearly 80 percent of the approximately $14 trillion worth of total global ABSs, collateralized debt obligations (CDOs), and other alphabetic concoctions or "structured" assets. Everyone was paid handsomely. In total, issuers raked in a combined $300 billion in fees. Fees can be made for all types of securitized assets, but the more convoluted they are, the riskier and more lucrative they become.

By the fall of 2008, those ABSs, CDOs and all their permutations would be known as "toxic assets." They were considered by many to be the major cause of Big Finance's failures and losses. Toxic assets became devoid of value, not because all the subprime loans stuffed inside them tanked, but because there was no longer demand from investors. This basic supply-and-demand concept is something our government apparently didn't understand when it offered to take the toxic assets off the banks' books.

THE CRUELEST LIE OF ALL

There are those who blame lending, and certainly subprime lending was terribly predatory. Conservatives, however, toward the end of 2008, began to blame the people getting the subprime loans and the Democrats for pushing through the Community Reinvestment Act (CRA) in 1977, which sought to end discriminatory home-lending practices.

CRA "led to tremendous pressure on Fannie Mae and Freddie Mac— which in turn pressured banks and other lenders—to extend mortgages to people who were borrowing over their heads. That's called subprime lending. It lies at the root of our current calamity," the conservative columnist Charles Krauthammer wrote on September 26, 2008, in his nationally syndicated column. Translation: the Democrats allowed Poor People to do this. And innocent Wall Street paid the price.

Krauthammer continued, "Were there some predatory lenders? Of course. But only a fool or a demagogue—i.e., a presidential candidate—would suggest that this is a major part of the problem."

Since late 2008, plenty of "fools and demagogues" have, in fact, proved Krauthammer wrong. But for a while, conservative stalwarts such as Fox News' Neil Cavuto and newspaper columnist George Will echoed the idea that it wasn't greed, but a 1977 regulatory law that brought down the economy.

Given that the value of subprime loans in the market is overwhelmed by the amount of the full federal bailout by a factor of 10 to one, that's not anywhere near reality.

The finance community's theory is one of selective Darwinism: Little people who take bad risks deserve the consequences. Companies that take bad risks are a welcome addition to the fallen competitor list. Banks that survive the chaos can reposition themselves at the top of the financial piles, and deserve all the federal bailout money, and assistance in growing even bigger, that they can get.

When all is forgotten and we've moved on to our next financial crisis, there will be certain fingers frozen in time pointing at the subprime loans as the cause of the calamity. Big Finance would prefer that. But the truth is that the subprime loan tragedy was merely the catalyst that exposed the mega-tiered securitizations of securitizations, the massive leverage chain derivatives attached to nothing concrete, and the ineffective regulatory restraints. All of which led us down the rabbit hole of the Second Great Bank Depression.

This story was excerpted from Nomi Prins' book, It Takes a Pillage: Behind the Bailouts, Bonuses, and Backroom Deals from Washington to Wall Street *(Wiley, 2009).*

HOW WALL STREET THIEVES, LED BY GOLDMAN SACHS, TOOK DOWN THE GLOBAL ECONOMY

BY LES LEOPOLD

FOR ALL THE damning evidence you'll ever need about Wall Street corruption, take a look at the recent report from the Senate Permanent Subcommittee on Investigations, "Wall Street and the Financial Crisis: An Anatomy of a Financial Collapse." The 650-page indictment reveals the myriad of ways Wall Street lies, cheats, steals and defrauds on a routine basis. Unfortunately, it's too technical to be widely read. So here are the CliffsNotes.

This study, broken into four case studies, forms a biblical tale of how toxic mortgages were born, nurtured and spread like the plague throughout the land, making money for the financial philistines every step of the way.

The first case study focuses on Washington Mutual (WaMu), the nation's largest savings bank, and its overt strategic decision to go big into selling high-risk, high-profit mortgages. Here you will find a detailed description of every type of dangerous mortgage foisted onto the public. Your blood pressure also will climb when you read how the bank used focus groups to help its mortgage brokers find better ways to sucker customers into risky mortgages even though the applicants had qualified for and wanted safer, fixed-rate mortgages.

The report also details outright fraud committed by brokers—forging documents, making phony loans, stealing money—who then were rewarded again and again by the bank for their high sales records, even after they were caught! Nobody cared because the loans quickly were sold to Wall Street—the riskier the loan, the higher the interest rates and the fatter the commissions.

The second case study recounts the pathetic tale of the Office of Thrift Supervision, the regulatory agency that was supposed to halt WaMu's shoddy and corrupt practices. The report shows that OTS knew of these deceptive practices in great detail for five full years and still failed to stop the pillaging. Why? Because OTS's top regulators didn't believe in regulation. Banks should regulate themselves. OTS only wanted to help. And one way it helped was by deliberately impeding other regulators like the FDIC from enforcing stronger regulations on WaMu.

The third case study focuses on the two largest rating agencies (Moody's and Standard and Poor's). Here we learn how the rating agencies prostituted themselves, turning trick after trick for the big Wall Street banks, doling out favors (AAA ratings) to thousands of "innovative" securities based on the junk mortgages that WaMu and others originated and packaged. Then, when it became obvious to everyone that the crap was still crap, they drastically downgraded thousands of toxic assets overnight. The result was a rapid and deep collapse of all financial markets.

The last case study is the most pornographic as it strips bare two investment banks, Deutsche Bank and Goldman Sachs. The report accuses them of packaging and selling toxic securities, while at the same time, betting that those securities would fail. Furthermore, the report argues forcefully, that "Investment banks were the driving force behind the structured finance products that provided a steady stream of funding for lenders originating high risk, poor quality loans and that magnified risk throughout the U.S. financial system."

The subcommittee found that Goldman Sachs, the envy of all Wall Street, was corrupt to its core. Not only is it accused of creating toxic assets and unloading them on its own customers, but the report also accuses GS of betting that the very assets they were selling would fail. They profited by selling the junk and then profited even more when the junk they were selling lost value.

'PUTTING OUR CUSTOMERS FIRST'

The path of looting and destruction starts in 2006-2007 when the leadership of Goldman Sachs became convinced that the housing market was in decline and that they had to get rid of all their mortgage-related securities in a hurry. How do you get rid of crap? You package it together, slice and dice it and get your favorite rating agency strumpets to kiss it with AAA-ratings. Then you send your sales force out on a mad scramble around the world to find customers.

Once the junk was packaged and sold, GS placed billions of dollars of bets that the mortgages contained or referenced in the securities would crash and burn. The more they crashed, the more the bets paid off for Goldman Sachs. However, GS failed to reveal this crucial information to its customers. Rather it said that GS's interests were aligned with that of its customers, implying that GS was buying into the deal and holding the same garbage as the customers were buying. The report details many cases where GS bet big against what they were selling without providing this material information to its buyers.

The most egregious example of this swindle was the Abacus deal that GS cooked up with Paulson and Company, the hedge fund that bet billions that toxic mortgage-related assets would fail. Paulson approached GS with a plan to rig a bet that was sure to fail for the buyers and pay off big for Paulson. Without telling the buyers, Paulson was allowed to set the criteria for the selection of the toxic assets that were placed in the securities, and of course he picked the worst ones he could find.

To hide Paulson's role, GS needed an independent "portfolio selection agent" to pretend to be the final arbiter of what mortgage pools became part of the security. They soon found one and within a year, the buyers of the security lost a billion dollars and Paulson made a billion on his bet. Goldman Sachs got the fees for arranging the deal. However, they later had to pay a fine of $550 million to the SEC for failing to disclose Paulson's role. Meanwhile, Paulson became the most prosperous hedge fund manager in world.

DEFICIT PREDATORS

BY JAMES K. GALBRAITH

THE SUMMER OF the debt ceiling was one that only Salvador Dali could paint, a reality so twisted that one almost yearned for the simple verities of the War on Terror. In both cases, one had to be a "hawk" to be taken seriously—a formidable bird that preys on the unsuspecting.

The debt ceiling was first enacted in 1917 on the eve of the Great War. To fund that effort, Wilson needed to issue Liberty Bonds. This was controversial, and the debt ceiling was cover, passed to reassure the rubes that Congress would be "responsible" even while the country went to war. It was an exercise in bad faith and has remained so.

Today this bad-faith law is pressed to its absurd extreme, to force massive cuts in public programs as the price of not reneging on the public debts of the United States. What happened over the summer in Congress was an effort to subvert the authority of the government to meet and therefore to incur obligations of every possible stripe. It was an attack on the concept of government itself. In Washington, this assault on government had elite and media support because it could conceivably force the parties to solve the government's "fiscal crisis."

What fiscal crisis? The United States has many problems: high unemployment, a foreclosure catastrophe, a slowing economy and the ongoing challenges of infrastructure, energy and climate change. But the fiscal crisis was a figment, made up of wise men's warnings repeated endlessly and linked to the faulty projections of technicians who believed cutting government would achieve economic recovery.

Many believe fervently in the resilience of the private sector and think that government is just a burden. Some are pure predators: resource magnates, media magnates, banking magnates. Others have blinded themselves to the role government actually plays in sustaining the advanced networks, human protections and social systems that make up our lives, and imagine that one can go back to the world of subsistence farming, church charity and credit from the corner store.

In broad terms, today's government does four major things:

- Provides for the national defense
- Purchases goods and services from the private economy for a wide

range of public purposes, most of them individually quite small-scale in relation to GDP

• Regulates a wide range of private-sector activity, for safety, health, environmental and other purposes, including financial stability—or so one should hope

• Administers Social Security, Medicare and Medicaid, as well as other pension and health benefit programs

On what grounds are any of these functions too large? We could surely end unnecessary wars and dispense with bloated military spending. But these are security judgments, not broad economic ones. In other words, I would not cut a single dime of Pentagon spending that was actually necessary to defend the United States, in order to supposedly to lower the interest rate on federal debt.

By the same reasoning, why should we cut transportation, or public health, or environmental protection, or scientific research, or bank inspectors or funds that support the public schools? One can argue these matters program by program—and one should. But there is no economic case for placing an overall limit, and it is obvious that the hundreds of thousands of public sector workers who have lost their jobs since 2009 were doing good and useful things that are now missed. If sacking teachers and firefighters was good for the economy, we would be having a stronger recovery than we are.

Finally, there's Social Security, Medicare and Medicaid. Unlike the military or the transportation program, Social Security is not a government-purchasing program. It takes nothing directly from the private sector. Along with Medicare and Medicaid, Social Security is a powerful protector of the entire working population—young and old. It redistributes purchasing power, in loose relation to past earnings, in a way that meets the basic needs of a large number of Americans who would otherwise be destitute or medically bankrupt.

What economic purpose would cutting such programs serve? To do so would again redistribute incomes. Many of the future elderly would be much worse off. Many would die younger. Survivors and the disabled would suffer as well. In return, what would the federal government and the country gain? A release of real resources to the private sector? Social Security does not take real resources from the private sector! Lower interest rates? The idea is absurd, and not just because interest rates are low today. Interest rates are set in a way that has no relationship at all to the scale of Social Security, Medicare or Medicaid.

The right steps would be to lower—not raise—the Social Security early retirement age, permitting for a few years older workers to exit the labor force on better terms than are available to them today. This together with a lower age of access to Medicare would work quickly to rebalance the labor force, reducing unemployment and the futile job search among older workers while increasing job openings for the young. Unlike all the pressures to enact long-term cuts in these programs, it would help solve one of today's important problems right away.

Instead, we have the false claim of a fiscal crisis, an arbitrary and cruel effort to enact massive cuts in public services on one hand and in vital social insurance programs on the other, and a refusal to stand on the strong ground of the Constitution against those whose open and declared purpose is tear that document and the public credit to shreds.

During the summer of sound and fury, the pundits and politicians in Washington refused to say what was really true. That cuts to Social Security, Medicare, Medicaid and all the legitimate and necessary functions of government would be for millions of Americans the catastrophe itself.

A version of this essay appeared on New Deal 2.0.

WHY THE WEALTHIEST AMERICANS ARE THE REAL JOB-KILLERS

BY JOSHUA HOLLAND

THAT THE WEALTHY are "job creators," and therefore have interests that must be defended by the public at large, is a talking-point that, however facile, is so popular it slips effortlessly from the lips of conservatives every day.

It can be deployed for any purpose—not only in calling for more tax breaks for the rich, but also when opposing public interest regulation, consumer litigation and worker protections. Rep. Michele Bachmann, (R-MN), even used it to deflect attention from the "gay rehabilitation" services her clinic allegedly offers. When asked about it by ABC News, Bachmann merely acknowledged, "we do have a business that deals with job creation."

It's also complete nonsense; the opposite of the truth. Sure, the wealthy create a few jobs—people who offer exclusive services or sell them high-end goods. But the overwhelming majority of jobs in this country are "created" by ordinary Americans when they spend their paychecks.

Consumer demand accounts for around 70 percent of our economic output. And with so much wealth having been redistributed upward through a 40-year class-war from above, American consumers are too tapped out to spend as they once did. This remains the core issue in this sluggish, largely jobless recovery. The wealthy, in their voracious appetite for a bigger piece of the national pie, are the real job-killers in this economic climate.

Don't take my word for it. The *Wall Street Journal* recently reported that "the main reason U.S. companies are reluctant to step up hiring is scant demand, rather than uncertainty over government policies, according to a majority of economists" the paper surveyed. That jibes with what business owners themselves are saying. The National Federation of Independent Businesses released a survey of small businessmen and women that found widespread "pessimism about future business conditions and expected real sales gains."

New York Times reporter David Leonhardt wrote that, "We are living through a tremendous bust. It isn't simply a housing bust. It's a fizzling of the great consumer bubble that was decades in the making."

> *The auto industry is on pace to sell 28 percent fewer new vehicles this year than it did 10 years ago—and 10 years ago was 2001, when the country was in recession. Sales of ovens and stoves are on pace to be at their lowest level since 1992.*

Leonhardt cited worse-than-expected retail sales and a study conducted by the New York Federal Reserve Bank that found "discretionary service spending"—which excludes housing, food and health care—to have dropped 7 percent, more than twice the decline we saw during previous recessions.

Average American households' economic malaise started long before the current downturn, as those at the top started grabbing an ever-increasing share of the pie in the 1970s.

Paul Buchheit, a professor with City Colleges of Chicago, crunched some numbers using IRS data and found that "if middle- and upper-middle-class families had maintained the same share of American productivity that they held in 1980, they would be making an average of $12,500 more per year." Studies have shown that when wealthy people grab more post-tax income they're more likely to bank it than to spend it, so much of that $12,500 also represents lost demand, and hence less jobs. Wealthy Americans' avarice is a job-killer.

American households compensated for their flat incomes first by sending millions of women into the workforce—the single-earner household is largely a relic of the past—and then by running up lots of debt. In the 1970s, Americans socked away between 8-12 percent in case hard times hit, but the national savings rate declined precipitously as the top earners started grabbing an outsized share of the nation's income. By the 2000s, it was less than 2 percent.

As a result, we were among the least prepared citizens in the developed world to handle the crash—we didn't have a rainy-day fund put away.

The fact that we're broke means that businesses are facing less demand for their goods and services than they otherwise would, and have less need to hire a bunch of employees. And that dynamic explains why it's the wealthiest Americans who are the real "job killers."

HOW WALL STREET GREED FUELS THE FORECLOSURE CRISIS

BY YVES SMITH

IN THE WAKE of the global financial crisis, terms like robosigning, foreclosure mills and securitization became part of the American lexicon. While the terms are abstract, the tragedy isn't. Families at the kitchen table ignore the phone, fearing a representative of their unpaid lender on the other end. Horror stories abound of foreclosures by banks relying on fraudulent procedures. Millions have lost their homes. Communities have been shattered.

Instead of taking the crisis seriously, lawmakers and regulators too often make excuses for banks and blame the borrowers. Or they talk dismissively of isolated incidents instead of widespread abuse. In reality, the violations are pervasive. And much of it arose through a form of financial alchemy called securitization.

Securitization—the bundling of mortgages—allowed mortgage industry participants to collect handsome fees throughout a long mortgage supply chain. The mortgage broker selling the loans collected fees, as did the banks that funded "warehouses" where the mortgages were held prior to being bundled for sale to investors. The mortgages went through yet more parties to protect investors from the possibility that the originators might go bankrupt (as many later did), with a fee nick at each transfer. Ratings agencies and the lawyers advising on these deals took fees. And the investment banks selling them to investors took their cut too.

Amid the push to extract even more profit, lending standards plummeted. Predatory lenders steered people into mortgages with features they weren't told about, like costly resets after two years, or promised them conservative 30-year fixed-rate mortgages but presented the papers for toxic ARMS at closing. And they put more of these risky mortgages into securitizations than their agreements with lenders permitted. The whole securitization industry ran roughshod over the law and abandoned established procedures.

This mess didn't happen overnight. Securitization had been around since 1970, and private label securitization started to become a meaningful activity in the later 1980s. For well over a decade, the industry complied with the complex agreements governing these deals and state and federal law. Mortgage servicing was once a decent, even attractive business. But three things went terribly wrong.

First, starting in the 2002-2003 refinancing boom, the originators and packagers of mortgages started cutting corners on the carefully crafted procedures for notes (borrower IOUs) to be conveyed to securitization trusts. There is supposed to be an unbroken chain of transfers, deliveries and acceptances of the mortgage note from the originator to the sponsor to the depositor and finally to the trust. To comply with special tax rules created just for these securitizations, the transfers had to be completed by a date certain. And the agreements were set up to be rigid to force the participants to comply. In this world of structured credit, strict adherence to the procedures mattered. Failure to dot the i's and cross the t's would impair the investors' rights. The implication was that if things weren't done correctly, it would be impossible to remedy matters legally after the fact.

But greed overtook caution, and abuses grew rampant. In an overwhelming number of cases, the notes weren't transferred properly to the trusts. The critical intermediary transfers might be skipped, or the notes were left with the originator or another party early in the transfer chain (tantamount to paying for a car but failing to transfer title). These changes didn't simply violate the contracts that govern the securitization; they also made it impossible to foreclose legally, making the investors vulnerable if borrowers challenged a foreclosure. So many servicers and foreclosure mills have resorted to deception—like claiming the notes were lost and using so-called lost note affidavits, attesting that they really had complied—or engaged in forgeries and document fabrications to create the needed paper trail to give the servicer the right to foreclose.

Second, the banks replaced public mortgage registries with a giant private registry known as Mortgage Electronic Registration Systems (MERS). Historically, public mortgage records were filed at county records offices, a slow and cumbersome process for mortgage industry members, since members would have to record a series of transfers at the local courthouse. A standardized, centralized database was a good idea in theory, but bankers focused on the profits to be made in speeding up the process. The MERS system started in the late '90s, but it did not begin to be widely used until the early 2000s.

MERS has been implemented in a slipshod, reckless way, without even a state-by-state legal review as to whether this new approach would be permissible across the U.S. Moreover, the database is lacking in basic procedures to assure the integrity of its information, such as tough password controls and audit trails. So it is not only opaque, its more than occasional errors and doubtful status of some of its procedures have raised serious doubts about the integrity of land records in the U.S.

The third thing that went wrong was the global financial crash, which left a record number of foreclosures in its wake, far higher than ever contemplated when these securitization deals were designed.

In the ongoing foreclosure crisis—which is far from over—the courts have largely acted as collection agencies for the banks. The banks remain largely unaccountable for abuse and fraud, buying off regulators and politicians alike. Thankfully, in the wake of the robosigning scandal, many judges have been appalled by the abuse of well-established legal procedures and are pushing back against bank abuses.

There are no easy answers here. Federal regulators seem to think a head-in-the sand approach will succeed, when servicers are often unable to foreclose due to their inability to prove in court that they have the right to do so. Many members of the public are upset with borrowers who stay in homes, waiting for the eviction notice, when the lengthy period between default and foreclosure is more often than not the bank's doing. Securitization industry managers and executives are in denial, often surprisingly ignorant of how this mess was created by the industry and not subject to easy remedy. It may be that things have to become much worse before this country develops the political will to bring a miscreant securitization industry to heel.

This essay was compiled from various pieces written by Smith for Naked Capitalism.

HOW BANKING BECAME AN OLIGOPOLY INSTEAD OF A COMPETITIVE BUSINESS

BY LYNN PARRAMORE

SO WHY DOESN'T competition punish banks that gouge customers? Because banking is not a competitive industry.

Banking has become an oligopoly. That's a lot like a monopoly, where one firm controls an industry. Only, in an oligopoly, you have two or more firms calling the shots. And those big dogs love to do things contrary to the notion of a free market, like colluding to raise prices. Here are the signs that competition has left the building in the banking industry.

CONCENTRATION OF POWER

The last time big banks blew up the economy, causing the Great Depression, they got broken up. Thereafter, tight regulation protected small banks. But in the mid-'80s, bigger banks started to gobble up little ones in a massive trend of consolidation. The biggest banks controlled a larger and larger share of deposits.

Concentration of deposits is the best measure of competition in the banking industry. The number of depository organizations in the U.S. fell from 15,416 in 1984 to 8,191 in 2001, a drop of 46.9 percent! Worse, the share of deposits held by the biggest five banks swelled to 23 percent in 2001 from just 9 percent in 1984. Sound like a competition-driving trend to you?

If you think 23 percent is a big piece of the pie, consider this: In June 2008, before the Lehman collapse, the share of deposits held by the five biggest banks had soared to 37 percent. That figure has only risen since then. By 2009, the top five banks (Bank of America, Chase, Citi, Wells Fargo and PNC) boasted nearly 40 percent of all deposits. They got all these deposits not because they offered amazing service, but because they ate up smaller banks. This increasing concentration of deposits suggests that banks have been getting steadily less competitive over the last 30 years. Which allows nasty things to happen.

Exhibit A: When B of A announced its new debit card fee, it performed a maneuver common in oligopolies known as "price leadership." In this form of tacit collusion, the lead dog in the industry announces a price increase, signaling to the other big dogs that it's cool for them to do the same. The other dogs might not place fees on debit cards, because that would look too obvious.

But they find ways to keep pace with the leader, like hiking fees on ATMs or charging for checking accounts.

Collusion is the enemy of competition.

COST V. RETURNS

Another telltale feature of oligopolies is a yawning gap between the cost of performing a service or making a product and how much a firm charges for it.

Chase CEO Jamie Dimon warned us that if regulators tried to prevent the banks from charging certain kinds of fees, they would find the money elsewhere, just like a restaurant might charge more for the burger if it can't charge for the soda.

What Mr. Dimon doesn't want you to realize is that the restaurant industry and the banking industry are quite different. Joe sets a price for his burger based on the cost of food, overhead, etc. In the restaurant industry, food costs are about 35 percent of the price of a menu item. If Joe's burger costs $10, then you could expect that the meat, bun and condiments cost $3.50. The rest goes to cover the other costs and a slender margin for profit. According to the National Restaurant Association, a restaurant makes about 4 cents on every dollar you spend. The industry is highly competitive, and restaurants fail all the time, most within their first year of operation. Survivors need a sound business plan, good management and products that consumers want to buy. The gap between costs and what restaurants charge must be small, or else you'll head to Bill's Burger Heaven.

The banking industry operates in a different universe. Charges for products and services and their costs often have very little relation to each other.

Case in point: Commercial litigator Lloyd Constantine noted recently in the *New York Times* that banks were challenged by an antitrust lawsuit in 1996 for charging dubious fees to stores for debit card transactions. The banks were forced to lower the fee, but the Fed knew it was still much too high. Later on, when ATM cards were first used at stores as debit cards, there was no fee at first because getting rid of checks was hugely profitable for banks. But, as Constantine put it, "Bank of America, Chase and their Visa/MasterCard partners wanted to have their burgers and eat them, too." So they started charging high fees. When the Dodd-Frank Act ordered the Fed to find out whether the banks could actually justify these high fees on the basis of costs, the Fed concluded that banks were grossly overcharging. The banks lowered fees from 44 cents to 21 to 24 cents per transaction. But the Fed said they should actually be only 7 to 12 cents.

Ridiculous cost v. returns gaps are another sign that banking isn't competitive.

RISK OF FAILURE

In a free market, businesses fail; half go under in the first two years. They fail for all kinds of reasons. Maybe they were underfunded. Or they weren't cost competitive. Or their management sucked. Whatever the reason, they fail. One day the business is there, and the next it's gonzo.

Again, the banking industry sails right past this free-market logic.

"Too big to fail" sums up what happens nowadays to the biggest banks even when they commit fraud against consumers, poison them with toxic products, neglect their duties to shareholders and blow up the economy. They are rescued with public money. Not so at Joe's Burger Joint. If Joe picked customers' pockets and sold burgers that made them throw up, then Joe would probably see a padlock on his door.

But bad management at banks is highly profitable. Just ask recently booted B of A execs Sallie Krawcheck and Joseph Price. The bank gave Krawcheck a severance package that includes a year's salary of $850,000 plus a payment of $5,150,000. Price got $850,000 and a payment of $4,150,000.

B of A CEO Brian Moynihan took over from Ken Lewis, an exceptionally crappy manager who exited the door with $125 million. Moynihan defended his bank's debit card decision and made noise about his loyalty to shareholders and customers and his bank's "right to make a profit." But as former bank regulator Bill Black has pointed out, it was "Moynihan's incompetence and moral blindness that allowed B of A to commit tens of thousands of felonies in the course of foreclosing through perjury on those who were often the victims of Countrywide's underlying fraudulent mortgages."

Moynihan collects a $2 million annual salary. As a base.

WHAT TO DO?

Just going from one big bank to another won't help. Your only recourse is to move your money to a credit union or a healthy small bank. By doing this, you can invest in Main Street and you might even end up with fewer fees. Choices will remain limited as long as Too Big to Fail continues. But it feels good to take your money out of the banks that caused the financial crisis and are still harming the economy.

OCCUPY THE WAR MACHINE
BY ROBERT GREENWALD AND DERRICK CROWE

THE OCCUPY MOVEMENT has been a massive success so far, putting the spotlight on the corporate takeover of our economy and politics. The protesters' opposition to the malign influence of big banks has received quite a lot of press, but one motivator for the people in Zuccotti Park and at other occupations across the country has received relatively little attention: opposition to war profiteers' stranglehold on Washington, DC.

While millions of Americans lack jobs, the heads of the biggest war industry corporations are living large, and using our tax dollars to keep job-killing war spending going. Seven of the Pentagon's top 10 contractors are headed by CEOs in the richest 0.01 percent (individuals with an annual income above $9.14 million) and all of the 10 are in the richest 0.1 percent. Most of these men's fortunes come from taxpayer dollars, and they use our money to buy our elected officials out from under us. Here are just a couple of examples:

Lockheed Martin is the Pentagon's number-one contractor. According to Forbes.com, Lockheed CEO Robert Stevens made $21.9 million last year, placing him in the richest 0.01 percent of Americans. His company's annual report shows they got 83.7 percent of their revenue ($38.4 billion out of $45.8 billion in total revenue) from the federal government in 2010. That massive payout was undoubtably tied to $26 million they spent on lobbying in 2009-2010. Stevens uses his company's massive, taxpayer-funded revenue stream to persuade Congress to keep his wallet nice and fat at our expense.

Northrop Grumman's CEO, Wes Bush, does even better on the taxpayer dole. As the Pentagon's number-three contractor, his company made 92.2 percent of their total revenues from federal contracts ($32.1 billion out of $34.8 billion). Out of that pile of cash, Bush took home $22.8 million in 2010, again putting the military contractor CEO in the richest 0.01 percent. The $30.9 million his company spent in 2009-2010 lobbying the government definitely paid off for him as well.

Collectively, the military industry's lobbying influence is truly massive. According to Reuters (August 11, 2011):

> *According to a database maintained by the Center for Responsive Politics, a total of 843 lobbyists represented 279 defense industry clients in 2011 so far. Lockheed Martin, Boeing, General Dynamics, Northrop*

Grumman and Raytheon [the top five military contractor companies] are some of the top spenders on Capitol Hill.

But for the 99 percent of Americans being throttled by the employment crisis, all that taxpayer-funded lobbying and military spending did not pay off. Every time the military contractors think they face slightly reduced allowances, they squeal about "jobs, jobs, jobs," but the economics are crystal clear: compared to any other way of spending the money, military spending costs jobs. While more than 9 percent of Americans cannot find work, and five people are seeking jobs for every one opening, we need spending that creates jobs, now.

Instead, the steady flow of our cash into the hands of war profiteer CEOs empowers them to purchase a broken consensus in Washington, DC, keeping us in wars the American people don't want. Afghanistan, anyone? The public hates that war, with opposition in the most recent CNN poll sitting at 63 percent. Most Americans want troops brought home rapidly. With a massively powerful lobby representing a corporate sector that says, "Afghanistan is our business plan," it's not hard to tell why we're stuck in a war that's not making us safer and that's not worth the costs.

The decade-long outrage about wars waged against popular will is a major part of the energy driving the Occupy movement. Tired of seeing loved ones killed for no good reason, and their taxes spent on keeping war tycoons drinking the good champagne, the occupiers have specifically named wars for profit among their grievances and have called for a swift end to the wars in Iraq and Afghanistan.

From the Declaration of the Occupation of New York City:

> *They continue to create weapons of mass destruction.*
> *... They have squandered our public treasure, over half of federal discretionary spending, into the military and security state, while waging immoral and illegal wars opposed by the people of the United States and the world.*
> *They have wasted trillions of dollars on these wars, much of it spent on contracts outsourced to private mercenary corporations directly affiliated with members of government.*

We're tired of being played for suckers by super-rich men paying off politicians to keep the war dollars rolling. The Occupy movement is onto their game. We're sick and tired of wars that don't make us safer and that kill our loved ones and our jobs. We want our country back from the war profiteers. The first piece of it we are taking back is the streets, but we won't stop there.

OCCUPY COLLEGE
BY TAMARA DRAUT

I GREW UP IN a blue-collar, middle-class family in Middletown, Ohio. My dad worked at the local steel factory as a machinist, and my mom was an office manager at the local orthodontist's office. I had a good life growing up—we took vacations every year to Myrtle Beach, four kids and six suitcases crammed into a Chevy. We always had healthcare and didn't really lack for anything. My parents were able to pay for me to go to a state college out of their own pocket. I focused on my studies, graduated in four years and left college with zero debt.

Today, my story isn't possible for a new generation. That steel factory, which once employed about half of the town's workers, now has jobs for less than one-fifth. College tuition at my alma mater has nearly tripled since I graduated in 1993. My mom lost her job and now makes half of what she made before, and she was without healthcare for two years before becoming eligible for Medicare.

All the factors that allowed my parents to give me a better life are gone. There are no good jobs anymore for folks without college degrees. Going to college requires taking on five-figure debt. So it's no surprise to me that it is a new generation—the first to have the American dream pulled out from under them—that is finally spurring us all to question our nation's path and the state of our democracy. Today's millennials are directly experiencing the culmination of 30 years of political and economic inequality.

Today the average college grad leaves school with just over $24,000 in debt, an amount that eats up $276 every month if you stretch the payments out over 10 years and it's a government loan with a 6.8 percent interest rate. Of course, one out of five students also carries more costly private loans, where interest rates are in the double digits and fees add to the balance. This debt-for-diploma system is what counts as opportunity in America today. And it is animating much of the frustration and passion of the Occupy Wall Street movement.

A handmade sign at Zuccotti Park summed it up perfectly: "I went broke trying to become middle class." Far too many of today's twentysomethings are earning less than their parents did at the same age—a downward slide that was true even before the Great Recession left a jobless generation in its wake. Today, young men earn 90 cents for every dollar their fathers earned in 1980.

Young women make more, about $1.16 for every dollar their mothers brought home in 1980—gains driven by better job prospects, more college degrees and longer working hours.

But those overall trends mask a big divergence between the college haves and the college have-nots. Over the course of a generation, only young people with bachelor's degrees have seen substantial increases in their earnings—cold comfort to the legions of twentysomethings struggling to pay back their student loans while working in jobs that don't require a degree, or with no job at all.

This problem—downward economic mobility for a new generation—didn't just happen. It was the inevitable outcome of 30 years of failed policies fueled by the needs and interests of major multinational corporations and an ever-expanding trove of rich and politically connected individuals. Our economic destiny was not predetermined by globalization or technological change; it was determined by how our political system—including both parties—responded to those major forces, or in some cases failed to respond. And that observation is what the Occupy Wall Street protesters (and the spinoff Occupy College movement) have so powerfully articulated.

There are plenty of good ideas for getting our nation back on track. The best of them would squarely address the economic plight facing young people today. Many people are calling for us to use this window of opportunity to invest in our crumbling infrastructure, but what about our stagnating human infrastructure? How can the government justify charging students nearly 7 percent while it charges the banks nothing? Short of returning to a grant-based college aid system that restores the purchasing power of Pell grants, we should immediately reduce the federal student loan interest rate to a level lower than what the Fed offers banks through the discount window (currently less than 1 percent). It would provide immediate relief and send a strong signal that We the People are finally treating our children better than we treat banks.

Next, we need to address the double-digit unemployment rate for youth by directly putting young people to work. Our nation needs to deliver something big and bold so that this generation—and those that follow it—know that the country has not left them behind.

Reprinted with permission from the November 14, 2011 issue of The Nation.

EXPANDING THE OCCUPATION FROM WALL STREET TO THE NATURAL ENVIRONMENT

BY LISA KAAS BOYLE

THE OCCUPY WALL Street Movement reflects a growing realization that our democracy has been usurped by corporate power that drowns out the voices, votes and concerns of average Americans. While the corporate hijacking of our democracy is most obvious in the realm of finance, there is an analogous, but lesser known corporate hijacking of environmental policy.

As a nonprofit environmental attorney, I have been very concerned about the growing power of corporations to railroad existing environmental laws and prevent new environmental safeguards. The Supreme Court's decision in *Citizens United* further tipped the balance toward corporate interests in exploiting our natural resources and away from protecting those resources for this and future generations.

I'm calling for the Occupy Wall Street movement to expand from the streets and into our precious natural environment in response to this assault on democratic governance. Yes, we should all be angry that our economy was destroyed by the games played on Wall Street, but we must also realize that the very air we breathe, the water we drink and the land we farm is at risk when we cede power to corporations over individuals. There is just too much money in too few hands. Without fundamental campaign finance reform giving power back to the people, not just to the .05 percent who buy our leadership, there is no hope for just and democratic decision-making in any policy arena from banking to environmental protection.

The collapse of our economy has huge implications for our natural environment. When our government fails to collect adequate tax revenues and penalties from the wealthiest corporations and individuals, we are left with few financial resources to fund public services. That means less money to keep parks open; less money to monitor coal mining operations; less money to test water; less money to detect and enforce environmental crimes; less money to clean up toxic waste; and less money to preserve the wilderness.

And when government doesn't have any money in the public coffers to serve the public in a fair and democratic fashion, who does it turn to, to fund programs? You guessed it, the same corporations that don't pay enough taxes or penalties for their bad actions; the same corporations that fund the elections of the decision-makers. The corporate sponsorship of public services with the corporations' vast under-taxed resources compounds the problem of undue corporate influence on government policies and actions. Let me give you one small example.

The recent National Oceanic and Atmospheric Administration/United Nations Environment Program International Marine Debris Conference was funded through the riches of Coca-Cola and the American Chemistry Council (ACC), a lobbying group for the petrochemical/plastics industry. Sixty to 80 percent of the trash or debris in our oceans is plastic. Plastic pollution accounts for nearly 100 percent of the trash problem at sea since it is non-biodegradable, absorbs toxins from the water, breaks down into smaller bits, and enters our food chain when consumed by sea life.

Although almost all the talks given at the conference were about plastic pollution in our oceans, the term plastic pollution does not appear even once in the resulting "Honolulu Strategy Document" from the conference. This is not surprising, since the ACC sat on the peer-review panel to write the document.

"Marine debris" is described not as mainly plastic, but euphemistically as "anthropogenic, manufactured or processed solid material." The solutions to the problem of "marine debris" are as could be expected, not on the supply side of non-biodegradable single-use plastics being manufactured and marketed, as this interferes with the business interests of the sponsors of the NOAA/UNEP environmental conference, Coca-Cola and the ACC, but on the cleanup side at the expense of volunteers and local governments after the pollution has entered the environment.

There are many more examples of corporate-influenced environmental policy. We have put ourselves at the mercy of corporations whose interests are not aligned with the preservation of our environment, nor with good job creation here at home. As Van Jones says, a few jobs on an oil rig are not enough. We need all kinds of jobs: teaching jobs, park rangers, solar installers, environmental crime detectives, riverkeepers, whale-watching boat captains, new technology jobs, healthcare providers, organic farmers. It is only the least sustainable industries like the fossil-fuel industry that stand to lose in a transfer of power to the majority of people. So if you care about democratic decision-making and the future of this planet, lend your voice and your clever signs to expand the Occupy movement from Wall Street and into our precious natural environment.

This story first appeared on the Huffington Post.

DISASTROUS DECISIONS BY THE HIGH COURT

BY JOSHUA HOLLAND

PERHAPS THERE WERE truly free markets before the industrial revolution, where townspeople and farmers gathered in a square to exchange livestock, produce and handmade tools. In our modern world, such a market does not exist. Governments set up the rules of the game, and those rules have an enormous impact on our economic outcomes.

In 2007, the year of the crash, the top 1 percent of American households took in almost two-and-a-half times the share of our nation's pre-tax income that they had grabbed in the 40 years following World War II. This was no accident—the rules of the market underwent profound changes that led to the upward redistribution of trillions in income over the past 30 years. The rules are set by Congress—under a mountain of lobbying dollars—but they are adjudicated by the courts.

The Supreme Court, with a right-wing majority under Chief Justice John Roberts, has become a body that leans too far toward the "1 percent" to be considered a neutral arbiter. So whether they know all the ins and outs of the court's profound rightward shift or not, those protesting across the country as part of the Occupy movement are motivated by the court's corruption as well.

While conservatives constantly rail against judges "legislating from the bench," it is far more common for right-leaning jurists to engage in "judicial activism" than those of a liberal bent. That's what a 2005 study by Yale University legal scholar Paul Gewirtz and Chad Golder found. According to the scholars, those justices most frequently labeled "conservative" were among the most likely to strike down statutes passed by Congress, while those most frequently labeled "liberal" were the least likely to do so.

A 2007 study by University of Chicago law professor Thomas J. Miles and Cass R. Sunstein looked at the tendency of judges to strike down decisions by federal regulatory agencies, and found a similar trend: the Supreme Court's "conservative" justices were again the most likely to engage in this form of "activism," while the "liberal" justices were most likely to exercise judicial restraint.

The most notorious case of activism by the Roberts court was its ruling in *Citizens United v. Federal Election Commission,* which overturned key provisions of the McCain-Feingold campaign finance law, rules that kept corporations—and their lobbyists and front groups (as well as labor unions)—from spending unlimited amounts of cash on campaign advertising within 60 days of a general election for federal office (or 30 days before a primary).

At a 2010 conference, former Rep. Alan Grayson, D-Florida, put the potential impact of *Citizens United* in stark terms. "We're now in a situation," he told the crowd, "where a lobbyist can walk into my office ... and say, 'I've got five million dollars to spend, and I can spend it for you or against you. Which do you prefer?'"

To arrive at their ruling, the court's conservative majority stretched the Orwellian legal concept known as corporate personhood to the limit, and gave faceless multinationals expansive rights to influence our elections under the auspices of the First Amendment.

"They wanted to hear the possibility that that's the way the constitution would read to them," said Grayson. "So they picked an issue out of the air that nobody had conceived of [as a First Amendment case] because 100 years of settled law meant that corporations cannot buy elections in America, and they not only allowed corporations to buy those elections, but they made it a constitutional right."

Early on, the plaintiffs themselves had decided not to base their case on the First Amendment. It was the conservative justices themselves who ordered the case re-argued fully a month after a ruling had been expected, asking the lawyers to present the free speech argument that they'd earlier abandoned.

In his dissent, Justice Stevens noted that it was a highly unusual move, and that the court had further ruled on a constitutional issue that it didn't need to consider in order to decide the case before it—the diametric opposite of the principle of "judicial restraint." He charged that the conservative majority had "changed the case to give themselves an opportunity to change the law."

While *Citizens United* is arguably the Roberts court's most widely criticized ruling, it was not the only time it has bent over backwards to protect the interests of corporate America and the 1 percent. Legal reporter Dahlia Lithwick, writing in *Slate*, condemned the court's "systematic dismantling of existing legal protections for women, workers, the environment, minorities and the disenfranchised." Those who care about spiraling inequality, she wrote, "need look no further than last term at the high court to see what happens when—just for instance—one's right to sue AT&T, one's ability to bring a class action against Wal-Mart, and one's ability to hold an investment management fund responsible for its lies, are all eroded by a sweep of the court's pen."

The takeaway is that those camping out in town squares across the country need to direct their energy not only at Wall Street, but also at its enablers—in Congress, and ultimately, at the high court.

VII.

MEDIA

AND

CULTURAL

RESPONSES

INTRODUCTION

A LARGE PART of Occupy Wall Street's success is rooted in its creativity as a movement. Its openness and vision comes from a collective willingness to think outside the box. As such, it has attracted myriad visionary thinkers, performers and other creative types, whether they be the super-famous, or the neighbor who lives down your block.

With so many artists present, the protests have been peppered with incredibly diverse types of performances, speeches and actions—music, poetry, visual and performance art among them. Their involvement has captured the attention of both traditional and pop culture media, whose coverage of Occupy has been alternately vilifying, misrepresented, celebratory and co-optive. Even when the mainstream press gets it wrong, though, it's clear that the longer Occupy exists, the longer it infiltrates and informs the culture at large: a triumph any way you slice it.

WHAT THE MAINSTREAM MEDIA IS MISSING

BY SARAH SELTZER

MANY MAINSTREAM NEWS outlets can be described as flummoxed at best, condescending at worst, when it comes to their coverage of a new movement that is leaderless, has no list of demands and aims to be as much a state of mind as an organization; a multifaceted sea-change rather than a single entity.

It's been a long time since our country saw the rise of a social movement this broad and ambitious, one not devoted to a single issue. There's no rulebook for covering it as one covers a campaign, or a company. For a powerful corporate media addicted to the "view from nowhere" approach—he-said, she-said style reporting that pretends to be entirely neutral—trying to adjust to the movement is not going so well.

It's no wonder that a *New York Times* reporter at the first "spokes-council" meeting was booed (although allowed to stay)—the *Times'* coverage has been bemused and sneering at times.

EXTREME OPPOSITION AND HIPPIE-BASHING

Let's start at the extreme end of anti-OWS propaganda. From printing enlarged photo spreads detailing fistfights in the downtown vicinity to running huge headlines like "Enough!" and "Zoo-Cotti," the *New York Post's* intense dwelling on the protests, it seems, is rivaled only by the paper's interest in the Kardashian divorce and local sports franchises.

But this angry attack reveals that, contrary to claims of uselessness and insignificance, the occupation has burrowed deep down into the skin of the decision-makers at the notoriously reactionary and sleazy Murdoch-owned tabloid. Still, the *Post's* response, while frustrating because of the paper's popularity in the city, arises from a clear bias that almost any reader with basic media literacy can understand. What's more disturbing are the sins of omission from outlets that are supposed to be neutral.

SINS OF OMISSION

On the first night that Occupy Oakland was getting tear-gassed in the streets, I flipped through my TV channels to see if anyone was reporting on the chaos. On MSNBC, there was mention of previous incidents in Oakland, but nothing live. Everywhere else I saw only discussion of the GOP primary.

Meanwhile, the drama unfolded on Twitter and on livestreams, as photos of smoke-filled streets, videos of projectiles being hurled into peaceful crowds, and most horrifyingly, footage of the injured Scott Olsen amassed online in close to real-time. It was riveting, as much as any television feed might be. It was definitive proof that in this case the revolution (and the backlash) would not, in fact, be televised. It would be tweeted.

A DESIRE FOR CONFLICT

Here's something else that's being omitted from coverage, that isn't as dramatic as police beatings and tear gas: what's happening at 60 Wall Street, an open atrium (another privately owned public space) that has become a preferred meeting spot for many of Occupy Wall Street's busiest working groups and soon, its "spokes-councils."

There is no anarchy here, although there are anarchist-style decisions being made. There is no chaos, and the conflict is worked out on an individual level. Media critic Felix Salmon wrote an excellent post for his Reuters blog on October 31, taking on his colleagues' coverage of the movement, with this need for conflict as a sticking point: "Journalists love conflict, of course, and so when they cover OWS there's a tendency to try to gin up the story with imaginary beefs—OWS hates the Jews! Goldman has declared war on OWS's bankers! Etc. This is not helpful," he wrote.

NOT BUYING LEADERLESSNESS

On November 7, the *New York Times* Public Editor Arthur Brisbane asked a group of his media expert colleagues: "How should the *New York Times* cover this movement that resembles no other in memory?" In particular, the respondents were absolutely sure that any devotion to "leaderlessness" is a lie being passed off by a secret cabal to deny their own existence.

The 99%

In a follow-up column Brisbane continued on this absurd track: "The push to establish origins and leadership would help surface the [movement's] demands ..." Once again, the *Times* is behaving as though beneath the amorphous movement lie its puppetmasters with a point-by-point platform—and all the *Times* needs to do is to sniff it out, old-school reportage style. Brisbane also noted that the *Times* must "remember to capture the strong dissenting perspective of those who view Occupy Wall Street dimly." Something tells me that won't be a huge hurdle to overcome.

Here's the truth—Occupy Wall Street is actually succeeding, thus far, without a core group of leaders but with an ever-growing group of point-people contributing ideas. As one protester told *Crains New York* it's a "leaderful" movement, with more "leaders" joining each day. Yes, there are some things about Occupy Wall Street and its offshoots that resemble other old-school lefty movements. But this absolute dedication to horizontalism, is real. And the messiness involved in decentralizing the movement's authority in a society structured around traditional leadership models is a big reason it deserves to be taken seriously.

AN ABSURD THRESHOLD FOR 'NEUTRALITY'

Occupy Wall Street's overarching message (income inequality and reckless financial institutions are bad) is particularly pertinent for media professionals, who have seen their sector shrink, their workload increase and many of their jobs reduced to "contractor" status—no health insurance for you. The disenfranchisement of the 99 percent is all too real.

And yet some reporters, having been caught holding signs at protests, have been fired, while others have to attend rallies clandestinely or refrain from chanting or using the people's mic to maintain their alleged neutrality. Neutrality, for many outlets, remains the hard and fast rule, when it's no secret anymore that pure objectivity doesn't exist, that journalists are people with opinions.

This kind of insistence on "neutrality'" leads to statements like "Occupy Wall Street activists are protesting against what they say is a growing inequality," when in fact, the facts are out there and the numbers document that yes, in no uncertain terms, inequality *has* grown. Hiding the fact that smart journalists actually have opinions and exercise their rights—and the right to protest is as essential as the right to vote—adds to the perception of a "secret liberal bias" that only hurts the media in the end, leaving journalists prey to James O'Keefe style-stings.

MAKE YOUR OWN MEDIA

In this vacuum, do-it-yourself and indie media have shone. From freelancers and progressive writers who have found themselves arrested and tear-gassed as they stand with marchers to young people with cellphones and cameras and Twitter accounts, more media is being made about Occupy Wall Street than any movement that's come before. There are newspapers and gazettes being produced by occupiers and friends of occupiers, and blogs and tumblrs about women, people of color, queer people and individuals' experience within the movement.

Journalist Russ Baker writes of "traditional" media outlets covering Occupy Wall Street: "We need to move on to something new, and better." Maybe we already have.

MTV COMES TO OCCUPY WALL STREET

BY JULIANNE ESCOBEDO SHEPHERD

READY OR NOT, here comes MTV. Thus far, the network has produced or announced two separate programs devoted to the Occupy Wall Street protests—reality programs, naturally.

First up: a search for "sexy, young Occupy Wall Streeters" for its long-running show "The Real World."

The open casting call, sent out via Craigslist, immediately provoked ire from OWS allies on Twitter. No one, it seemed, thought it was a good idea.

Then MTV aired an episode of its long-running documentary program, "True Life," which focused on three young protesters over the course of two weeks at Zuccotti Park, in an episode titled, "I'm Occupying Wall Street." A widely seen advance preview focuses on protesters the night before Brookfield Properties was set to clear out the park: it shows them working together to gather all of the trash and recycling to successfully prevent the "cleanup."

At the same time MTV conducted a marketing study of millennials (ages 18-29) and found:

• Nearly three-quarters of those ages 18 to 29 feel "things are unfair for my generation"
• Nearly half (45 percent) have postponed a major life milestone
• 93 percent feel the current economic situation is having a personal effect on them
• 72 percent do not trust the government to take care of their well-being
• 62 percent fear for their parents' ability to retire in this economy
• 66 percent wish there was some leader, outside of a political one, who could speak to their generation's needs

It's tempting to hand-wring over MTV's interest in Occupy Wall Street—particularly its youngest protesters. First, there's the obvious: MTV is owned by Viacom, which represents the type of corporate concentration some people at Occupy Wall Street are protesting. Meanwhile, reality show stars notoriously work for lower wages than trained actors, driving down standards while making the top tier richer.

But what if MTV is not just jumping on what it deems a "hot new trend," and is actually using its considerable power for good? How can Occupy Wall

Street allies use that for the positive? Consider this: in the 1990s, MTV was markedly more activist, outspoken and politically aware, reflecting the mood of the generation. The network was at the forefront of the shift from the conservative Reagan-Bush eras to the brighter, more vibrant Clinton years—in fact, it helped usher it in, with Clinton speaking to Town Halls aired on the station leading up to the 1992 election, and a voter-registration movement called "Choose or Lose" that got eligible youth to the polls.

But it wasn't simply the station's explicit social activism that helped change the culture. The same year MTV launched its "Choose or Lose" campaign, a groundbreaking new reality show called—yes—"The Real World," brought to light the pressing issues of the era: racism, homosexuality, AIDS, activism, sexuality and religion, as experienced through the cast. Certainly the standards for reality television have plummeted greatly (concurrent with the George W. Bush era) in the 19 years since "The Real World" first aired—but couldn't OWS use the platform to articulate what America's protesting? Zuccotti Park has human mics to communicate messages ... imagine MTV as digital mic, one with the potential to reach millions. And if the mainstream media continues to belittle and misrepresent the protesters as "kids," wouldn't it be nice to be one of said kids and prove them wrong?

Here's another reason not to feel too cynical about MTV's interest in Occupy Wall Street. The network generally has a lock on the 18-34 age group, but its real viewers are tweens, a demographic that right now has not experienced any type of mass American protest in their lives. At its most cynical evaluation, MTV is in the business of marketing coolness to youth, and the fact that Occupy Wall Street—a wholly organic, worldwide protest movement—could be considered (or portrayed) as something that is "cool," is nothing short of marvelous. Occupy Wall Street is constructed so that anyone with general overlapping beliefs can participate; if some show up just because it's *de rigueur*, as several celebrities at OWS have been accused, it's not the worst thing in the world. Kanye West may have ventured to Zuccotti Park wearing gold and Gucci, but the fact that West even knew what it was is symbolic of the impact OWS has had.

Christopher Nolan is rumored to be filming shots for the next Batman film at Zuccotti Park. Actor/comedian Russell Brand documented his first trip to the protest on his blog, writing, "It was apparent that they have colonized more than the formerly anonymous square, they have colonized the international agenda."

Occupy Wall Street has trickled up. It's making its mark in the pop culture—something the Tea Party will never do.

10 CRAZIEST THINGS SAID ABOUT OCCUPY WALL STREET

BY LYNN PARRAMORE

Answer a fool according to his folly, or he will be wise in his own eyes.
—Proverbs 26.5

WHAT AN EMBARRASSMENT of riches we found in compiling this list. The following selections are by no means comprehensive, but here, in no particular order, are 10 of the craziest things we've heard so far about the movement that has taken an abusive system by its lapels and said: "Enough already!"

1. WHAT, ME WORRY?

The out-of-touch medal must go to Wall Street financiers whose tenuous grasp of reality leads them to conclude that the protests have nothing to do with them. You might think that the name of said protest would serve as a hint. But apparently obtuseness is as plentiful as arrogance on Wall Street. The smartest guys in the room have taken a smoke break.

In a recent *New York Times* report, one Wall Street champion sums up his view: "'I don't think we see ourselves as the target,' said Steve Bartlett, president of the Financial Services Roundtable, which represents the nation's biggest banks and insurers in Washington. 'I think they're protesting about the economy. What's lost is that the financial services sector has to be well capitalized and well financed for the economy to recover.'"

What's lost, Mr. Bartlett, is your mind if you think that the protests have nothing to do with you and your rapacious clients.

2. THE ANTI-SEMITIC MEME

David Brooks earns a slot here for promoting this nasty little meme, having launched it on the op-ed page of the *New York Times*, no less.

After dismissing the protests as "inconsequential," he observes that "this uprising was sparked by the magazine *Adbusters*, previously best known for the 2004 essay, 'Why Won't Anyone Say They Are Jewish?'—an investigative report that identified some of the most influential Jews in America and their nefarious grip on policy."

Hmm. The movement seems to be "consequential" enough to panic Brooks into scaring up a seven-year-old magazine article in support of his smear campaign. Accusations of anti-Semitism are a tired ploy of conservatives who have severe allergic reactions to popular movements. Perhaps if Brooks actually attended any of the gatherings and marches, he might ask the Jewish OWS protesters how they feel about his charge. They are plentiful in the 99 percent.

3. THE BILLIONAIRE'S LAMENT

It took the high-rolling NYC mayor, whose fortune has levitated from sale of his "Bloomberg boxes" to Wall Street, to accuse the protesters of picking the wrong target. Guess you gotta defend your constituency! In a mind-bender of an interview with radio host John Gambling, Mayor Bloomberg complains of unfeeling attacks on the impoverished souls toiling in the financial district. "The protesters are protesting against people who make $40,000 and $50,000 a year and are struggling to make ends meet."

Really? It should be pretty obvious that the protesters are not pointing the finger at Wall Street receptionists. The median salary of a stockbroker is $80,000 per year, and of course it only goes up from there. Memo to Mayor: Gargantuan Wall Street salaries helped tank the economy. And even as regulators have tried to rein in bonuses, banksters simply jack up base pay rates. At Goldman Sachs, the base salary for managing directors has jumped to $500,000 from $300,000 since the crisis.

If that's "struggling," we'd like to sign up for it.

4. THE COMMUNIST CONSPIRACY KOOKS

Deserving of a whole list all his own, the certifiable Glenn Beck serves up the latest in a long history of right-wing attacks on anything that ordinary people do to improve their lot. In the world according to Beck, the protesters are card-carrying Communists who wish to destroy the global economy.

But that is not all. They are planning the "violent overthrow of the United States government" and are bent on killing Democrats, Speaker Pelosi, and basically "everybody." Warming to his theme, Beck offers a sinister prediction: "Capitalists, if you think that you can play footsies with these people, you're wrong. They will come for you and drag you into the streets and kill you … they're Marxist radicals … these guys are worse than Robespierre from the French Revolution … they'll kill everybody."

Never mind that the protesters are nonviolent and express no allegiance to any political group. If you like your lunacy served undiluted, it's hard to beat Beck.

5. THE MUSLIM BROTHERHOOD COMETH

Wherever you find wingnuts, chances are you'll stumble on somebody obsessed with the Muslim Brotherhood, the Cairo-based Islamist group that looms larger in the psyche of American paranoids than it does in that of Egyptians. But to a certain stripe of conservative, the Brothers are poised to take over the planet. Starting with sunny Orlando.

The *Tea Party Tribune* alerts readers to what "may be a move by a Muslim activist to take over control of 'Occupy Orlando,' in the 'spirit of the Arab Spring.'" This suspicion gives rise to grave—if somewhat incoherent—concerns: "Is it really possible for a 'strange' group of Muslim Brothers to take their anti-American, anti-Jewish hatred into our country and be welcomed, even into meetings with President Obama … ah … yes, it's happening right under your nose, folks! And it may be happening in Orlando, Florida."

The "intel" proving this nuttery consists of a video featuring Tom Trento, the leader of anti-Muslim group United West, following around American-Muslim attorney Shayan Elahi at an Occupy Orlando gathering. (The *Florida Independent* reports that GOP Senate hopeful Adam Hasner calls Trento a "good friend." Yuck.) Helping readers to "connect the dots," Trento links the man's presence to references to the Arab Spring on the Occupy Orlando website. Bingo! The whole movement must be a nefarious plot for the Muslim Brotherhood to take over America. "Something to think about," says Trento.

Yep. And the fact that Trento is bonkers.

6. SECRET FUNDING

Aggravated by the well-established fact that right-wing billionaire David Koch has backed the Tea Party, conservatives are predictably trying to claim that liberal billionaire George Soros is secretly financing Occupy Wall Street.

It's no surprise that Rush Limbaugh would jump on this wagon. But Reuters lent credibility to this baloney with a widely criticized report. The evidence? Reuters reporters Mark Egan and Michelle Nichols claimed that some people sort of said something about Soros: "There has been much speculation over who is financing the disparate protest, which has spread to cities across America and lasted nearly four weeks. One name that keeps coming up is investor George Soros, who in September debuted in the top 10 list of wealthiest Americans. Conservative critics contend the movement is a Trojan horse for a secret Soros agenda." (Note: this excerpt is reprinted from Alex Pareene's Salon report, as the original story seems to have been scrubbed). Egan and Nichols go on to claim that Soros gave some money to the magazine *Adbusters* a while back (Pareene debunks this) and "some of the protesters share some ideological ground" with the billionaire. So there!

The news wire reversed the story when more thorough journalists cried foul. Then it tried to bury the whole shameful episode. But here's betting on Dawn of the Dead returns of the lie throughout the right-wing media machine.

7. COSMIC CONVERGENCE

On to the "Dirty Hippies/Druggies" caricature. (We might easily paint Wall Street as playground for cokeheads and hookers, but we will refrain.)

Perhaps the suggestion that the protests are Woodstock Redux suggests a lack of imagination more than insanity. But pundit Lowman S. Henry, writing for the PennLive.com news organ of Central Pennsylvania, drives this meme all the way to Crazyville: "The Occupy Wall Street protest is the latest incarnation of the Haight-Ashbury gang transported from San Francisco to New York. Loosely gathering under a mutual disdain for the nation's financial community, the group appears to be a hybrid between Woodstock and a college political science class. The lawlessness and arrests have it tilting more toward the former." There's more. According to Henry, the protesters have been paid to call for a change in "cosmic consciousness" by union organizers. Moreover the public has been horribly deceived by the media into believing that Occupy Wall Street is a "spontaneous outpouring of Plebian anger aimed at the rich in America." The idea!

Henry sure looks like an expert on psychedelics. What we'd like to know is, what's he smoking?

8. ALL THE PRESIDENT'S PROTESTERS

Spend five minutes at Zuccotti Park, and you will notice that many of the protesters are openly critical of Obama—as they are of a whole swath of politicians. Nevertheless, people like presidential hopeful Herman Cain are painting the movement as a tool of the Obama reelection campaign. Cain plainly admits that his evidence for this is exactly zilch. But does that stop the Herminator? Of course not!

In a *Wall Street Journal* interview, Cain asserts: "I don't have facts to back this up, but I happen to believe that these demonstrations are planned and orchestrated to distract from the failed policies of the Obama administration. Don't blame Wall Street, don't blame the big banks, if you don't have a job and you're not rich, blame yourself ..."

Sounds like 99 percent crap to us.

9. THIS IS WHAT IGNORANCE LOOKS LIKE

The rejection of business-as-usual politicking among Occupy Wall Street protesters has quite a few knickers in a twist. Observing the recent Occupy the London Stock Exchange rally, Slate's Anne Applebaum blanks out on her country's own history and accuses the protesters of undermining democracy:

> *In New York, marchers chanted, 'This is what democracy looks like,' but, actually, this isn't what democracy looks like. This is what freedom of speech looks like. Democracy looks a lot more boring. Democracy requires institutions, elections, political parties, rules, laws, a judiciary, and many unglamorous, time-consuming activities, none of which are nearly as much fun as camping out in front of St. Paul's cathedral or chanting slogans on the Rue St. Martin in Paris.*

Mm-kay. Last time we checked, American democracy kicked off when protesters demonstrated in the streets against an unjust system. They distributed pamphlets. Gathered at rallies. You know, roused the rabble.

Applebaum might wish to peruse the Declaration of Independence, which OWS's Declaration of the Occupation of New York City echoes in many ways, such as its focus on abuses of power. The author of the original document, Thomas Jefferson, thought that a rebellion every 20 years or so was just the thing for a democracy:

"I hold it that a little rebellion now and then is a good thing and as necessary in the political world as storms in the physical … It is a medicine necessary for the sound health of government." —Thomas Jefferson to James Madison (Jan. 30, 1787).

And just when did using the loo at McDonald's become glamorous?

10. CONSERVATIVES LIKE US

The Occupy Wall Street protests have become sort of a Rorschach test in which people tend to see their own grievances and philosophies. That's one of the strengths. But staffers at the American Enterprise Institute? Whoa! But it's true. The conservative think tank sent a couple of fresh-faced, polar-fleeced staffers to find out just what the heck was going on down in Zuccotti Park. Surprised at how "articulate" and "concerned" the protesters seem to be, the staffers chat up protester Edward T. Hall, who seems to advocate state's right in matters like health care. Conclusion? The entire movement is "a bunch of people that are conservatives, they just don't know it."

Finding evidence of their free-market fundamentalism everywhere in the camp—from its "order" to its water filtration system—the staffers praise the can-do spirit and "entrepreneurship." They ride away—is that a taxi or a limo?—resting easy that the movement will soon embrace the wisdom of Ayn Rand. Their feeling of solidarity is not altogether silly. Until they rise up the think-tank career ladder, they, too, are in the 99 percent.

OCCUPATION AS PERFORMANCE ART

BY SARAH SELTZER

WHEN THE MAYOR of Denver asked the local Occupy group to name a leader for negotiations, they named a dog, a collie, as their leader, humorously drawing attention to their dedication to group decision-making. In New York, clowns dressed in rodeo and matador outfits scaled the Wall Street bull, while sympathetic literati did a marathon reading of Herman Melville's "Bartleby, the Scrivener," and musicians played impromptu sets.

While some will inevitably express scorn for the countercultural trappings of the Occupy movements, the reality is that these trappings—from the people's mic to music and painting to a library and zombie makeup artistry—are garnering positive reactions from dissidents beyond the establishment Left, affirming the oft-repeated adage, "If I can't dance, I don't want to be part of your revolution." In fact, impromptu Zuccotti Park dance parties abound.

A long-term occupation needs morale to survive, and the morale granted by artists isn't just in the immediate vicinity, but everywhere people are paying attention.

The list of celebrity artists involved in Occupy goes on and on: Jeff Mangum, Talib Kweli and Tom Morello have played sets. Sean Lennon and Rufus Wainwright treated protesters to an ironic cover of Madonna's "Material Girl." Hip-hop legend Russell Simmons and actor Mark Ruffalo show up to support activists and tweet thoughts regularly, saying the movement has inspired them. Katy Perry and Russell Brand, Kanye West, Pete Seeger, David Crosby and Graham Nash, Lupe Fiasco, underground artists and Oscar winners alike are flocking to the occupations.

The staggering number of involved artists is comparable to previous movements, but different in the fact that many of the artists are there not to perform but to absorb. This isn't just about publicity, but about the heart of the movement itself, which is growing in organic and creative ways. The Internet and technology are allowing everyone involved to create media and art without sponsorship or fame to get them noticed.

Elisa Kreisinger, a filmmaker and creator of feminist video remixes, notes that she witnessed a protester refuse to do an interview for a Fox News team because, she thinks, protesters are capable of making their own narrative, via YouTube, Twitter, independent media and more. "I think we're finally creating the type of media coverage we want to see and no longer have to depend on commercial networks to do it for us," she says. "Additionally, people who aren't necessarily artists are able to participate and that's an important distinction. The relatively low barrier to participation in the protest as well in media creation sustains civil disobedience, helping its presence spread among on- and off-line populations."

Indeed, much of the "art" coming out of the occupation is playful, straddling the realm between homemade media-making and provocative artistic statements. A group of artists are engineering an "Occupennial," while groups of musicians have organized on Facebook to play for the protesters downtown.

Shamus Khan marched down to Wall Street with a group called "Artists and Writers Exhausted by Capitalism and Inspired by the Occupation." He notes: "There is a kind of performance art to what's going on down there. It's about expression, about challenging alienation, about giving voice to one's experience. All of these things are resonant with artists and writers. And if we think of this as performance art that changes the world, how can't that be inspiring?"

This quality of "permanent performance art"—from the stark visual power of the sleeping bags in the park to the tent cities and the homemade signage—has allowed the movement to reach past the usual suspects, capturing the imagination of a wide variety of Americans who may not ascribe to a rigid political philosophy but are eager to take action against the oppression they witness every day.

SEVEN NEW ANTHEMS FOR THE OCCUPATION

BY JULIANNE ESCOBEDO SHEPHERD

CONTEMPORARY MUSICIANS ARE always being accused of not being political enough. They aren't Nina Simone or Woody Guthrie, the complainers grouse, they aren't Joan Baez or Joe Hill. Particularly in times of strife—say, 9/11 up to now—there is a warped perception that today's songwriters simply aren't concerned with contemporary events, and that the alleged narcissism of this generation has rendered political music moot. In the last 10 years, there have been approximately 2,000 think-pieces written about this non-fact.

But the Occupy movement is pulling musicians out of the woodwork, with many artists big and small dropping by to show support and perform. With that in mind, here are the best, most political songs by some of our favorite musicians who've lent their support to Occupy Wall Street, proving that bashing working musicians as apolitical is straight-up wrong.

1. KATY PERRY, "WHO AM I LIVING FOR?"

Perry joined her husband Russell Brand and life magnate Russell Simmons at Occupy Wall Street on October 23, but it wasn't the first time the pop superstar has made explicit her political leanings. In June, she spoke up for universal health care, telling *Rolling Stone*:

> *I think we are largely in desperate need of revolutionary change in the way our mindset is. Our priority is fame, and people's wellness is way low. I saw this knowing full well that I'm a part of the problem ... the fact that America doesn't have free healthcare drives me fucking absolutely crazy, and is so wrong.*

Certainly the revolution she was looking for is represented in OWS, which she promoted on Twitter to her more than 11 million followers. But her candied pop hits aren't completely devoid of political undertones. In "Who Am I Living For?" from her 2010 album *Teenage Dream*, over a dramatic, dubstep-influenced beat, she sang, *I am ready for the road less traveled/Suiting up for my crowning battle ... I can see the writing on the wall/I can't ignore this war ...*

Full of biblical allusions, the song is about finding the courage to be part of some kind of resistance. Whether or not it's about Perry's Christian upbringing, as some have suggested, it's a righteous anthem for the brave souls currently sleeping in tents at Occupy Wall Street, and a reminder that Jesus was himself a revolutionary.

2. JOHN LEGEND & THE ROOTS, "WAKE UP EVERYBODY!"

John Legend and the Roots' cover of the 1975 revolutionary song by Harold Melvin and the Blue Notes is pitch-perfect and super-relevant. *The world won't get better if we just let it be*, the chorus goes, *we gotta change it, you and me*. Released on the performers' expressly political album *Wake Up!* (2010), it's just an extension of a long career of outspokenness and opinion the Roots have had from the beginning—and Questlove has been very supportive of Occupy Wall Street. He told Urban Daily:

> *It's taken 99% of the people long enough to finally wake up ... A lot of people think revolution and change will be the next man's fight. They want to hang back and see what happens and it doesn't work that way. You've got to get your hands and knees inside the mud. You have to be a part of the change you want to see.*

3. KANYE WEST & JAY-Z, "MADE IN AMERICA"

Kanye West got a lot of flack for going down to Occupy Wall Street after a shopping trip in Soho (with Jay-Z and Beyonce), wearing a 1 percent outfit of Gucci and gold chains. While his latest album with Jay-Z, *Watch the Throne*, is essentially all about being part of the 0.25 percent, contextualize it: those songs are based in triumph about being formerly impoverished African-American men who became wealthy and successful in the face of impossible odds.

Still, not all of the album is this way: "Made in America" tells their tale in a more sympathetic fashion. Ebullient singer Frank Ocean's hook (*Sweet baby Jesus, we made it in America*) sounds mournful, incredulous and thankful, while the rappers' brags are tempered by their narratives—that West went from struggling with his beats to lacing up his mother with a nice car, and that Jay-Z was a young gun cooking crack, but now hopes to pass on his legacy to his child.

It's not riot music, but it represents the aspirational undertones of most rap music from its very beginnings; fetishization of consumer goods in rap is so prevalent because so many of its practitioners, or the people it represents, have so little. In that sense, let *Watch the Throne* be a 1 percent album dedicated to the 99 percent.

4. TOM MORELLO (AS THE NIGHTWATCHMAN), "WORLD WIDE REBEL SONG"

Morello's the guy most people out here know, a modern saint of political music and recent recipient of MTV's newly created O Award for Occupy Wall Street. The Rage Against the Machine guitarist has shown up at Wall Street and Occupy Los Angeles—in fact, he seems to appear at any significant progressive political protest, making his folk alter ego, the Nightwatchman, into a sort of Woody Guthrie for our time.

Speaking of Guthrie, that's exactly who he covered on October 13 in Liberty Plaza, doing "This Land is Your Land" for an enthusiastic crowd, before launching into his class-war anthem, "The Fabled City." But a more recent call to protest comes in the form of "World Wide Rebel Songs," off his 2011 album of the same name: *Pirates, blood suckers and bank men/Got us picking through the crumbs/Raise your voices all together/Motherfucka here we come!* Which is *so* fun to sing, and underscores a fundamental truth: protest music is at its best when it's a good time.

5. LUPE FIASCO, "STATE RUN RADIO"

This political rap star has been at Occupy movements all around the U.S., and has donated (and personally dropped off) supplies in Chicago and New York. His latest album, *Lasers*, depicts the A in the title as an anarchy sign, and that's about what you get when you talk to him about politics. (His infamous "Obama is the biggest terrorist" statement, for example.)

"State Run Radio" both alludes to the end of his record contract and the dependence of corporate radio stations on major labels (and vice versa), and uses the concept as a prescription for class war, rapping, *We interrupt this broadcast/to bring you this special message about the forecast/the future's cloudy and it's rainin on the poor class.* See you in the trenches, Lupe.

6. JANE'S ADDICTION, "IDIOTS RULE"

Perry Farrell, leader of Jane's Addiction, pulled his kids out of school to take them to Occupy, though he didn't perform. In honor of the band's reunion, it seems appropriate to pull out a classic jam from its back catalog. "Idiots Rule," from debut album *Nothing's Shocking*, expresses just the right amount of sarcasm for the Internet generation: a sassy, upbeat sax, jovial slap-bass and Farrell gleefully singing about the yahoos who comprise much of government. And they wrote it in 1985! Some things haven't changed ... yet.

7. TALIB KWELI, "DISTRACTION"

The ever-political rapper from Brooklyn actually free-styled "Distraction" at one of his Occupy Wall Street visits, making it perhaps the first song that was actually born in the movement. He used his first visit there in early October—which he later said made him "proud to be an American"—to rail on rappers he perceives as misguided, celebrity-worshiping culture and the ironic colonial impulse of Anglo-Saxon America. (*Steal the land from the Native American and make our missiles Tomahawks, touche Talib.*)

But it really is a good rap on paper, in which he flips his lyrics quite cleverly: *The people so thirsty, what they seeing is mirages/But this passion Photoshopping and your YouTube collages/Coming through like Collossus/Exposing the false prophet.*

There's plenty more where that came from, as these are just the folks who've made it to Occupy so far—but hey, if people down at Occupy Oakland or Occupy London are playing Rihanna, doesn't that automatically make it protest music? It's about what gets people motivated to fight.

VIII.

VISION: WHAT COMES NEXT

INTRODUCTION

ARE WE READY for a new vision of America? Can demands as bold as human dignity, economic equality, and social justice gain traction in our corporatized, compromised, and co-opted world? Will specific proposals, like a financial transaction tax, gain the broad support required for success?

The thinkers and visionaries in the following pages share their sense of the deeper meaning of what is happening, how we are transforming, and the change that is coming through Occupy Wall Street. They ask us to see with new eyes, to face difficult realities, and to brace ourselves for an unpredictable and difficult process of transformation. They call upon us to be witnesses and truth-tellers; communicators and catalysts. Most of all, they challenge us to recognize the preciousness of this moment, which comes perhaps only once or twice in a lifetime. And to continue the Occupation, together and everywhere.

GANDHI'S WINGS: OCCUPY WALL STREET AND THE REDISTRIBUTION OF ANXIETY

BY ROB JOHNSON

It's my home—last night I dreamt that I grew wings
I found a place where they could hear me when I sing
                                        —"Wings" by Josh Ritter

OCCUPY WALL STREET is about anxiety, and the courage of young people to fly into conflict on Gandhi's wings. This is the noble legacy of civil disobedience on display at Zuccotti Park. We are seeing that anxiety channeled by courage can transform a society.

What does anxiety look like? You can see this drama played out as the demonstrators meditate surrounded by police whose anxiety is palpable, perhaps because the police cannot figure out which side they should really be on. You see it and hear it and feel it from all of the media pundits who are trying to "figure out," discredit, or dismiss OWS. You see it in the angry denunciations emanating from Wall Street financiers who beat their breasts and cling to the image of their legitimacy because they work so hard that they deserve their top 0.1 percent style mega incomes.

NOTHING TO EAT AT THE ESTABLISHMENT CAFÉ

Rather than serving as the trusted nerve center, the discipline, and the arbiters of monetary value, our leading financiers tear apart our productive base and blow themselves up. Then they yank the chain of their portfolio of "owned" Senators and Congressmen to bail themselves out. The elected officials, in turn, pay the media companies for election advertisements with their campaign war chest garnered from Wall Street, and we are all told that our constructive outlet as citizens is through the electoral process. Is that some kind of joke? Have you ever gone to a restaurant found nothing on the menu you wanted to order?

Only those who pass the plutocratic primary ever make it on the ballot on election day. That is where we are as a nation. For the rest of us, watching this corrupt logic unfold gives new meaning to Ronald Reagan's adage that government is the problem not the solution. The critiques of the Democratic left and the Republican right are strikingly similar. Our leadership and institutions are unresponsive to the concerns of the people. But the young protesters at Zuccotti Park and encampments across the nation have simply gotten up from the table. They have walked out of the restaurant and are making their own meals now. That is what OWS is. Home cooking when everything is broken at the establishment café.

These young people have repudiated a system that has little to offer them. They are rising up against environmental degradation. They are challenging the devastating breakdown in financial regulation. They are saying "no thanks" to legislation protecting health care monopolies marketed as great reforms. They are condemning a toxic food industry that sabotages our health as the colors and chemicals tantalize and poison us. And they are refusing to swallow a military juggernaut that consumes lives and hundreds of billion dollars while we close schools. These young people have decided not to accept letting our society be crushed by an epidemic of mortgage overhangs and 30 percent credit card interest rates. They have opted not stand by as our elected representatives work with their campaign donors, pretending that the Wall Street bonuses are earned and banks are sound and business as usual can continue.

This inhuman economic and power logic impacts us all, and the protesters serve to heighten our awareness that the social contract has broken down. The truth has been revealed. That our large American-based multinational enterprises do not need healthy or well-educated Americans to profit. That CEOs do not want to pay taxes from their mega salaries when they can afford their own private security, private education and private transportation to escape the rubble that they have let the country become under their leadership. That all the while, the executives ransack their companies, aided and abetted by Wall Street collaborators who peddle off balance sheet schemes, complex derivatives, and stock buy backs, and then act as though it is a mystery that the pace of innovation is dwindling.

THE REDISTRIBUTION OF ANXIETY

As money poisons the veins of our political organism, as courts rule that money is speech and only millions in your pocket will give you a voice, is it any wonder that our jobless, debt-ensnared young people see this foul scene and understand that the greater danger to their future lies in not protesting the world we are putting on their shoulders? They have shrugged off Atlas. The protestors see something our leaders do not: Without protest, the future looks like a Brazilian favela for many. To alleviate the anxiety of that vision is to bear the anxiety of change. The protesters know they must face police brutality and the ridicule from those who drove us in the ditch. Resistance to change is organic and these brave and clever and peaceful young people are bearing their anxious birthright and redistributing the burden of anxiety to those who have left the nation in tatters.

When Martin Luther King delivered his famous speech on the immorality of the Vietnam war at New York's Riverside Church, "A Time to Break the Silence," he set off a rash of criticism from every establishment institution, black or white, in our entire nation. His legacy reminds us that anxiety is the sister of change. Anxiety is not always a mark of something wrong. It can be signal something that is overdue and needed. But can that anxiety of conflict be any more troubling than for our young people to believe they have to abide this discredited American political economic model indefinitely into the future? It is in the tilting balance of those anxieties that we can see now that "A Change is Gonna Come." The road will be painful and perhaps bloody. But the journey is now irreversibly underway. Though they may never acknowledge it, even the one percent should be grateful for that. These peaceful protesters may insure that anxiety does not erupt into a violence from which the wealthy and powerful themselves could not escape. Instead, we are all gratefully riding on the intuitive wisdom of these young people, who, like Dr. King, chose to fly on the ghost of Gandhi's wings.

A longer version of this essay appeared on AlterNet.

A NEW DECLARATION OF INDEPENDENCE: 10 IDEAS FOR TAKING AMERICA BACK FROM THE 1 PERCENT

BY ALEX PAREENE

HERE'S WHERE WE are in the course of human events right now: 14 million Americans are jobless and millions more are underemployed. Those still working have seen wages fall after 30 years of stagnation. The 1 percent of top wage earners could buy and sell the rest of us without so much as a low balance warning on their checking account apps. The tenth-of-1 percent earns millions more every year in barely taxed capital gains and derivatives while everyone else struggles to pay down trillions of dollars of debt. Massive, growing income inequality is now belatedly acknowledged by political and media elites, but many of them seem befuddled as to its cause and importance.

It is our belief that many of the problems facing Americans today can be directly connected to the unchecked power and complete unaccountability of the 1 percent, a group that benefits from every unequal boom of the modern era and escapes each disastrous bust unscathed. The 1 percent is insulated from the negative effects of its disastrous policies by its paid representatives in government. The elite 1 percent ensures the slavish loyalty of its political handmaidens by flooding their campaign coffers with money squeezed from the 99 percent as deposits, fees and interest.

What unites the outraged 99 percent is that we have all "played by the rules," only to learn belatedly that the game was rigged. Having been promised modest rewards for working within the system, by taking on debt or voting the party line, we find ourselves, bluntly, shit out of luck. Let the facts be submitted to a candid world:

For the young, higher education was said to be a ticket to class mobility, or at least a secure career. Instead, middle-class students have taken on billions of dollars of inescapable debt during a prolonged jobs crisis. Lower-income students are blatantly ripped off by usurious scam artists working for educationally dubious for-profit schools. Even those seeking to join the professional class, through medical school or law school, find themselves with mountains of debt and dwindling job prospects. The rapidly rising cost of higher education pushes bright students into lucrative but socially destructive fields, like finance. Prestigious universities are still largely the finishing schools of the elite, with the most common and pernicious form of affirmative action being that given to the children of the 1 percent most likely to write schools the biggest checks.

For progressives, years of working within the political system to elect Democrats led to a congressional majority that was still more responsive to major corporate donors and powerful industry lobbies than to grass-roots liberal activists—or even organized labor, once the party's most powerful and respected ally. The crimes of the Bush administration remain uninvestigated, the national security state remains unchecked in scope and size, the military-industrial complex ensures that Dwight Eisenhower's prescient speech remains relevant 60 years later, and the useless tactics of triangulation and one-way bipartisanship remain inexplicably popular among the Democratic Party establishment.

For millions of middle-class and striving blue-collar American families, the promise of homeownership as the world's safest investment became another money-making bubble for Wall Street that remains Main Street's intractable mess. Those members of the middle class unfortunate enough to do as an industry of wise men counseled them and invest in the stock market and real estate have seen the fruits of a lifetime's worth of labor evaporate in multiple busts and crashes that the wise men always escape from economically intact. The mere specter of limited relief for underwater homeowners inspired 1 percenter rage so all-consuming that they bankrolled a "populist" movement to channel it. Minority homeowners defrauded by unscrupulous lenders are blamed for an international recession sparked by the venal and simply foolish behavior of megabanks.

The 1 percent aims to exploit a fiscal crisis caused by its own reckless behavior by wiping out pensions earned (and paid into) by public employees and tearing up fairly negotiated union contracts. Meanwhile, they use their media outlets, political foundations and lobbying shops to foment resentment of unionized workers whose crime is benefiting from a system that corporations and conservatives worked to completely dismantle for private employees a generation ago.

The threat that our modest social welfare system for the elderly will be sacrificed to the gods of austerity has already led significant numbers of young people to assume that there will be no Social Security in place by the time they reach what used to be referred to as their retirement years. And that belief is tacitly encouraged by the "moderate" members of the austerity club, who seek to maintain a system of low taxation of the 1 percent in the face of declining income for the 99 percent by gradually phasing out the services government provides for the majority. The austerity sages are considered the most serious and wise in all of the nation by our corporate press, which defines "the center" of every national political debate as "whatever the elites want."

The weight of the 1 percent upon us has become unbearable and intolerable. We therefore respectfully submit our own Demands.

In Liberty Plaza in Lower Manhattan, in Oakland's Oscar Grant Plaza, and at other parks and public squares across the nation (and the world), Occupiers are daily creating the more perfect democracy they'd like to see. As part of that process, groups and individuals and intellectuals and pundits have put forth proposed "demands," to address the myriad problems laid out above. From Occupy Wall Street's principles of solidarity to the General Assembly's proposed New New Deal to Robert Reich's list of essential progressive reforms to the Working Group of the 99 Percent's Petition of Grievances, we've read the proposals and humbly offer our own, for ways to begin to make the richest nation on the planet fair for those of us who can't afford a congressman.

Our list is meant to be the beginning of a conversation, not a final product.

1. DEBT RELIEF

Total household debt in America is $13.3 trillion—114 percent of after-tax income. That millions of working Americans owe every penny they make to hugely profitable financial institutions is absurd and grotesque.

We demand immediate relief for the 99 percent, particularly the poor and young students and college graduates. The Debt Jubilee is an ancient idea, and an attractive one in an era of growing economic feudalism, as the poor increasingly devote all their labor to repaying the rich. It is not in the national interest to force the impoverished to become wage slaves to pay off insurmountable debts owned to payday lenders and hugely profitable bankers.

Every other rich nation on earth heavily subsidizes higher education. We force mere kids to mortgage their futures, then ensure that the debt follows them the rest of their lives, regardless of their living circumstances. Student loan debt hurts not just the graduate but everyone else in society, too: The cost of healthcare would surely decrease, and the availability of primary care for disadvantaged populations increase, if new doctors were not regularly graduating school $200,000 in the red.

And real and widespread relief for homeowners in crisis is urgent. Even millions of homeowners who "did everything right" find themselves underwater, or illegally foreclosed upon by banks running roughshod over the rights of homeowners by robo-signing fraudulent foreclosure documents by the thousands. Banks servicing mortgages are (rightfully) more worried about getting sued by the owners of securities made up of Americans' debt than they are about getting in any sort of trouble for bullying or illegally seizing the homes of regular people. Everyone should get a shot at a renegotiation of their mortgage, at fair rates, and with support from the government.

2. A SUBSTANTIAL JOBS PROGRAM

Most American cities are filled with beautiful old buildings and monuments and parks dating back to the recovery programs of the New Deal, as well as increasingly decrepit bridges and roads and structures that have been neglected by the last couple of decades of shrinking infrastructure investment. A real, direct jobs program, done in the WPA style, would rebuild our cities and towns in addition to putting thousands of people back to work.

3. A HEALTHCARE PUBLIC OPTION

Medicare is probably the single most popular government program in the country, which is no surprise, because government-subsidized healthcare tends to be the most popular government program in every nation that has implemented it.

If a true single-payer system would be too disruptive, we can put the building blocks in place by giving people a public option. Expanding the pool of Medicare recipients to include healthy younger people paying into it would instantly improve the program's fiscal outlook. Nationalizing the underfunded Medicaid system would instantly reduce the deplorable inequity of our healthcare system, too. If this new Medicare could negotiate drug prices—like the Veterans Administration, our wonderful, totally socialized healthcare program for one group of Americans—it would save even more. (Hey, why not combine the proposal with debt relief for young doctors?)

4. REREGULATE WALL STREET

Taking the "unsophisticated" broad view, it seems painfully obvious that Wall Street deregulation undid the stabilizing effects of 1930s-era Wall Street regulation. We're on a boom-and-bust cycle, and a shrinking number of growing megabanks now regularly threaten the entire world economy. It's hard to imagine that we wouldn't be better off with a worldwide network of small, independent credit unions than massive financial institutions daily innovating new and more arcane methods of shifting vast sums of imaginary capital around, but in lieu of smashing the banks with brickbats why not just reinstate the rules that effectively limited their behavior for 40 years or so? Bring back Glass-Steagall. Pass the Volcker rule, too. Ban banks from trading derivatives. Limit their behavior and tax their earnings.

5. END THE GLOBAL WAR ON TERROR AND REIN IN THE DEFENSE BUDGET

Brown University estimates that our wars in Afghanistan, Iraq and Pakistan have cost 236,000 lives and $4 trillion. Millions more people are displaced refugees. If 10 years of war have weakened al-Qaida, we should draw down. If it hasn't, we should seriously rethink our tactics. Regardless, there's no way the world's sole remaining superpower can justify spending more than every other country on Earth combined on its military. There's no coherent reason why the Pentagon's budget should be rising inexorably every year, while the rest of the country grows shabbier and poorer. Spending more on defense now than we did at the height of the Cold War is insane.

The billions spent yearly to rain death on faceless strangers thousands of miles away should be the first program on the chopping block if we're serious about tackling the deficit. That money could better be put to use both here at home and abroad. USAID and the State Department could surely do more to defeat those Who Hate Us For Our Freedom with that money than the Defense Department has so far managed to.

6. REPEAL THE PATRIOT ACT

Speaking of expensive wastes of resources that are also in direct violation of the nation's founding principles, let's dismantle the expansive domestic surveillance state, hurriedly established at a panicky period of national crisis and then enshrined as permanent without a word of serious debate.

The extra-constitutional "delayed-notice search warrants" given to law enforcement by the Patriot Act have been used far more for fighting the war on drugs than the war on terror, which is to be expected from a law that was essentially a massive laundry list of tools and privileges that prosecutors and FBI agents had wanted for years that had thus far been denied to them by pesky constitutional checks on their powers. The government even has its own secret legal readings of the act, allowing it to do secret things we can know nothing about.

The government now has vast powers to track and spy on us for whatever reasons it chooses, and both parties are mostly fine with that. When the NSA was found to be engaging in illegal domestic wiretapping and data mining, Congress responded by granting them more domestic wiretapping and data mining powers. As we've moved further from those panicky days that birthed the Patriot Act, the law and its associated unaccountable domestic surveillance state have, perversely, become more normalized. Those in favor of limited government should be the most alarmed at this.

7. TACKLE CLIMATE CHANGE

We may be rapidly approaching the catastrophic point of no return when it comes to preventing major, devastating climate change. To keep warming below "dangerous levels," one recent study says, we'd need to "reverse the rise in emissions immediately and follow through with steep reductions through the century." Immediately—like now.

Frustratingly, even half-measures have found no support in Congress, where the industries doing the polluting have far more clout than mere scientists or human beings who'll be alive in a future period of mass extinctions, hunger, flooding and drought. At the very least—and this is literally the very least the government should be doing right now to combat climate change—a price should be put on carbon emissions, either in the form of a direct tax or as part of a cap-and-trade scheme. This is a policy so self-evidently beneficial to the vast majority of mankind—it taxes a bad thing, so that corporations do less of the bad thing, while also giving the government revenue to spend on good things—that cap-and-trade's defeat in Congress says just about all there is to say about the corrupting power of industry money on the government process.

8. STOP LOCKING EVERYONE UP FOR EVERYTHING AND END THE DRUG WAR

The American incarceration rate dwarfs that of our closest competitor, Russia, at 743 per 100,000 residents. A full quarter of the world's prison inmates are

American prison inmates. One in 100 American adults are behind bars. These staggering numbers have been repeated over and over again for years by activists, reporters, academics and even the very rare courageous politician, but the prison system just keeps growing, and growing, and growing.

The problem is that there is no political will to do anything about it. In fact, locking people up tends to be a popular campaign platform. In some locales, felons are both denied voting rights and also counted as residents of their prisons for the purposes of congressional apportionment, causing a perverse incentive to lock up more inmates. Tens of thousands of inmates are in long-term solitary confinement, which is essentially torture by another name.

As violent crime rates have fallen, the prison population has continued to grow, because of longer terms and mandatory sentencing and denial of parole. The U.S. holds its prisoners longer than any other nation in the world, and because rehabilitation comes a distant second to punishment in our prisons, recidivism is common. (It doesn't help that, across the nation, ex-felons can't qualify for welfare or subsidized housing or find work.) We're actively creating a massive, mostly black and Hispanic underclass of permanent prisoners and future prisoners. America desperately needs more juvenile diversion programs and well-funded rehabilitation and education programs for those currently in the system.

A major contributor to our mass incarceration state is the "War on Drugs," which after years of waging we've yet to win.

Full legalization of marijuana would lead to many fewer people being jailed for victimless crimes and immediately destroy a critical income stream for gangs and increasingly violent drug cartels. Legalizing marijuana would also give states and cities a desperately needed infusion of tax revenue. (Legalization or decriminalization of other drugs would be similarly beneficial, but a good deal more controversial.) Those who commit nonviolent drug offenses should never be sent to prisons for years. Those currently in prison for nonviolent drug offenses should be freed and rehabilitated into society.

9. FULL EQUALITY FOR THE QUEER COMMUNITY

Gay marriage is a no-brainer—rights granted to a majority are being denied to a minority based on arguments founded solely on bigotry—and should be recognized nationwide.

Let's not forget, too, that gay, lesbian, bisexual and transgendered Americans are denied other rights, including, in most states, protection from workplace discrimination and housing discrimination. I suspect lots of Americans don't even know the LGBT community lacks those basic protections, and that is itself an outrage.

10. FIX THE TAX SYSTEM

There are a million ways the tax code could be made fairer, simpler and more progressive, and most of those ways are opposed by powerful entrenched interests. But it is an inescapable fact that for most of the 20th century, federal income tax rates were very high on the wealthy—very, very high, in fact—and most of that period also happened to be a time of widespread prosperity for rich and middle-class Americans alike. The experiment in slashing taxes on the rich seems to have failed everyone but the rich.

The system as it currently stands forces states to fund essential services with the most regressive taxes possible, mainly sales taxes, in order not to scare businesses elsewhere. The current system allows hugely profitable transnational corporations to get away without paying anything, to make killings "overseas" while operating at imaginary losses domestically. Warren Buffett, as we all know, is paying less than his secretary.

So let's create a millionaire's tax bracket, and a financial transactions tax. Let's close the carried interest tax loophole and raise the estate tax and taxes on capital gains. Let's get the highest marginal tax rate back up to, at the least, Reagan-era levels. Let's stop all being held hostage, as a nation, to the fanatical anti-tax doctrine of the 1 percent.

This story first appeared on Salon.

WHY BANK TRANSFER DAY IS ONLY THE BEGINNING OF SOMETHING HUGE

BY ANDREW LEONARD

ON OCT. 9, Kristen Christian, a 27-year-old art gallery owner in Los Angeles, created a Facebook page urging her friends to move their money out of the big banks on Nov. 5. The suggestion hit a nerve. By Nov. 4, 77,015 "friends" had declared their intention to "attend" Bank Transfer Day.

That doesn't necessarily mean that 77,015 people all pulled all their money out of the likes of Chase, Citibank, Wells Fargo and Bank of America all at once. Saturday is hardly an ideal day to get banking business done, and the process of switching over one's account to a new bank or credit union is not something that can be accomplished—yet—with a flip of a switch. And of course, clicking your intent to do something on Facebook is a far cry from actually, well, doing it.

It's also not clear that the big banks will take a big hit from Bank Transfer Day. [Editor's Note: Tracy Van Slyke, co-director of the New Bottom Line, told AlterNet that since launching the group's "move our money" tools, individuals, congregations, union members and even business owners have moved $50 million out of the big banks.] The usually sensible economics commentator Felix Salmon goes so far as to assert that "the big banks are blithely unconcerned about people withdrawing their funds on Saturday ... I'm not kidding myself that doing so is going to harm the big banks at all."

In purely numerical terms, Salmon might be right, but there's a larger sense in which he is almost surely wrong. The simple fact that one ordinary citizen using social media tools can start a grass fire of protest that captures massive media attention and connects hundreds of thousands of people to useful information is an encouraging sign of where our society is headed. Every single person who actually goes ahead with a switch of banks is casting a potent vote in the long-range democratization of finance. Even if the banks shrug it off, people who go ahead and change their bank will probably feel better about themselves. Just because it's a psychotherapeutic cliché doesn't mean it's wrong: Taking action is empowering.

And something is clearly happening here. According to a press release from the Credit Union National Association, "at least 650,000 consumers across the nation have joined credit unions in the past four weeks."

CUNA estimates that credit unions have added $4.5 billion in new savings accounts. More than four in every five credit unions experiencing growth since Sept. 29 attributed the growth to consumer reaction to new fees imposed by banks, or a combination of consumer reactions to the new bank fees plus the social media-inspired Bank Transfer Day.

$4.5 billion here, $4.5 billion there, and pretty soon you are talking about real money, even for JPMorgan Chase. In all of 2010, credit unions added only 600,000 new customers. But even more telling has been the decision by the big banks to abandon their plans to institute fees for debit-card use. Whatever the reasons for their capitulation, it's hard to describe that about-face as representing a "blithe disregard" for how their customers are feeling.

Tracing out the cause-and-effect connections here are tricky. Bank overreach, Occupy Wall Street and Bank Transfer Day are all feeding into and reinforcing each other. If Bank of America hadn't announced plans to charge a $5-a-month fee for debit card use and Occupy Wall Street hadn't pointed an accusing finger at the financial sector with such a powerful media-amplified voice, Kristen Christian's Bank Transfer Day might never have advanced beyond her own family and friends.

But now the genie is out of the bottle. Because it didn't stop on Nov. 5. The movement to go local, go independent, and make sure that our money serves our own values rather than the bottom line of huge banks will only gain energy as word spreads, and small victories accumulate.

This story first appeared on Salon.

NURSES STEP UP CALL FOR GLOBAL FINANCIAL TAX

BY ROSE ANN DEMORO

BEFORE THERE WAS an Occupy Wall Street, there was a sea of red on Wall Street, and in Washington cheek to jowl with Wall Street's main lobbying arm, the U.S. Chamber of Commerce, and at Congressional offices across the country. Registered nurses and members of National Nurses United, in red scrubs, were demanding immediate action with a tax on Wall Street financial speculation to provide desperately needed revenue to heal our economy.

The call for a financial transaction tax (FTT), sometimes called a "Robin Hood tax," has inspired a global movement, uniting international labor federations, environmental activists and non-governmental organizations. They have already persuaded more than a dozen nations to adopt an FTT, and prodded most European Union countries, including conservative governments in Germany and France, to favor it as well. As the campaign for an FTT, a small charge on bonds, derivatives, currencies and similar speculation that targets the big banks and investment firms, has exploded internationally, it remained under the radar in the U.S. until NNU helped rekindle the call for a tax on Wall Street transactions earlier this year.

NNU leaders, seeing the broadening decline in health status and living standards directly linked to the seemingly intractable economic calamity—from ailments linked to poor nutrition to patients rejecting needed medical care because of cost—reasoned that a tax on Wall Street could help fund such critical needs as health care for all, jobs at living wages, and full funding for quality public education. Some major U.S. economists and organizations including the AFL-CIO, Oxfam, Institute for Policy Studies and Public Citizen have long supported implementation of a tax on Wall Street financial transactions that are now largely untaxed. Citing the work of eminent economists, NNU says a meaningful FTT could raise up to $350 billion every year to help reframe the economy.

This past spring, NNU, with the support of labor and consumer allies, began a highly visible public campaign for the tax as a major way to make Wall Street begin to pay for reviving the economy it crashed. The big banks and investment houses did so through reckless gambling with family mortgages, worker pensions and other misdeeds that were the prime cause of the 2008 crash and resulting crumbling conditions in Main Street communities with devastating consequences for the health and welfare of American families.

In June, NNU brought thousands of nurses in their red scrubs and friends to Washington and to the doors of the New York Stock Exchange to sound the call for an FTT. From July through mid-September, NNU members held multiple actions from coast to coast, including soup kitchens, health clinics, sit-ins, and street theater, culminating in a national day of action on September 1 with thousands of nurses calling on 60 congressional offices in 21 states. NNU signs, urging "Tax Wall Street" become a highly visible banner throughout the nation.

Just a few weeks later, tens of thousands of other Americans began their own form of protest against Wall Street's excesses—a prairie fire now known as Occupy Wall Street. Many Occupy Wall Street protesters have also endorsed the call for a tax on Wall Street. Calls for an FTT now ring the airwaves, and can be found not just in obscure blogs, but in the columns of leading writers in all of the major U.S. media. And the nurses' campaign continues to grow.

In early November, nurses from four continents gathered at the G-20 Summit to tell world leaders that time is running out: Real revenue is needed now and a global FTT is the answer. They came to put particular pressure on President Obama and Treasury Secretary Timothy Geithner, who have been major barriers to international action on the FTT, with Geithner actively lobbying European finance ministers to oppose it. On that same November day, 2,000 people, including hundreds of RN members of NNU joined by the AFL-CIO and other unions, environmental and community groups, and participants from the Occupy Wall Street movement, marched on the White House and Treasury Department to step up the push on the Obama administration.

Marchers paused to see a parade of three "bankers" carrying mock golden parachutes and a contingent of nurses spelled out a special message to the Treasury Secretary with individual letters: "HEAL AMERICA, TAX TIMMY'S FRIENDS." Wall Street firms, including banks and their trading arms, have actually reported "more profit in the first two-and-a-half years of the Obama administration than they did during the entire Bush administration ... with very little regard for Main Street," reported the *Washington Post* on November 6.

All the pressure has apparently had an effect on the Obama administration which, for the first time, several media outlets reported, was easing its opposition to an FTT, at least for Europe. Demands for a U.S. FTT continue to grow, propelled by a social movement that converges with the Occupy Wall

Street actions swarming across the U.S. With the constellation of the Occupy protests and the broad international movement, the moment for achieving a meaningful FTT, and the critical revenue it can provide to help revive struggling economies, has never been greater.

"Protests matter. Pressure matters," wrote John Nichols in *The Nation,* writing about the shifting sands in the White House, and the erupting support for an FTT, that includes not just NNU, but extends even to billionaire Bill Gates and the Pope. "The nurses aren't just making noise," Nichols wrote. "It looks like they're changing the debate, altering the policies of the most powerful players in Washington and perhaps the world."

WHY OCCUPY WALL STREET HAS ALREADY WON

BY ELIOT SPITZER

OCCUPY WALL STREET has already won, perhaps not the victory most of its participants want, but a momentous victory nonetheless. It has already altered our political debate, changed the agenda, shifted the discussion in newspapers, on cable TV, and even around the water cooler. And that is wonderful.

Suddenly, the issues of equity, fairness, justice, income distribution, and accountability for the economic cataclysm-issues all but ignored for a generation—are front and center. We have moved beyond the one-dimensional conversation about how much and where to cut the deficit. Questions more central to the social fabric of our nation have returned to the heart of the political debate. By forcing this new discussion, OWS has made most of the other participants in our politics—who either didn't want to have this conversation or weren't able to make it happen—look pretty small.

Surely, you might say, other factors have contributed: A convergence of horrifying economic data has crystallized the public's underlying anxiety. Data show that median family income declined by 6.7 percent over the past two years, the unemployment rate is stuck at 9.1 percent in the October report (16.5 percent if you look at the more meaningful U6 number), and 46.2 million Americans are living in poverty—the most in more than 50 years. Certainly, those data help make Occupy Wall Street's case.

But until these protests, no political figure or movement had made Americans pay attention to these facts in a meaningful way. Indeed, over the long hot summer, as poverty rose and unemployment stagnated, the entire discussion was about cutting our deficit.

And then OWS showed up. They brought something that had been in short supply: passion—the necessary ingredient that powers citizen activism. The tempered, carefully modulated, and finely nuanced statements of Beltway politicians and policy wonks do not alter the debate.

Of course, the visceral emotions that accompany citizen activism generate not only an energy that can change politics but an incoherence that is easily mocked. OWS is not a Brookings Institution report with five carefully researched policy points and an appendix of data. It is a leaderless movement, and it can often be painfully simplistic in its economic critique, lacking in subtlety in its political strategies, and marred by fringe elements whose presence distracts and demeans. Yet, the point of OWS is not to be subtle, parsed, or nuanced. Its role is to drag politics to a different place, to provide the exuberance and energy upon which reform can take place.

The major social movements that have transformed our country since its founding all began as passionate grassroots activism that then radiated out. Only later do traditional politicians get involved. The history of the civil rights movement, women's rights movement, labor movement, peace movement, environmental movement, gay rights movement, and, yes, even the Tea Party, follow this model. In every instance, visceral emotions about justice, right, and wrong ignited a movement. Precise demands and strategies followed later. So the critique of OWS as unformed and sometimes shallow may be correct, but it is also irrelevant.

Just as importantly, most of those who are so critical of OWS have failed to recognize inflection points in our politics. They fail to recognize that the public is responding to OWS because it is desperate for somebody to speak with the passion, and even anger, that has filled the public since the inequities and failures of our economy have become so apparent.

Will the influence of OWS continue? Will it continue to capture the imagination of the public? Will it morph into a more concrete movement with sufficiently precise objectives that it can craft a strategy with real goals and strategies for attaining them? These are impossible questions to answer right now.

Could it launch a citizen petition demanding that a Paul Krugman, Joseph Stiglitz, or Paul Volcker be brought into government as a counterweight to or replacement for the establishment voice of Treasury Secretary Tim Geithner? Maybe. Could OWS demand meetings with top—government officials? Could it demand answers to tough questions—from the specific (explain the government's conflicting statements about the AIG-Goldman bailout) to the more theoretical (why "moral hazard" is a reason to limit government aid only cited when the beneficiaries would be everyday citizens)?

There is much ground to cover before real reform, but as a voice challenging a self-satisfied, well-protected status quo, OWS is already powerful and successful.

This story first appeared on Slate.

The 99%

ORGANIZE AND OCCUPY
BY STEPHEN LERNER

THE ACTIVISTS OF Occupy Wall Street have captured the imagination of the world, focusing a spotlight on economic inequality and the role of big banks and corporations in hijacking democracy and plundering the economy. What is fascinating is that they have succeeded where so many of us have failed, and they have done it by violating many of the cardinal rules that have dominated past thinking about how to raise and popularize issues of inequality and out-of-control corporate power. They didn't focus-group, poll and then milquetoast the message to appeal to the middle. They didn't stay away from conflict, arrests and disruptions out of fear of alienating potential supporters. Nor did they play it safe and set out modest demands and goals so they would seem "reasonable" in the hope that they could influence the politics of the country from the margins.

In some ways, Occupy has more in common with the mass industrial strikes of the 1930s than with most current political and union organizing. It may seem counterintuitive to compare strikes of the old industrial economy to the wired world of online organizing, tweeting and instant YouTube videos, but there are strong parallels. Just as the auto strikes and plant occupations of the 1930s continued until they achieved their objectives, the occupiers have said their movement will go on indefinitely, and it won't be won in a day, or through a few demonstrations, or by electing more sympathetic politicians alone. They have a center of activity, the Occupy site, which like a picket line in a mass strike is a place anyone can show up at any time to help and get involved. And they have spread their energy far and wide, knowing they can't win just by being at Wall Street, any more than garment, auto and steelworkers could have won by striking just one plant at a time.

Most important, they have been crystal clear and uncompromising in naming the bad guys: Wall Street and the big banks. Just as workers knew that they had to beat GM and U.S. Steel back then, so Occupiers know we must beat Wall Street if we are to win a fair economic and political system now.

I've spent the past month participating in meetings, marches and actions across the country from Boston to Chicago to Los Angeles to Jefferson, Missouri, with students, unemployed Americans, union members and other folks fed up with the gross inequality and lack of opportunity in our economy. And what I have seen again and again is that more people than we ever believed possible are showing up and sitting down, risking arrest in long-planned as well as spontaneous actions in unlikely places from Bismarck, North Dakota, to Jackson, Mississippi. All of this has been magnified by a massive level of media attention. By supporting but not trying to control or co-opt Occupy Wall Street, groups long committed to challenging inequality and the power of big banks can join and strengthen a movement already changing the direction of our country, in a mutually reinforcing relationship.

Over the summer, as Occupy was being conceived, community groups, unions and other organizations, many part of the New Bottom Line—which includes the Alliance for a Just Society, Alliance of Californians for Community Empowerment and National People's Action—were planning actions across the country starting in September. The actions, involving nonviolent civil disobedience unfolding as weeks of overlapping events, took aim at Wall Street, big banks and runaway corporate power. In Washington State, sit-ins at JPMorgan Chase in Seattle and actions in three other cities coincided with hundreds crashing a meeting of the state's business elite at the posh Suncadia resort. The action quickly spread to San Francisco, Los Angeles, Boston, Chicago, New York, Minneapolis, and on to Denver and Honolulu.

Just as Occupy Wall Street in New York was starting to penetrate the nation's consciousness, community groups led by Right to the City in coalition with local unions staged a week of actions in Boston. Thousands marched on Bank of America, and twenty-five were arrested in a sit-in. That night many marchers joined when Occupy Boston was launched, and the next day hundreds gathered in support as people moved into a home that sat empty after a foreclosure. Occupy Boston helped make the march on Bank of America a national story, and the excitement of that march and sit-in helped establish and grow Occupy Boston.

In Chicago, union and community groups joined to "take back Chicago." On October 10 marchers gathered at multiple locations, with unions and Occupiers merging at the Board of Trade to lead one of the feeder marches for a 7,000-strong march through the Loop to a gala for the Futures Industry Association. That march ended with a mass sit-in where dozens were arrested. National People's Action members were arrested at the Mortgage Bankers Association meeting, and members of Action Now were arrested delivering garbage to Bank of America.

Coinciding with events in Chicago, Minnesotans for a Fair Economy worked with labor and community groups to engage thousands of people in dozens of actions at banks, the school board and the Occupy Minneapolis site. The week of action painted a picture of how big banks are devastating African-

American neighborhoods through foreclosure and hurting schools in poor neighborhoods. Immigrants' rights groups led a protest against Wells Fargo's support for anti-immigrant politicians. Close to 1,000 people sat down in the streets outside Wells Fargo as the bank closed its office tower so a delegation couldn't enter the building to withdraw their money. Minnesotans then marched to Government Plaza, where the local Occupy group is based, and community and union groups stood with Occupy as the county sheriff backed down from arresting protesters camped out in the plaza.

And in New York City, New York Communities for Change called for divestment from JPMorgan Chase, and its long-planned "Millionaires' March" down Park Avenue was joined by a contingent from Occupy Wall Street. The media coverage made it hard to tell who was leading what, because everything was part of an overlapping movement.

That's the beauty of this moment: we can supercharge the impact of Occupy and the work of unions, community groups and others if we continue to support one another and learn from one another.

In 1937, when the Flint workers escalated their campaign and rose to national prominence, the elites tried to isolate them by calling them radicals, communists and anarchists. They claimed that the workers' actions would destroy the economic system. Given the Occupy movement's sudden rise, it's no surprise that the 1 percent have started leveling the same attacks today. What really frightens them is that the other 99 percent have realized that we do indeed need to destroy a system rigged in favor of Wall Street, big banks and giant corporations and replace it with one that provides opportunity and social and economic justice for the rest of us. And that we're prepared to engage in sustained, dramatic, nonviolent action to make it happen.

Reprinted with permission from the November 7, 2011 issue of The Nation.

NO DEMAND IS BIG ENOUGH
BY CHARLES EISENSTEIN

LOOKING OUT UPON the withered American Dream, many of us feel a deep sense of betrayal. Unemployment, financial insecurity and lifelong enslavement to debt are just the tip of the iceberg. We don't want to merely fix the growth machine and bring profit and product to every corner of the earth. We want to fundamentally change the course of civilization. For the American Dream betrayed even those who achieved it, lonely in their overtime careers and their McMansions, narcotized to the ongoing ruination of nature and culture but aching because of it, endlessly consuming and accumulating to quell the insistent voice, *I wasn't put here on Earth to sell product. I wasn't put here on earth to increase market share. I wasn't put here on earth to make numbers grow.*

We protest not only at our exclusion from the American Dream; we protest at its bleakness. If it cannot include everyone on earth, every ecosystem and bioregion, every people and culture in its richness; if the wealth of one must be the debt of another; if it entails sweatshops and underclasses and fracking and all the rest of the ugliness our system has created, then we want none of it. No one deserves to live in a world built upon the degradation of human beings, forests, waters and the rest of our living planet. Speaking to our brethren on Wall Street, no one deserves to spend their lives playing with numbers while the world burns. Ultimately, we are protesting not only on behalf of the 99 percent left behind, but on behalf of the 1 percent as well. We have no enemies. We want everyone to wake up to the beauty of what we can create.

Occupy Wall Street has been criticized for its lack of clear demands, but how do we issue demands, when what we really want is nothing less than the more beautiful world our hearts tell us is possible? No demand is big enough. We could make lists of demands for new public policies: tax the wealthy, raise the minimum wage, protect the environment, end the wars, regulate the banks. While we know these are positive steps, they aren't quite what motivated people to occupy Wall Street.

What needs attention is something deeper: the power structures, ideologies and institutions that prevented these steps from being taken years ago; indeed, that made these steps even necessary. Our leaders are beholden to impersonal forces, such as money, that compel them to do what no sane human being would choose. Disconnected from the actual effects of their policies, they live in a world of insincerity and pretense.

It is time to bring a countervailing force to bear, and not just a force but a call. Our message is, "Stop pretending. You know what to do. Start doing it." Occupy Wall Street is about exposing the truth. We can trust its power. When a policeman pepper-sprays helpless women, we don't beat him up and scare him into not doing it again; we show the world. Much worse than pepper spray is being perpetrated on our planet in service of money. Let us allow nothing happening on earth to be hidden.

If politicians are disconnected from the real world of human suffering and ecosystem collapse, all the more disconnected are the financial wizards of Wall Street. Behind their computer screens, they occupy a world of pure symbol, manipulating numbers and computer bits. Occupy Wall Street punctures their bubble of pretense as well, reconnects them with the human consequences of the god they serve, and perhaps with their own conscience and humanity too. Only in a hallucination could someone imagine that the unsustainable can last forever; in puncturing their bubble, we remind them that the money game is nearing its end. It can be perpetuated for a while longer, perhaps, but only at great and growing cost. We, the 99 percent, are paying that cost right now, and as the environment and the social fabric decay, the 1 percent will soon feel it too. We want those who operate and serve the financial system to wake up and see before it is too late.

We can also point out to them that sooner or later they will have no choice. The god they serve, the financial system, is a dying god. Reading various insider financial Web sites, I perceive that the authorities are flailing, panicking, desperately implementing solutions they know are temporary just to kick the problem down the road a few years or a few months. The strategy of lending even more money to a debtor who cannot pay his debts is doomed, its eventual failure a mathematical certainty. Like all our institutions of exponential growth, it is unsustainable.

Once you have stripped the debtor of all assets—home equity, savings, pension—and turned every last dollar of his or her disposable income toward debt service, once you have forced the debtor into austerity and laid claim even to his future income (or in the case of nations, tax revenues), then there is nothing left to take. We are nearing that point, the point of peak debt. The money machine, ever hungry, seeks to liquidate whatever scraps remain of the natural commons and social equity to reignite economic growth. If GDP rises, so does our ability to service debt. But is growth really what we want? Can we really cheer an increase in housing starts, when there are 19 million vacant housing units on the market already? Can we really applaud a new oil field, when the atmosphere is past the limit of how much waste it can absorb? Is more stuff really what the world needs right now? Or can we envision a world instead with more play and less work, more sharing and less buying, more public space and less indoors, more nature and less product?

So far, government policy has been to try somehow to keep the debts on the books, but every debt bubble in history ultimately collapses; ours is no different. The question is, how much misery will we endure, and how much will we inflict, before we succumb to the inevitable? And secondly, how can we make a gentle, nonviolent transition to a steady-state or degrowth world? Too many revolutions before us have succeeded only to institute a different but more horrible version of the very thing they overthrew. We look to a different kind of revolution. At risk of revealing the stars in my eyes, let me call it a revolution of love.

What else but love would motivate any person to abandon the quest to maximize rational self-interest? Love, the felt experience of connection to other beings, contradicts the laws of economics as we know them. Ultimately, we want to create a money system, and an economy, that is the ally, not the enemy of love. We don't want to forever fight the money power to create good in the world; we want to change the money power so that we don't need to fight it. I will not in this essay describe my vision—one of many—of a money system aligned with the good in all of us. I will only say that such a shift can only happen atop an even deeper shift, a transformation of human consciousness. Happily, just such a transformation is underway today. We see it in anyone who had dedicated their lives to serving, healing and protecting other beings: people, cultures, whales, children, ecosystems, the waters, the forests, the planet.

In the ecological age, we are beginning to understand that we are connected beings, that the welfare of any species or people is aligned with our own. Our money system is inconsistent with this understanding, which is dawning among all 100 percent of us, each in a different way. I think the ultimate purpose of Occupy Wall Street, or the great archetype it taps into, is the revolution of love. If the 99 percent defeat the 1 percent, they, like the Bolsheviks, will ultimately create a new 1 percent in their place. So let us not defeat them; let us open them and invite them to join us.

If Occupy Wall Street has a demand, it should be this: Wake up! The game is nearly over. Jump ship while there is still time. In my work I meet many people of wealth who have done that, exiting the money game and devoting their time to giving away money as beautifully as they can. And I meet many more people who have the skills and good fortune to earn wealth if they wanted to, but who likewise refuse to participate in the money game.

So if I sound idealistic, keep in mind that many people have had a change of heart already.

Some might call these ideas impractical (though I think that nothing other than a change of heart is practical), and seek to issue concrete demands. Unfortunately, though no demand is big enough, yet equally any demand we would care to make is also too big. Everything we want is on the very margin of mainstream political discourse, or outside it altogether. For example, it might be within the range of respectable policy options to tighten standards on industrial-scale confinement meat operations; but how about ending the practice completely? Congress wrangles about whether or not to reduce troop levels by a few thousand here and there, but what about ending the garrisoning of the planet? Any demand we could make that is within the realm of political reality is too small. Any demand we could make that reflects what we truly want is politically unrealistic.

Shall we fight hard for something we don't even want? It is fine to make demands, but the movement cannot get hung up on them, much less on practicality, because any remotely achievable demand is far less than what our planet needs. "Practical" is not an option. We must seek the extraordinary.

We might come up with a list of demands, something we can all stand behind, albeit each with a secret reservation in his or her heart that says, "I wanted more than that." I encourage those in the movement to recognize such demands as stepping-stones, or landmarks perhaps, on the road to an economy of love. Let us never mortgage a greater to a lesser. The means of the movement, more than the ends, will be the genesis of what comes after the debt pyramid collapses. Occupy Wall Street is practicing new forms of non-hierarchical collaboration, peer-to-peer organization and playful action that someday, maybe, we can build a world on.

We must learn the lessons of Egypt, where a people's movement started with the amorphous demand to end intolerable conditions, and as it discovered its power, soon turned to demand the ouster of the president. That demand would have been too big at the outset, too impossible; yet at the end it proved to be too small. The dictator left, the protesters went home without creating any lasting structures of people power, and while some things changed, the basic political and economic infrastructure of Egypt did not.

Occupy Wall Street should not be content with half-measures, even as it encourages and applauds the tiny hundredth-measures that might come first. It should not let such concessions sap the strength of the movement or seduce it into neglecting to foster its organizational network. Occupy Wall Street is the first manifestation in a long time of "people power" in America. For too long, democracy has, for most people, meant meaningless choices in a box. The Wall Street occupation is stepping out of the box.

Our job is to take a stand for a world that is truly beautiful, fair and just, a planet and a civilization that is healing. For a politician or a financier, even a small step in this direction takes courage, for it goes against the gradient of money and all that is attached to it. I think the task of Occupy Wall Street is to provide a context for that courage, and a call to that courage. With each step taken, the necessity of far larger steps will become apparent, along with the courage to take them.

To those holding the reins of power, let us say, We will be your witnesses and your truthtellers. We will not allow you to live in a bubble. We will not go away. We will show you who you are hurting and how. We will make it awkward to do business, until your conscience cannot stand it any longer. We know, in the beginning, many of you will try to escape us; perhaps you will leave Wall Street for suburban corporate offices on private land where there is no "street" for us to hit. You might also retreat further into your ideologies of globalism and growth that deny the obvious. But nothing will stop us, because our tactics will constantly shift. In one way or another, we will speak the truth and we will speak it loudly. Where speaking the truth becomes illegal, we will break the law. We will not wait to be invited. We will enter, in some way, every physical and ideological fortress.

The truth is dwindling rain forests, spreading deserts, mass tree die-offs on every continent; looted pensions, groaning burdens of student debt, people working two or three dead end jobs; children eating dirt in Haiti, elders choosing between food and medicine ... the list is endless, and we will make it no longer possible to hold it in disconnection from the money system. That is why we converge on Wall Street, and anywhere that finance holds sway. You have lulled us into complacency for long enough with illusions and false hopes. We the people are awakening and we will not go back to sleep.

This piece originally appeared on Reality Sandwich/ Creative Commons.

BACK TO THE FUTURE? GENERATION X AND OCCUPY WALL STREET

BY LYNN PARRAMORE

THE YEAR WAS 1974. My family was gathered around the shrine of the living room television. I was four years old, aware only that something momentous must be happening to draw such rapt attention. A jowly, vaguely menacing-looking man with dark hair was reading a speech.

"What is it, Daddy?"

"The president is getting kicked out on his butt."

My introduction to the world of politics was learning that the leader of my country was a no-good crook. Welcome to Generation X.

People wonder why those born between 1965 and 1980 tend to be nihilistic and wary of commitment. Why many of us keep an ironic distance between ourselves and just about everything. That's because so many aspects of the culture we inherited were a form of lie told to us daily. And unlike previous generations, we never really got a hero. No FDR. No Camelot. Just one jerk after another trying to sell us snakeoil with a smile. The only president who even made an attempt to do things honestly, Jimmy Carter, was branded a fool.

Plenty of us rolled the dice as entrepreneurs because we didn't trust the suit-and-tie corporate scene any more than we trusted politicians with combovers. Left alone as latchkey kids, we turned away from all that, creating our own worlds (the Internet) and cocooning ourselves in shallow pop culture, our very own Land of the Lost. As we reached adulthood, many of us sat alone at our computers, accepting all too often Reagan's invitation to disconnect from our government and get on with the business of accumulating and consuming to fill the great emptiness.

For a moment, it looked like Barack Obama might finally give us something to believe in. But we weren't terribly surprised when that didn't work out, either. Among progressives, Gen-Xers may have been the least trusting of the sweet-talking pol from Chicago. Baby Boomers were stirred by the lingering hopes of their youth. Millennials had not yet faced betrayal by a politician they looked up to. But Gen-Xers suffered no such delusions. We never really looked up to anybody. We've tended to travel pretty lightly in this world.

Our grandparents saw ordinary people rise up in the '30s and '40s to demand—and receive—fair wages, Social Security and equitable growth over the next 40 years. Our moms and dads witnessed the great advances for women and minorities born from the rebellion of the '60s. Those generations before us saw with their own eyes that the people could join together and fight back to gain something powerful for themselves. They understood that entrenched systems could be challenged, and even conquered.

Gen-Xers never got to learn this. We learned how to blow up digital aliens with a joystick.

Occupy Wall Street, can we believe in you? Can you help us break through the recesses of memory and connect with those earlier triumphs in our country's history? Can you take us on a cross-generational back-to-the-future ride and inspire us with your passion and your startling energy? Can you remind us that we don't have to wait for the next politician, the next charismatic leader to get things done? That we can actually do it ourselves?

Be patient with us. We tend to be individualistic, and we need to learn how to form the sustained bonds needed for long-term activism. Lots of us don't do so well sitting through meetings that last hours discussing laundry and trash. In the face of crackdowns and violent attempts to kill this movement, we need to know that you're not going away. We have been manipulated in too many ways, by too many systems. We have scars.

Truthfully, you need us. Smaller than other generations, we are still 50 million souls. We are well-educated, technically adept and ethnically diverse, more so than those who came before us. And we are hungry, so hungry for a better world.

We need you, too. We've seen that look in the eyes of the '60s children when they told us stories of joining protests in their youth. The era-envy we felt! We wanted to taste possibility so badly that tens of thousands of us flocked to Prague in the '90s after the Velvet Revolution, just to see what history-in-the-making looked like. We saw the poet-president guiding a new society and wistfully thought, "Why can't this happen at home?"

The first time I went down to Liberty Plaza, I didn't trust what I was seeing. "Just another wasted effort," I thought. But I came back, and in the first general assembly that I joined (and admittedly made it only halfway through), my eyes began to tear as I listen to the amplified voices of the people's mic. When I shouted along, I was a part of this. Other generations may not easily understand just how difficult that is for Gen X—feeling part of something. A long-jaded heart opens up slowly and painfully.

But that's what you've done. You've taken us somewhere we have never traveled.

The 99%

Let's do this thing together. It's not like Gen-Xers don't have a lot to be pissed off about. In fact, we excel in being pissed off. The years of our birth marked the beginning of so many declines in American life, real wages, worker's rights, manufacturing, etc. We are sick of downgrading the future. We don't have pensions; they're chipping away at our Social Security; our houses (if we have them) are underwater; our healthcare sucks; and the last time we worked a 40-hour week was—never. Frankly, we never lost the fear that we'd end up flipping burgers like the slackers they told us we were. In fact, in a world of chronically high unemployment, we often fear we won't be able to do even that.

You, with your fresh thoughts, can you teach us to close our in-boxes and march with you? To get off the treadmill of endless work and consumption, to slow down and keep pace with you? To stand firm in the face of violent assaults and propaganda and a global financial monster bent on strangling us?

Yes, let's do this thing together. Let's link arms with every generation to oppose the demonic force of unfettered capitalism, a system of such appalling evil that it must deny basic human values in order to justify itself. Let's get the Baby Boomers who remember how to organize. And let's call in the children of the Depression who know how to fight labor battles. Let's talk to the college students who are trembling right now to inherit a world that has been so desperately screwed up. Let's bring in the trade unions and the churches and the community groups and the university professors and even the Silicon Valley guys who think that a high-speed connection beats a human connection.

Let's grow this thing together, no matter what happens. Let's learn from one another and prove that the 99 percent will not be silenced. Maybe we can figure out how to divide the 1 percent. Or conjure strategies the established media won't expect. Or make sure the politicians choke on every lie they tell us. Or just continue to talk and think about what kind of society we actually want to live in.

Let's channel this elemental energy into something that lasts. For then Generation X will no longer be popcorn venders at the intermission of history.

We will be making it. With you.

TO CHANGE THE COUNTRY, WE JUST MIGHT HAVE TO CHANGE OURSELVES

BY DON HAZEN

THE EMERGENCE OF what we know as Occupy Wall Street, or the 99 Percent Movement, has taken nearly everyone by surprise, producing a transformation of public consciousness. There is little doubt that something striking has taken place, far from our normal range of expectations. As a result, many thousands of progressives, excited that the logjam in American politics has been psychologically broken, are still wondering exactly what has happened and why. Suddenly the style and conventional wisdom of traditional progressive models for social change have been pushed aside in favor of "horizontalism," general assemblies, "culture jamming," and many unconventional ways of doing politics.

THE ANTECEDENTS OF OWS

The DNA strands of some of these alternative approaches can be traced to Europe's Situationist International movement of the 50s and 60s, which combined radical politics with avant-garde art, and helped lead to a general strike in France in 1968. There are echoes, too, of American progressive movements that rose in response to the inequality, corporate excesses, and corruption of the Gilded Age and the Roaring 20s. There are also reverberations from early in the union movement in the large-scale industrial strikes of the 1930s, and also with the civil rights movement, and the women's movement's model of consciousness raising. Powerful acknowledgement must be given to the Arab Spring, for igniting the world's imagination. In Egypt, power was contested that seemed incontestable; protestors didn't have the answers beyond the end of Mubarack—still they came and stayed.

Strong antecedents can also be found in the student-led anti-war movement of the late 1960s, which was also about dehumanizing corporate power. Then, many male students faced being drafted to fight in a destructive and despised war. These young people and their families strongly pushed back, saying, "Hell no, we won't go!" Many of today's millennials are also fighting back against circumstances that affect them directly. They took on large debt to prepare them for jobs that aren't there. Student debt is more than one trillion

The 99%

dollars, while unemployment for young people is at Depression levels. Students can not declare bankruptcy on student loans—those crushing debts will follow them forever. Many of these young adults see their futures at stake. Not surprisingly, they want a solution—either the jobs that would enable them to pay off their loans, or forgiveness of debt incurred under false pretenses.

Nevertheless, what has burst out of a small park in Lower Manhattan feels like a new manifestation of the will for ordinary people to challenge dangerous and daunting forces that have come to dominate their lives. With its global reach and advanced technological and media tools, OWS may well usher in a whole new political and cultural era. Still, no one can say just where this thing will go and what the future will bring. And therein lies much of the power of OWS, and for some, the frustration. Pundits and organizers across the ideological spectrum have tried to understand the phenomenon, and explain it by fitting it into what we already know about how the system works, because not knowing is a source of great anxiety in our society, in the media, in the establishment, and even among progressives.

But as Eve Ensler, global activist and author of the *Vagina Monologues* says, "What is happening cannot be defined. It is happening. It is a spontaneous uprising that has been building for years in our collective unconscious. It is a gorgeous, mischievous moment that has arrived and is spreading. It is a speaking out, coming out, dancing out. It is an experiment and a disruption." Of course, nothing concrete has changed yet. But the possibility of change— really, the necessity of change—is now in the middle of our nation's politics and public discourse. This alone is an incredible achievement because a few short months ago, many millions of us essentially had no hope.

WHY HAS THE TRIED-AND-TRUE FAILED US, AND OWS SUCCEEDED?

We may well ask why so much progressive organizing and billions of dollars of investments in social change over the past 20 to 30 years has failed to slow down the right-wing, corporate-dominated juggernaut or catch the public's imagination. And how is it that remarkably, what is succeeding in front of our eyes breaks what we thought were the hard and fast rules of political relevance. We had come to think that we needed the development of charismatic leaders operating within vertical organizational models, with heavy emphasis on fundraising and electoral politics. But that is changing. Reality is undergoing an adjustment.

Micah Sifry, writing at the website Tech President, wondered why this and why now. "Did OWS succeed simply because it was non-hierarchical in method, had smart framing in tune with public anger about the economy and Wall Street, and made really effective use of social media?" If so, he asked, "Why didn't a very similar effort, called 'The Other 98 Percent' take off last year? Why didn't the U.S. Uncut movement, a spin-off of an ongoing street protest movement in England, take off here this past winter? Why didn't Van Jones' new Rebuild the Dream movement, which was launched this summer with the backing of MoveOn, labor and the progressive netroots, take off?"

Long-time organizer Andrew Boyd described a few key elements to Sifry. One is the powerful tactic of occupation itself, with the personal commitment and determination of people on the ground to see it through. "Continuous occupation creates a human drama" and a demonstration of dedication that matters. "People await the next episode. Will the cops kick them out? Will they outlast the weather? Will they participate in the elections?" Another reason is the lack of demands: As Boyd says, it puts OWS in the morally potent "right vs wrong box," instead of in the "political calculation" box. Still another is the authenticity of OWS. As Sifry notes, "Occupy Wall Street isn't slick. It isn't focus-grouped. It isn't something professional activists would do ... As the authors of the Cluetrain Manifesto wrote more than a decade ago, we instinctively know the difference between a human voice and a corporate voice. I know it may sound strange to say this, but could it be that the reason that so many progressive social change projects fail to connect with ordinary people and move them to action, is because they seem too corporate in style? Think of all those hand-scrawled signs on scraps of cardboard vs a thousand professionally printed signs from a union shop—which is more authentic?"

But there is something simultaneously much harder to grasp *and* incredibly easy to digest if one is able to suspend disbelief, to stop thinking in all the ways we have been taught and trained to respond in American politics. And get ready for a wild ride.

A GENERATIONAL SHIFT

Even though OWS involves people of a wide range of ages, there has been a fundamental generational shift. Millennials have a different view of how to do things, with values and knowledge gained from leaders across the world. They have absorbed quite naturally the fundamental approach of horizontalism—

or perhaps better labeled participatory democracy—field tested in places like Argentina, Spain and Greece.

As Marina Sitrin, a veteran of political organizing in Argentina ten years ago and an early OWS participant explains:

> *2011 has been a year of revolutions—uprisings—and massive social movements—all against an economic crisis and crisis of representation. Most all of these new movements have taken directly democratic forms, and are doing so in public spaces, from Tahrir Square in Egypt, to the plazas and parks of Spain, Greece, and increasingly the United States. The words horizontal, horizontalidad and horizontalism are being used to describe the form the movements are taking. Horizontal, as it sounds, is a level space for decision making, a place where one can look directly at the other person across from you ... Horizontalism is more than just being against hierarchy ... it is about creating something new together in our relationships. The means are a part of the ends. The forms of organizing manifest what we desire; it is not a question of demands, but rather a manifestation of an alternative way of being and relating.*

On a practical level, what this means is that Gen Xers and Boomers have much to learn from the different approaches to politics represented by OWS. Instead of focusing on traditional power structures, the OWS operation seems like the "wisdom of crowds" combined with a fundamental sense that top-down power can't really ever change anything, because it will always, by its nature, reproduces the system it is trying to change.

For decades, we progressive Boomers (I am one) and Gen Xers have continued doing things the way we always have, believing that if we only organized a little better, raised more money, were a little smarter, tweaked the message just so, that success would be ours. But we could not discover how to make a dent in the political hegemony of banks and corporations, in the political corruption, in unjust laws that protect the powerful. Life in the social and economic realms has declined over the past decades—for the working class, poor people, people of color, students, and increasingly the middle class. Meanwhile, more and more corporate money is invested to game the system. The Supreme Court's decision in *Citizens United* was the last nail in the coffin, giving yet more influence over our "democracy" to the 1 percent.

OWS represents a challenge to many established orders. It challenges a large professional class of highly-educated progressives who learned to work the funding system and to create a broad, comfortable and self-reinforcing progressive establishment. While millions suffer with joblessness, houses under water, and student debt, many in the progressive establishment are well paid, and thriving, fighting a battle on many fronts that it seems we are doomed to continue to loose. Why? Perhaps it is because our system and way of doing things mirrors the oppressive system in many ways. There is nothing revolutionary about movement professionals trying to negotiate with the Obama administration to tweak one policy or another. Or spending time convincing Americans to sign another petition or offer financial support, things I personally promote, so I do not write this from a place of any superiority, nor do I have an immediate clear idea of how to change it, except that we must try.

BUILDING ON WHAT WE HAVE DONE

Our old ways of doing things are going to be challenged and questioned everyday. We have to be bold enough to resist running for establishment cover and use this teachable moment to take a hard look at what we have wrought. If we believe in our values, we have to adapt and change. At the same time, and this is crucial, we have to take stock of what we have built, which is significant. There are infrastructures in place that will help the OWS movement go forward. We must be creative and gutsy in imagining how to weave together the new with old, and not throw out the baby with the bathwater. For Boomers, let's remember that our early efforts of crossing many dividing lines—of race, gender, class sexual orientation—provides the historical backbone of what the OWS movement is building on, 40 years later. It just may be that this generation is doing a better job than we did.

Moving forward, we have to distribute resources more broadly. We must bring people into productive roles who have been left out. None of this will be easy. But it could be amazing, and even more importantly, essential. Because if we are going to catch this tidal wave, if we are going to contribute to this huge fight against unbridled global capitalism, we must accept the anxiety and uncertainty of doing things differently. And many of us will. Already, many of us do sense that this is the best chance we will have in our lifetime to reinvigorate our democracy, create a livable world for ourselves and future generations, and help millions, young and old, pull themselves from the grinding everyday pain of poverty and powerlessness.

WE ARE THE CHANGE

Joining the change will require reassessing both our habits and our organizations. And a fair question is, just what does that mean? I don't pretend to have the answers. But there are places to start. We can examine our privileges, share power, insist that resources be spread much further than they are now. We can think about relating better to all, not just to those in our political and social circle. As a daily practice, we can better value the people on whose work we depend, those who collect our garbage, deliver our food, clean our offices, do our laundry. And for the future of the earth—we can challenge and change some of our greedy habits and remind ourselves of how easy it is to abuse the environment when we are privileged.

Many of us have been toiling for years, struggling for social change, for inspirational and accurate media coverage, for fairness and equality. We have been doing it the way we thought was right, and we should give ourselves credit for persistence, for not giving up. But, we do find ourselves at a crossroads. Embracing the new has risks, and feels confusing, perhaps even threatening.

Eve Ensler has a way of artfully articulating the elements of key moments. She writes: "If we are not afraid, if we open ourselves, we all know everything has to change. We need places to announce and actualize this change. Places are crucial. The ingredients involve stepping out of your comfort zone, giving up more than your share, telling your story and listening to others, not thinking in an obvious linear way, trusting the collective imagination to be more empowered and visionary than your own, refusing to participate in the violent destruction of anything. That includes taking anything that isn't yours, taking more than you need, and believing you have a right to dismiss or ignore or belittle anyone with less power or money or education. Believers ... will be beaten with batons and pepper sprayed and dragged off. But no one can evict or silence what is emerging in Zuccotti Park." Or from the thousands of sister and brother "occupations" in the U.S. and across the globe.

It's clear. The movement that is OWS can't do it alone. They need, we need, millions of us, to be willing to step up, and change ourselves and change the world in the process.

CONTRIBUTORS

Lisa Kaas Boyle *is an environmental attorney. She co-founded the Plastic Pollution Coalition, where she serves as Director of Legal Policy.*

Mikki Brunner *is a multimedia writer living in New York City.*

Melanie Butler *is a NYC-based activist and Coordinator of CODEPINK's Truth Set Free campaign.*

Derrick Crowe *is political director at Brave New Foundation and runs the Rethink Afghanistan and War Costs campaigns.*

Rose Ann DeMoro *is executive director of National Nurses United.*

Tamara Draut, *vice president of policy and programs at Demos, is the author of* Strapped: Why America's 20- and 30-Somethings Can't Get Ahead.

Charles Eisenstein *is a writer, speaker and the author of* The Ascent of Humanity *and other books.*

Tom Engelhardt, *co-founder of the American Empire Project and the author of* The American Way of War: How Bush's Wars Became Obama's, *as well as* The End of Victory Culture, *runs the Nation Institute's TomDispatch.com. His latest book, just released is* The United States of Fear.

Eve Ensler *is a Tony award winning playwright, performer and activist.*

Thomas Ferguson *is professor of political science at the University of Massachusetts, Boston and author of* The Golden Rule: The Investment Theory of Party Competition and the Logic of Money-Driven Political Systems.

James K. Galbraith *is the author of* The Predator State: How Conservatives Abandoned the Free Market and Why Liberals Should Too. *He teaches at The University of Texas at Austin.*

Tana Ganeva *is AlterNet's Managing Editor.*

Leo W. Gerard *is the international president of the United Steelworkers union. He is a member of the AFL-CIO Executive Committee and chairs the labor federation's Public Policy Committee.*

Amy Goodman *is the host of "Democracy Now!" a daily international TV/radio news hour airing on more than 900 stations in North America. She is the author of* Breaking the Sound Barrier.

David Graeber *is a Reader in Social Anthropology at Goldsmiths University London. Prior to that he was an associate professor of anthropology at Yale University. He is the author of* Debt: The First 5,000 Years.

Robert Greenwald, *the president and founder of Brave New Foundation, is the director/producer of* Outfoxed: Rupert Murdoch's War on Journalism, *as well as many other films. He is a board member of the Independent Media Institute, AlterNet's parent organization.*

Arun Gupta *is a founding editor of* The Indypendent *newspaper. He is writing a book on the decline of American Empire for Haymarket Books.*

Kristen Gwynne *graduated from New York University with a degree in journalism and psychology. She covers Drugs at AlterNet, specializing in addiction and prescription pills. Gwynne grew up in the Philly area and is based in New York.*

Don Hazen *is executive director of the Independent Media Institute and executive editor of AlterNet.*

Joshua Holland *is an editor and senior writer at AlterNet. He is the author of* The 15 Biggest Lies About the Economy: And Everything Else the Right Doesn't Want You to Know About Taxes, Jobs and Corporate America.

Sarah Jaffe *is an associate editor at AlterNet. She has been reporting on economic justice, labor, and pop culture since 2002.*

Rob Johnson *is Director of the Institute for New Economic Thinking (INET). He served as Chief Economist of the U.S. Senate Banking Committee under the leadership of Chairman William Proxmire and was Senior Economist of the U.S. Senate Budget Committee under the leadership of Chairman Pete Domenici. He is co-founder of the Move Your Money campaign.*

Lauren Kelley *is an associate editor at AlterNet and a freelance writer and editor who has contributed to Change. org,* The L Magazine *and* Time Out New York. *She lives in Brooklyn.*

Rania Khalek *is an associate writer for AlterNet based in Washington, DC.*

Richard Kim *is the executive editor of TheNation.com.*

Naomi Klein *is an award-winning journalist and syndicated columnist and the author of the international and* New York Times *bestseller* The Shock Doctrine: The Rise of Disaster Capitalism.

Andrew Leonard *has been working at Salon as a technology reporter, editor, blogger and staff writer for 15 years.*

Les Leopold *is the executive director of the Labor Institute and Public Health Institute in New York, and author of* The Looting of America: How Wall Street's Game of Fantasy Finance Destroyed Our Jobs, Pensions, and Prosperity—and What We Can Do About It *(Chelsea Green, 2009).*

Stephen Lerner *serves on the Service Employees International Union's International Executive Board and is the architect of the Justice for Janitors campaign.*

Roberto Lovato *is a Bay Area-based writer with New America Media.*

Manissa McCleave Maharawal *is a doctoral student in the Anthropology department at the CUNY Graduate Center and a New York City based activist.*

Yotam Marom *is an organizer, educator, musician, and writer. He is a member of the Organization for a Free Society.*

Pam Martens *worked on Wall Street for 21 years. She spent the last decade of her career advocating against Wall Street's private justice system, which keeps its crimes shielded from public courtrooms. She has been writing on public interest issues for CounterPunch since retiring in 2006. She has no security position, long or short, in any company mentioned in her essay.*

Anna Lekas Miller *is a student, activist and political journalist living in New York City.*

J.A. Myerson *is an independent journalist who works with the Media and Labor Outreach Committees at Occupy Wall Street. His work has appeared on AlterNet, Truthout, In These Times, MSNBC, and Al Jazeera.*

Alex Pareene *writes about politics for Salon.*

Lynn Parramore *is a contributing editor at AlterNet, co-founder of Recessionwire, and founding editor of New Deal 2.0. She is the author of* Reading the Sphinx: Ancient Egypt in Nineteenth-Century Literary Culture *and has taught cultural theory and writing at NYU.*

Nomi Prins *is a senior fellow at the public policy center Demos and author of* Black Tuesday *(Createspace, 2011).*

Barbara Schneider Reilly *is a playwright, teacher and citizen of New York and Berlin.*

Jennifer Sacks *is a journalist living in New York and a proud member of the 99 percent.*

Sarah Seltzer *is a freelance writer in New York City and associate editor at AlterNet.*

Julianne Escobedo Shepherd *is AlterNet's Culture Editor. Based in Brooklyn, she has written about music, style, and pop culture for* Billboard, Spin, Interview, The New York Times, *and countless other publications.*

Yves Smith *is the founder and main writer of NakedCapitalism.com. She is the author of* ECONNED: How Unenlightened Self Interest Undermined Democracy and Corrupted Capitalism.

Eliot Spitzer *is the former governor of the state of New York.*

Adele M. Stan *is AlterNet's Washington correspondent. She also writes for the AFL-CIO Now blog.*

Nick Turse *is the associate editor of TomDispatch.com and a senior editor at AlterNet. His latest book is* The Case for Withdrawal from Afghanistan *(Verso).*